Professional Education for International Organizations

Dietmar Herz / Marc Schattenmann
Susan Lynn Dortants / Kristin Linke / Stefanie Steuber

Professional Education for International Organizations

Preparing students for international public service

PETER LANG

Frankfurt am Main · Berlin · Bern · Bruxelles · New York · Oxford · Wien

Bibliographic Information published by the Deutsche Nationalbibliothek
The Deutsche Nationalbibliothek lists this publication in the Deutsche Nationalbibliografie; detailed bibliographic data is available in the internet at <http://www.d-nb.de>.

ISBN 978-3-631-56007-5

© Peter Lang GmbH
Internationaler Verlag der Wissenschaften
Frankfurt am Main 2008
All rights reserved.

Printed in Germany 1 2 3 4 5   7

www.peterlang.de

Preface

This book presents the cumulative findings of a research project on "Professional Education for International Organizations"that the two of us led at the University of Erfurt for two years. To all those who worked on the project and to those whom we worked with, the project was best known by its acronym: PROFIO.

PROFIO started in July 2004, but the questions that fueled it had been on our minds for quite some time before. In the summer of 2000, we had been entrusted to take the lead in establishing Germany's first Master of Public Policy (MPP) degree program and what eventually became the Erfurt School of Public Policy (ESPP). From the start, it was clear that the program and the school should prepare talented students not only for careers in government or non-governmental organizations, but equally well for careers in international organizations (IOs). Therefore, our ideas about what it takes to get into an IO and to succeed there had influenced the design of the curriculum and the extra-curricular activities. These ideas, however, were mostly based on common sense, personal experience, and anecdotal evidence.

We were therefore very grateful when we were given the opportunity to receive funding for a larger research project that could shed more light on the matter and generate some robust empirical data. Without the financial support of the German Federal Ministry of Education and Research *(Bundesministerium für Bildung und Forschung, BMBF)*, such a project would probably have remained a pipe dream.

Another federal ministry, the German Federal Foreign Office *(Auswärtiges Amt, AA)*, provided important intellectual and moral support. We benefited greatly from our discussions with Ambassador Wolfgang Stöckl, Special Coordinator for German Personnel in International Organizations. The fact that the Foreign Office hosted the conference were the results of PROFIO were presented to an audience of experts on June 22nd and 23rd, 2006, underscores the productive relationship we had.

This book makes these results available to a wider audience. It presents the cumulative findings of half a dozen separate empirical studies and a number of additional research efforts that were conceptualized, planned, undertaken and written up by various researchers and research teams. Being cumulative, it is more than a compilation. It is a synthesis that allows one to look at the bigger picture. While we hope that the many cooks did not spoil the soup, but instead have made it all the richer, this process means that it is quite impossible to weigh the individual contributions precisely. Some have chopped the carrots, some have broiled the meat, and others provided the recipe.

In identifying the authors of this book, we were guided by the "Proposals for Safeguarding Good Scientific Practice"of the *German Research Foundation*. They state that "[a]uthors of an original scientific publication shall be all those, and only those, who have made significant contributions to the conception of studies or experiments, to the generation, analysis and interpretation of the data, and to preparing the manuscript, and who have consented to its publication, thereby assuming responsibility for it."[1]

We have named as primary authors those five individuals who have made significant contributions to all or most of the individual studies as well as to this final comprehensive report and who resume responsibility for it. As collaborators, we have listed all colleagues who have been recognized as authors of one of the individual studies that have formed the basis of this report and that have been published online:

– Dietrich, S., Herz, D., Dortants, S. L. & Linke, K. (2006). *Careers with the World Bank. A study on recruitment strategies and qualification requirements at the World Bank.* Retrieved from http://nbn-resolving.de/urn/resolver.pl?urn=urn:nbn:de:gbv:547-200601351

– Herz, D., Dortants, S. L. & Linke, K. (2006). *Careers with UNEP. A study on recruitment strategies and qualification requirements at the United Nations Environment Programme.* Retrieved from http://nbn-resolving.de/urn/resolver.pl?urn=urn:nbn:de:gbv:547-200601348

– Herz, D., Schattenmann, M., Dortants, S. L., Linke, K. & Steuber, S. (2005). *Careers with the EU. A study on recruitment strategies and qualification requirements of the institutions of the European Union.* Retrieved from http://nbn-resolving.de/urn/resolver.pl?urn=urn:nbn:de:gbv:547-200601351

– Herz, D., Schattenmann, M., Dortants, S. L. & Steuber, S. (2005). *Working for the OSCE. Careers in a non-career organization.* Retrieved from http://nbn-resolving.de/urn/resolver.pl?urn=urn:nbn:de:gbv:547-200601330

– Hoelscher, P., Herz, D., Dortants & Linke, K. (2005). *Studie zu Studiengängen und Bildungsangeboten Frankreichs, Belgiens und der Schweiz, die für eine Karriere in internationalen Organisationen ausbilden.* Retrieved from http://nbn-resolving.de/urn/resolver.pl?urn=urn:nbn:de:gbv:547-200601430

[1] http://www.dfg.de/aktuelles_presse/reden_stellungnahmen/download/self_regulation_98.pdf, retrieved May 10, 2007.

− Krause, C., Tschirschwitz, C., Herz, D., Dortants, S. L. & Linke, K. (2006). *Bericht über Studiengänge und Bildungsangebote im deutschspra-chigen Raum, die für eine Karriere in internationalen Organisationen ausbil-den.* Retrieved from http://nbn-resolving.de/urn/resolver.pl?urn= urn:nbn:de:gbv:547-200601418
− Studzinski, J., Herz, D., Dortants, S. L. & Linke, K. (2005). *Qualification requirement strategies at the European Space Agency (ESA).* Retrieved from http://nbn-resolving.de/urn/resolver.pl?urn=urn:nbn:de:gbv:547-200601376
− Studzinski, J., Herz, D., Schattenmann, M., Dortants, S. L. & Linke, K. (2005). *Evaluation of the "Carlo-Schmid-Program for internships in interna-tional organizations and EU institutions".* Retrieved from http://nbn-resolving.de/urn/resolver.pl?urn=urn:nbn:de:gbv:547-200601395

Generally, the leader(s) of the research team are named first, then the participating research associates in alphabetical order, except in those cases were there was a lead author. Because the individual studies were conceptualized from the start as steps on the way to this cumulative study and in order to keep the following text readable, we have refrained from quoting (ourselves) every time we have used data or text from these previous studies that should be considered pre-publications.

In addition to the great team of research associates who contributed to this study, we want to thank PROFIO's dedicated and resilient student assistants Lea-Valeska Giebel, Stephanie Beck, Andreas Hahn, and An-nika Meyen. During the final weeks of the editing process, Marc Schat-tenmann's student assistants Benjamin Richter, Theresa Arens, and par-ticularly Sören Krüger provided invaluable support.

We are also very grateful to our colleague Kai Ahlborn who dissected many of our early ideas and drafts with his customary but quite unusual analytical acuity and who helped us to pick the best people out of the big pile of applications.

For many valuable pieces of advice and support, we are indebted to Andreas Blätte who succeeded Marc Schattenmann as ESPP's Associate Director when the latter went on leave during the academic year 2005-06. Furthermore, we thank the Peter Lang Publishing Group for enabling us to turn this final research report into a real book.

Finally, our biggest thanks go out to the many people working at inter-national organizations and institutions of higher education who an-swered our questions and who must and will remain unnamed. Without them, we would not have had much to report about. It is our hope that this is a book for them: one which they will find useful in improving the education for and the practice of international organizations.

Erfurt, August 2007

Dietmar Herz & Marc Schattenmann

Contents

List of Tables

List of Figures

1. Introduction

What does it take to work for an international organization and to succeed there? How can universities prepare their students for a career in international organizations? These are the questions that are at the center of this book.

In the following introductory sections, we will fist recount how these questions grew out of a specific German context and concern, Germany's "underrepresentation" in international organizations, and how they have informed our research project on "Professional Education for International Organizations"(PROFIO), on which this book is based. A subsequent overview of the research previously done on this and related topics will permit us to identify the contribution we hope to make. In the course of this, we will clarify a few key terms used throughout the book. Finally, we will explain how the two big questions named above were transformed into more specific research questions and research objectives.

1.1. Germany's underrepresentation in international organizations

For quite some time now, the German government has realized that Germany is not strongly represented among the staff of many international organizations – at least not as strongly as the government would like to have it.[2] If one counts the numbers of staff members in the professional category and compares them to the budgetary contributions of different countries, Germany fares less well than others (see Table 1.1 for an example of the representation of various nations in the United Nations Environment Programme). This problematic situation is frequently referred to by the term *deutsche Delle* (German "dent"), a more specific term originally coined to capture the lack of Germans particularly in middle-management positions at international organizations, a situation which supposedly leads to a lack of Germans in top positions later on.[3]

The merits of measuring "adequate" representation in proportion to budgetary contributions are certainly debatable, but so are other plausible measures, e.g. representation according to population size, gross na-

---

[2] For more information, please see Deutscher Bundestag: Bundestagsdrucksachen 13/10793, 13/10300, 14/2158, 14/1937, 14/4952, 14/5048, 14/8347, 14/8185, 15/0517, 15/2652, 15/3635. Retrieved July 25, 2007, from http://dip.bundestag.de/parfors/ parfors.htm.
[3] This term was first mentioned in writing in a newspaper article: Blome, N. & Middel, A. (1999). *Deutsche Delle in Brüssel*. Retrieved July 20, 2007, from www.welt.de/print-welt/article578116/Deutsche_Delle_in_Bruessel.html.
However, it existed before that point in time as a spoken term.

Table 1.1. Distribution of nationalities at UNEP (professional categories)

Member States	Occupied professional posts in 2005 (n = 504)	Percent of occupied professional posts in 2005 (n = 504)	Payment/pledge in 2005 (amount in USD) (n = 58,961,600)	Percent of contributions
Kenya	32	6.35%	0	0
UK	28	5.56%	7,986,720	13.55%
Germany	25	4.96%	6,641,934	11.26%
Netherlands	25	4.96%	6,003,878	10.18%
US	25	4.96%	6,000,000	10.18%
Canada	18	3.57%	2,058,894	3.49%
Japan	17	3.37%	3,230,000	5.48%
Italy	16	3.17%	2,886,960	4.89%
France	16	3.17%	4,000,000	6.78%
India	12	2.38%	100,000	0.16%

Sources: UNEP (2005). Report of the Executive Director. Staffing in UNEP. Nairobi, UNEP. UNEP (2006). "Contributions to UNEP's Environment Fund 1973-2006." Retrieved March 2, 2006, from http://www.unep.org/rmu/en/Financing_of_UNEP/Environment_Fund/Table_Byyear/ index.asp

tional product, or number of votes within the organization. The two extreme alternatives – to strive for strict parity or to ignore nationalities altogether – are even more contentious, let alone impractical. In any case, the German Federal Foreign Office has made representation in proportion to budgetary contributions the key indicator for proper representation. For practical reasons, we have followed suit and have selected the budgetary contribution as the main point of orientation to talk about national representation in international organizations.

The relative underrepresentation of German staff members in many IOs is perceived as a political problem not simply because Germany is usually among those nations paying the most toward international and regional organizations in absolute terms. More importantly, Germany strives to be a major actor in the global political arena and often favors multi-lateral approaches. More German staff in international organizations could probably help to achieve these objectives better.

A number of reasons for this low level of representation are already known. They can be divided into objective reasons having to do with the available positions and subjective reasons dealing with the applicants themselves.

Objective reasons are the reasons why suitable applicants are not interested in working for international organizations. As a matter of fact, the working conditions at IOs often do not correspond to the expectations of highly qualified Germans. This applies to the length of contracts (especially since public officials in Germany have unlimited contracts and cannot be laid off), insurance coverage and other benefits available in the event that the contract is not renewed, the salaries in relation to the cost of living (wage levels in Germany continue to be much higher than in most other countries), and often with regard to the professional options of one's spouse. In most cases, there is not much the German government could do about these objective reasons. Usually, they have to be accepted as given.

Subjective reasons are related to the behavior and profile of the applicants. A first reason is quite simply that Germans tend not to apply for positions for which they do not fulfill all of the formal criteria, whereas applicants from other nations seem to be less scrupulous. A second reason – and the one that is of primary concern to us – is that German applicants are in some respects less qualified than the competition because of certain features of the German education system. At least some of the factors that make Germans less competitive can be linked to systematic causes rather than the individual strengths and weaknesses of a particular applicant. Among the factors that are directly related to the education that students interested in this field of work receive in Germany are the following:

– the lengthiness of German degree programs, which often causes applicants to be above the age limit;
– the rigidity of the educational system and labor market in Germany, which limits the ability of junior employees to gain sufficient experience and professional qualification before a certain age;
– the lack of necessary foreign language skills;
– and, finally, the tendency of selection procedures at international organizations to be oriented toward the French or Anglo-Saxon educational systems.[4]

In 1999, the "Stuttgart Appeal for more Internationality in Education and Personnel Policy" initiated a reform movement to increase the number of German staff members in entry-level positions by improving the

---

[4] http://dip.bundestag.de/btd/13/107/1310793.pdf, retrieved July 5, 2007.

awareness and interest of young people in this field of work.[5] The results of a study done at the German University of Administrative Sciences at Speyer in 2003 supported this appeal but focused more on the proper selection of personnel to be seconded to positions at international organizations.[6] This study showed that programs educating students for the national public sector simultaneously educate them for the international public sector as well. Then, at the beginning of the year 2004, the German parliament specifically requested the German government to begin a concrete initiative to improve the orientation of degree programs, internships, and continuing education offerings to better prepare young Germans for careers in international organizations.[7]

This is precisely where our research project comes in. By investigating career requirements of international organizations and comparing educational programs internationally, we wanted to get a clearer sense of how these improvements could actually be achieved.

One has to acknowledge that the German Federal Foreign Office has become very active in the field of international personnel policy in recent years, and that levels of representation are improving somewhat already through various policies and activities. But there is still room for improvement, particularly in the field of education.

We concur with many others that education is the key to long-term change, especially in light of the fact that many young Germans today have the goal of working at international organizations after their studies:

"Junior staff development is the strategic answer to the 'German dent' [underrepresentation of Germany in international organizations]. [...] Qualification for an international job begins while one is in school... [...] and continues while one is at university. [...] It is supplemented by experiences abroad and internships [...] and can be completed with a post-university, practically-oriented education."[8]

[5] Robert Bosch Stiftung (1999). *Stuttgarter Appell an Bund und Länder, Wissenschaft und Wirtschaft: Für mehr Internationalität in Bildung, Ausbildung und Personalpolitik.* Retrieved July 5, 2007 from www.berlinerinitiative.de/materialien/1999_stuttgarter_appell.pdf.
[6] Siedentopf, H., & Speer, B. (2004). Auslandserfahrung und Fremdsprachenkenntnisse in der Einstellungs- und Entsendepraxis des deutschen höheren Ministerialdienstes. Retrieved August 25, 2004, from http://www.berlinerinitiative.de/materialien/2004_studie_siedentopf.pdf
[7] http://dip.bundestag.de/btd/15/026/1502652.pdf, retrieved July 5, 2007.
[8] Claus, B. (2004). *Förderung deutscher Nachwuchskräfte für internationale entwicklungspolitische Organisationen: Chancen, Definzite und Reformbedarf (Analysen und Stellungnahmen (3/2003)).* Retrieved July 5, 2007, from www.die-gdi.de/die_homepage.nsf/FSdpub?OpenFrameset.

"One piece of evidence for the quality of an educational offering is that German applicants in international competitions perform above average. The deficits in this area – despite all the brochures and websites now available on this topic – are still due to the uncertainty of junior staff members concerning which type of education and which internships they should choose and also due to the lack of practical orientation of most programs."[9]

Despite the centrality of education, the number of degree programs in the fields of international relations, public policy, and humanitarian or development aid in Germany, Austria, and Switzerland is still quite low, especially compared to the offerings in the United States and United Kingdom. Furthermore, the educational traditions in German-speaking countries tend to have a strong theoretical focus and little room for knowledge application.

This is where the results of our research project should have great potential value by providing concrete analysis and recommendations for reform to currently offered degree programs or to to the development of entirely new offerings.

1.2. Looking for reasons: education, recruitment, personnel policies

Although Germany's underrepresentation has been a popular and widely debated topic for year now, very little quantitative or qualitative research has been undertaken to determine the causes and potential solutions to the problem.

One of the few examples to the contrary is a 1999 study by Beate Neuss and Wolfram Hilz on "German Personnel Representation in the EU Commission" which was commissioned by the Konrad Adenauer Foundation. Similar to the PROFIO project, its focus was on the actual ways in which employees are recruited and promoted in the professional category. It, however, did not include research on the employees' educational and professional backgrounds or the specific skills and qualifications employees need for a successful career at the EU. Its conclusions furthermore dealt primarily with determining the causes of the comparatively low number of Germans in the Commission and with proposing solutions to improve this situation. The following measures were listed in their "Measures for a strategic personnel policy":

[9] Ibid.

"– An improvement of the image of the Commission and EU officials;
– information for students about career opportunities with the EU and about the application requirements;
– the tracking and advising of interns and of applicants for permanent positions from the time when the job advertisement is posted until the new recruits are hired by the Commission;
– complete collection of information on all German employees in the Commission (A-level);
– a political decision about which positions are sought to be filled by Germans;
– the creation of a personnel pool consisting of federal- and state-level employees and/or consisting of employees in free enterprise and academia;
– European further training measures for officials;
easing of the transition between the federal and state level and EU institutions;
– the establishment of a German network;
– intensive personnel maintenance carried out by the Permanent Representation;
– continuous, coordinated lobbying for the filling of positions with German personnel;
– restructuring of European and personnel policy."[10]

In a sense, our project can be seen as a contribution to the further development of these proposals – specifically to the suggestion that students should be better informed about career opportunities and application requirements at the EU. The authors mention the great potential that lies in the reform of higher education and particularly in the creation of bachelor and master degree programs.[11]

Similar – though much shorter – studies were done of the United Nations System, the Bretton Woods institutions (World Bank and IMF), the OECD, and the European Commission. These were commissioned by the "Berlin Initiative for more Internationality in Education and Personnel

---

[10] Neuss, B., & Hilz, W. (1999). *Deutsche personelle Präsenz in der EU-Kommission.* Retrieved July 5, 2007, from www.berlinerinitiative.de/materialien/2001_europa.pdf, pp. 73-74.
[11] Higher education is the term that will be used in this report to refer to studies undertaken after high school, 'Gymnasium,' and the like. According to most definitions we are aware of, It is more specific than 'postsecondary' or 'tertiary education' but less specific than 'college' or 'university education'. We will further refer to the period of studies up to a bachelor's degree as 'undergraduate', the period up to a master's degree as 'graduate', and the period up to a Ph.D. as 'postgraduate education'. This may vary in the quotes of our interview partners, if they choose to use different terms instead.

Policy", which was created after the Stuttgart Appeal, and each presents a brief look (in 20 to 40 pages) at the extent to which Germany is underrepresented at these organizations as well as recommendations for improving this through specific personnel policies.[12] These publications served as useful sources for initial information on the numbers of Germans in these individual international organizations. Yet the PROFIO study went deeper by performing empirical studies of the recruiting mechanisms and personnel structures with special attention to the skills and qualifications necessary for being hired and later promoted in these organizations.

For obvious reasons, the optimization of the education and training for careers at the European Union has been a major topic of discussion among European students, instructors, and practitioners for many years. Already in 1976, the Collège d'Europe in Bruges hosted a large conference on how to best educate European civil servants with guest speakers from several EU institutions and member states. In Germany, a significant push came in the mid 1990s. In the wake of the treaties on European Union of Maastricht and Amsterdam, the German Foreign Office (in conjunction with the Federal Ministry for Education an and Research) called on German universities to submit proposals for post-graduate programs in European studies. In 1998, four "Master of European Studies" programs based on a common curriculum template were established with government support in Berlin, Bonn, Hamburg, and Saarbrücken.[13] Today, programs in European studies are offered all over Europe, and workshops and other meetings often take place for those involved in educating people on EU affairs to discuss what it means to have "European competency" and how this can best be acquired. This is an ongoing debate which shall not be reconstructed in this report, but which one can keep in mind while reading.

Careers in international organizations have been the topic of various reports by Burghard Claus of the German Development Institute in Bonn. He published papers that suggested improvements on the Junior Professional Officer program of the German government, how to form a network of Germans working at international organizations in the eastern part of the U.S., and recommendations to young people interested in jobs

[12]http://www.berlinerinitiative.de/materialien/2002_vn.pdf,
http://www.berlinerinitiative.de/materialien/2002_brettonwoods.pdf,
http://www.berlinerinitiative.de/materialien/2002_oecd.pdf,
http://www.berlinerinitiative.de/materialien/2001_europa.pdf, retrieved July 5, 2007.
[13] http://www.auswaertiges-amt.de/diplo/de/Europa/Karriere/Europastudien.html, retrieved July 26, 2007.

in the international development field.[14] We have taken his findings into account where relevant.

There is also a great deal of interest on the topic of staff representation at IOs in the United States of America. In 2001, the United States General Accounting Office published an extensive report called "United Nations: Targeted Strategies Could Help Boost U.S. Representation"[15]. This work is similar to that of Neuss and Hilz, but it is from the U.S. perspective and aimed only at the United Nations. Interestingly, the personnel policies of various other UN member countries were analyzed in a section titled 'Other Major Contributors Actively Promote UN Employment for Their Citizens', and somewhat surprisingly Germany was among the nations exemplified for their positive measures.

A more recent and more general contribution to this literature is *Working for Change: Making a Career in International Public Service* by Derick and Jennifer Brinkerhoff.[16] Although the topic itself is quite similar to the PROFIO project, the extent to which the contents are directly related and comparable is limited. "Working for Change" is a useful handbook for students desiring to learn more about career paths in development management, whereas the results of PROFIO should be more useful and relevant to politicians and educators than to students. One section of the book, however, deals specifically with 'Skills and Skill Building'. This chapter is directly relevant to the "curricular study" of the PROFIO project and discusses several of the same matters of education and training for careers in this field.

To summarize the findings of literature relevant to this research project, we can say that although there is a great deal of information on international organizations and – to a lesser extent – professional education in general, no work has been published specifically dealing with how to optimize or reform educational programs for the field of work in international organizations. There is some information on the international public service in general and personnel structures at some of the international organizations studied in this project (namely, the United Nations and the European Union), but this only sufficed as preliminary information be-

[14] Claus, B. (2004). *Förderung deutscher Nachwuchskräfte für internationale entwicklungspolitische Organisationen: Chancen, Definzite und Reformbedarf (Analysen und Stellungnahmen (3/2003)).* Retrieved July 5, 2007, from www.die-gdi.de/die_homepage.nsf/FSdpub?OpenFrameset.

[15] United States (2001). *Targeted strategies could help boost U.S. representation.* Retrieved July 5, 2007 from http://www.gao.gov/new.items/d01839.pdf

[16] Brinkerhoff, D. W., & Brinkerhoff, J. M. (2005). *Working for change: Making a career in international public service.* Bloomfield: Kumarian Press.

fore beginning our research project, as it did not answer the questions posed in our project. In particular, no published material could be found that described the competencies, skills, and educational backgrounds employees at international organizations must have or whether certain degree programs are better at preparing their students for this type of work. At least some of the IOs in question have performed internal studies, but firstly, their focus is different from ours, and secondly, often times these studies are confidential and not available to the public.

Of course, the literature that describes recruitment procedures at international organizations (much of which originates directly from the international organizations) was useful as background information for the PROFIO studies, but it was not written in the context of holistically preparing candidates for work in this field. Therefore, the results of the PROFIO project were generated and derived almost exclusively from the analysis of the data collected in our qualitative and quantitative empirical research (see Chapter 2 on Research Design for more information).

As our project is entitled "Professional Education for International Organizations," we feel obliged to say a few words about our understanding of these terms. They may seem self-explanatory to each reader, but may be so in different ways.

First, it must be clear what we mean by 'international organizations'. In this project, we have limited this to refer to international governmental organizations (IGOs) and not to international non-governmental organizations (NGOs) or multinational corporations. Even more parochially, our interest was limited to IGOs of which Germany is a member state. This does not mean, however, that the educational recommendations made in view of this selection of IGOs are irrelevant with regard to internationally operating NGOs or even multinational corporations.

From a personnel perspective, international governmental organizations (hereafter simply referred to as international organizations or IOs) can be divided into various categories based on the type of public services law they apply. These are as follows:
– The United Nations System with its sub-organizations and special programs,
– The institutions of the European Communities (European Union),
– International finance organizations,
– Organizations with specialized tasks.

It was according to this category system that various international organizations were selected to be examined in this study. The main objective was to obtain a broad sample from organizations with various personnel structures, recruitment procedures, and, most importantly, a wide range of tasks and responsibilities requiring employees of different types.

Secondly, it must be clear what we mean when we talk about 'professional education'. Especially in the context of the German educational system, the term is prone to create misunderstandings. Therefore, let us start by saying what we do *not* mean: 'professional education' does not refer to 'vocational education' or 'berufliche Bildung'.

What professional education refers to instead are study programs at the university level designed to prepare students for work in a specific field or 'profession', such as law, medicine, teaching, business management, engineering, and public administration.

In many countries – the United States is the most prominent example –, these study programs are offered by the corresponding "professional schools": law schools, medical schools, schools of education, business schools, etc. In other countries – Germany being a case in point – a different educational philosophy impeded the creation of professional schools; their functions were performed by other structural units within the University (the 'faculty') or not at all.[17]

In our view, the concepts of professional education and the professional school are so inextricably linked that talking about one means talking about the other. Therefore, if we ask ourselves if a professional *education* like that for lawyers or doctors can be created to train students for work at international organizations, we may as well turn to a text on professional *schools* for clarification.

Hans N. Weiler, who as professor emeritus of Education and Political Science at Stanford University and a past *Rektor* of Viadrina European University at Frankfurt/Oder is better positioned than most to compare the American and the German systems of higher education, is a leading advocate of the introduction of professional schools into the German system. His understanding of the professional school is as follows:

"We understand the professional school as a subdivision of the university that defines itself as an interdisciplinary and practically-ori-

---

[17] The German system produced many successes that were admired and imitated abroad (e.g. the "Diplom-Ingenieur" in the technical sector), but also a lot of mediocre programs that invited mischievous comments. Thirty years ago, for example, one author came to the conclusion that "nothing in the German system ensured a reasonable degree of competence. Such competence could be acquired, of course, but a professional degree could also be obtained without competence in either the disciplinary basis, or in the practical art of the profession. What a German degree stood for was very often a quasi-specialized, but actually rather general, philosophical erudition about one's field of studies [...]." (Ben-David, J. (1992). *Centers of learning: Britain, France, Germany, United States, Carnegie Commission on higher education sponsored research studies*. New York et al.: McGraw-Hill, p. 51.)

ented competence center at the highest level of scholarship and with a clearly defined profile. These centers can, in principle, offer programs either for basic or continuing education, but they typically focus on continuing education at the masters level. They have a particularly good chance of developing new and market-driven study programs than would be possible in the conventional study structure. One of the most intensive tasks of the professional school is in the area of further education. Here, as with vocational education offerings, curricular development is seen as the joint responsibility of the professional school and the corresponding area of society, whereby the fulfillment of this joint responsibility can take place in the form of critical discourse. In this way, the structure and content of a study program for teacher education and education research would take place in close cooperation with the public school system, just as the study program of a professional school of management would be developed in discussion with representatives of businesses and public administration. The following elements are constituent to the concept of the professional school: practical orientation, interdisciplinarity, and autonomy and recognition within the higher-education institution."[18]

As Weiler makes clear, the fact that professional programs tend to be closer to a specific field of work and more "market-driven" than 'traditional' programs must not be taken to mean that they are academic lightweights (a prejudice frequently encountered in Germany). As will become clear in the presentation of our empirical results and the recommendations we derive from them, we concur with the view that a 'professional' education is not inherently any less 'academic' than any other education. It all depends on the individual program and its standards.

We realize, however, that there are important differences between international public servants and the medical profession, for example. Most importantly, the breadth of tasks performed by employees of IOs is so enormous that grouping all employees in higher-level positions into one 'profession', could in essence span nearly the whole range of occupations that exist. Keeping this reservation in mind, later sections of this report will show that many similarities between the various groups of employees do exist and can be compounded into a relatively narrow set of skills common to essentially all international public servants. We therefore believe that this occupation (or group of occupations) can be considered to

[18] Weiler, H. (2003). *Professional Schools: Ein Bündnis von Anwendungsbezug und Wissenschaftlichkeit.* In *Hochschulreform in Europa - konkret. Österreichs Universitäten auf dem Weg vom Gesetz zur Realität,* edited by S. a. S. H. Titscher. Opladen: Leske+Budrich, pp. 1-2.

be a profession. This is one condition that must be fulfilled in order to design a relevant training or degree program in the form of 'professional education'.

It would be a fallacy, however, to assume that if there is a more or less well defined profession, there must be something like the ideal or perfect professional who provides the model after which all aspiring professionals must be carved. This fallacy has been a recurring topic in the literature on curriculum development for decades:

"A careful examination of the organizational structure in which the professional operates usually indicates that the educational goal of producing 'the professional' is unrealistic. There is division of labor in most professions such that persons with different interests and abilities are effectively contributing to the work. In the past professional schools have often talked about 'the ideal physician' or teacher or lawyer or nurse or engineer, who represented the model the school sought to produce. Often the faculty analyzed this 'ideal practitioner,' listing the competencies attributed to him. This list then became their educational objectives. It is clear now that most professions have become so complex that delivery systems have been developed utilizing a variety of persons working together to perform the complete functions of the profession. [...] In such cases, it is necessary for the professional school to analyze the several roles performed by different individuals and to consider how to devise educational programs that will prepare each one. The question should also be raised as to the extent to which it is feasible to prepare an individual to perform several or all of these roles. [...] Hence, several different occupational programs will need to be designed."[19]

Although we do not wish to prescribe how many study programs should be created to prepare students for careers in international organizations, we feel it is important for those responsible for designing and evaluating programs to understand the difficulties they might encounter. Throughout our report, we will mention conflicting ideas and problematic conditions that could hinder the realization of our recommendations.

1.3. Research questions and objectives

To put it quite bluntly and briefly, even if our aim was not to investigate what the 'ideal' applicant to international organizations is like and

---

[19] Tyler, R. W. (1971). *Basic principles of curriculum and instruction. Open University Set Book.* Chicago and London: The University of Chicago Press, pp. 231-232.

what institutions of higher education can best do to prepare their students to fit this desired profile, our goal was very similar: to investigate what qualifies someone to successfully apply and work with particular international organizations, and to see what institutions of higher education can best do to prepare their students to develop these qualities.

More specifically, we sought to answer the following five research questions:

(1) Which qualifications, skills, and expertise should applicants to international organizations have? What expectations are placed on applicants to and employees of international organizations? (In other words, success in being hired and/or promoted at IOs is based on what factors?) In the first part of our "labor market study", our focus was on the types of abilities employees at international organizations must have in order to successfully do their jobs. This included the identification of "career-boosting" factors. This refers both to those applying for jobs at international organizations (i.e., success in being hired by an international organization) and to those making their careers at international organizations (i.e., success in being promoted to continuously higher positions within an international organization). These factors go beyond the knowledge of subjects relevant to the position desired to include analytical and behavioral skills as well as personal attributes that play a role in one's ability to perform the tasks at hand.

(2) Which methods are or were most effective in acquiring these skills and competencies? After identifying these "career-boosting" factors we then set about determining to what extent it is possible to acquire these skills or abilities in one's university education. Here, we asked professionals at international organizations to describe where and how they learned what they know today: it may have been at school, during their studies, in internships, on the job, or in continuing education courses. We also attempted to find out which methods of instruction work best and, for those skills learned on the job, whether it is possible to integrate these into university coursework.

(3) To what extent do German candidates currently fulfill the requirements, and how do they measure up to their competitors from other countries? Our interview partners were requested to describe their experiences with Germans in the workplace and make general statements about their level of competency. This will be a somewhat brief section in our report, as the results are not empirically founded – different personal strengths and weaknesses cause difficulty in analyzing such findings, as most outcomes cannot be extrapolated to all or even most Germans.

(4) What can universities or other institutions of higher education do to pre-pare students for careers in this field in the most optimal way? By posing open questions on the possibilities for creating educational programs to qualify people for jobs at international organizations, we were able to answer this and other related questions, such as, "Does the education German univer-sities now offer to prepare students for this field of work compete on a global level?"

(5) How can existing degree programs for careers in international organiza-tions be improved or new programs designed to achieve these goals? We posed this question with all of our interview partners to obtain a wide variety of answers. Even those who currently administer study programs that are directly or indirectly related to this field of work had many ideas on what could be done differently or better along these lines. Several of the best practices listed below will deal specifically with recommendations for teaching these necessary competencies in a higher education degree pro-gram such as a master's.

The *structure* of this report alludes to the questions the research project attempts to answer. First of all, however, we will describe the methods and procedures with which we carried out our research (Chapter 2). Then, we will present the aggregated results of the labor market study (Chapter 3). The next two chapters contain the results of the curricular study, Chapter 4 for the United States, Chapter 5 for Western Europe. Fi-nally, we present our policy proposals or recommendations to politicians and educational administrators in Germany (Chapter 6). These are the measures we have determined that, if implemented, would help to im-prove Germany's representation in the personnel of international organi-zations. One can read this section without reading any of the others; how-ever, it is essential to read the entire report to understand the intercon-nections between our findings and our suggestions.

We understand that the approach and results of our research project might be controversial, in particular among those who have already de-signed educational programs similar to the ones we have examined. One could, for example, ask whether 'professional education' is a sensible idea for employees of international organizations, as their tasks and responsi-bilities include a wide variety of disciplines and fields. One could also ar-gue that existing educational opportunities suffice to qualify employees for work in this area. Another point of contention could be whether or not the skills we propose teaching in a master's or other study program should even be included in higher education, as these can also be learned on the job. We acknowledge these concerns and will address them in the following chapters of our report. We firmly believe, however, that it is not only possible but also desirable to reform or newly create educational offerings for this field using the recommendations and collection of best practices listed below, and it is our sincere hope that our findings will provide an incentive and opportunity to improve degree programs accordingly. This project will also help to advance the discussion of Germany's low representation in international organizations, as the current dialogue is too often based on opinions and seldom on solid empirical research. In the long run, it is feasible that the implementation of our ideas will actually alleviate the problem and contribute to an actual increase of the number of Germans successfully employed by international organizations. We would be pleased to see this occur, as it would make our efforts even more worthwhile.

2. Research Design

In the previous section, we have described how the two big questions that drove our research project – What does it take to work for an international organization and to succeed there? How can universities prepare their students for a career in international organizations? – and our parochial concern with Germany have led to five more specific research questions and objectives.

To achieve these objectives, two comprehensive studies were performed in the scope of the PROFIO project: a 'labor market study' and a 'curricular study'. On the one hand, we determined which knowledge, skills, and attitudes need to be developed for a successful application and job performance at international organizations and, on the other hand, we examined how study programs at higher education institutions in Germany and other countries already prepare students for international work. From the analysis of labor market demands and the examination of educational programs some general principles, or more specifically best practices, were drawn as guidelines for those responsible for design or redesign their educational programs.

The project combined two studies because we wanted a comprehensive analysis. Too frequently recommendations for educational programs reflect only interests of faculty, unverified requirements of the professions, or historic institutional emphases and interests. In a rapidly changing and expanding professional field such as the international public service, these will not suffice. Although curriculum design should not be governed by job descriptions and labor market demands alone, curriculum coordinators for professional education must be aware of the skills and knowledge professionals actually need in the workplace to ensure that the professional education provided is both more effective and more efficient with regard to students' employability. Therefore, to give proposals for future reforms in the German higher education system, it is inevitable to consider both the labor market demands and best practices in the education for international public service.

'Best practice' has been one of the buzzwords of public management for many years, but in our view, to search for 'best practices' is just a demand of common sense:

"It is only sensible to see what kinds of solutions have been tried in other jurisdictions, agencies, or locales. One looks for those that appear to have worked pretty well, tries to understand exactly how and why they might have worked, and evaluates their applicability to one's own situation. In many circles this process is known as best practices research."[20]

It should also be obvious that one must also take into consideration whether or not best practices are transferable to another country or system:

"Assuming that you have understood the essence of the generic smart practice very well, including its generic vulnerabilities, and have mapped the variety of supportive elements that could increase its odds of success, in the end, you must still ask: Assuming this practice is indeed smart in some contexts, is ours a context in which it can work well enough to warrant trying it? Answering this question intelligently entails looking at both the source contexts, where the practice appears to have worked well, and at your own target context, where it is being considered for adoption."[21]

In terms of transferability, it is clear that the educational systems and traditions in the U.S., Germany, France, and other countries in our study are different to some extent. We cannot go into detail here about the basic conditions and parameters in which higher education in these countries functions. There are countless sources of literature describing the history, structure, objectives, and principles of the different major systems. One often speaks of the "Humboldt ideal" when talking about German higher education, and the French model goes back to the times of Napoleon. The U.S., UK, Canada, Australia, and New Zealand all share the so-called "Anglo-Saxon" model, from which the bachelor-master-Ph.D. sequence is derived. Today, the Bologna Process is a movement toward the harmonization of higher education in 40 European countries.[22] This largely entails convergence with the Anglo-Saxon model in many dimensions. For now, it suffices to say that differences still exist between European and American degree programs, but that their standards and academic levels are mostly equal.

Last but not least, one must not overlook the eventuality that the best practice possible might not be practiced yet. In other words: even the best degree program out there (or the best teaching method, internship system, etc.) might still have room for improvement. After all, it is a genuine

---

[20] Bardach, E. (2000). *A practical guide for policy analysis: The eightfold path to more effective problem solving*. New York/London: Chatham House Publishers, p. 71.
[21] Ibid., p. 82.
[22] For more information, please see ec.europa.eu/education/policies/educ/bologna/bologna_en.html.

task of research not only to identify what works best, but also to say what might work even better.

2.1. The labor market study

The focus of the labor market study is to determine, among other things, the type of professional and non-professional qualifications successful applicants and employees possess and how they acquired them (in their studies, through extracurricular activities, at certain educational institutions, etc.). The study sought to collect detailed information on the educational and professional backgrounds of employees and to thereby gain insight into the recruitment process at international organizations and to understand which qualifications and skills are required by international organizations. Within the scope of the study the following international organizations were examined in more detail with regard to the goals described above:

– Organization for Security and Co-operation in Europe (OSCE)
– Institutions of the European Union
  – The General Secretariat of the Council of the European Union (GSC)
  – The European Commission
  – The European Parliament
  – The Committee of the Regions
– European Space Agency (ESA)
– United Nations Environment Programme (UNEP)
– World Bank[23].

In addition to these large-scale studies, we performed a smaller-scale study of the United agencies and programs in Kyrgyzstan: UNDP, UNFPA, UNICEF, UNAIDS, and UNODC.

There are various reasons why we chose to survey these international organizations. To consider the complexity of professional roles and task with which young academics might be confronted in their future professional life, different types or categories of international organizations were included in the survey. As international organizations have different goals, tasks, and instruments, it can be assumed that they require staff with diverse educational and professional backgrounds for a variety of jobs available. Therefore, to ensure that sufficient attention is paid to the diversity in the demands of the professional field, different types of international organizations were examined in this study. As mentioned in the

---

[23] The term "World Bank" refers specifically to two institutions: The International Bank for Reconstruction and Development (IRBD) and the International Development Association (IDA).

introduction, international organizations can be divided into various categories based on the type of public services law they apply. These are as follows:

- The United Nations System with its sub-organizations and special programs,
- The institutions of the European Communities (European Union),
- International finance organizations,
- Organizations with specialized tasks.

In our study we tried to examine at least one of each type of international organization. UNEP and ESA are understood as technical organizations with specialized tasks: UNEP serves as a focal point for environmental action within the UN System. Its main tasks are to facilitate international cooperation in all matters affecting the human environment; to ensure that environmental problems of wide international significance receive appropriate governmental consideration; and to promote the acquisition, assessment, and exchange of environmental knowledge. ESA is Europe's leading space science and technology organization. Its tasks are to define and put into effect a long-term European space policy of scientific research and technological development, and to encourage all member states to coordinate their national programs with those of the ESA. Studies on future projects, technological research, shared technical investments, information systems, and trainings programs are the ESA's basic activities. The OSCE was established to provide a multilateral forum for dialogue and negotiation in Europe. Further main priorities and tasks are in the fields of early warning, conflict prevention, crisis management and post-conflict rehabilitation. As a multilateral financial organization, the World Bank aims to combat poverty reduction and the improvement of living standards. It supports economic and social development projects around the world.

Furthermore, it was of particular interest to us to describe and compare the personnel structures and qualification requirements of international organizations in different socio-cultural and geo-political settings. For this reason, organizations located in both developing and industrialized countries were chosen to be examined in more detail. Working conditions, qualification requirements, and the employees' tasks and responsibilities at organizations based in a developing country may differ from those in an industrialized country.

Another criterion for making this selection included Germany's level of political interest in the organizations and/or the extremity of the difference between the percentage of employed Germans and the percent of

Germany's financial contribution to the total budget of the organization. As mentioned previously, according to the criterion of representation based on budgetary contribution, Germany is underrepresented in professional positions at the UNEP, OSCE, ESA and World Bank. Here, it is interesting to examine whether these organizations have set up specific qualification requirements which German applicants do not fulfill or whether there are other reasons for the low level of representation.

Overall, the comparative approach of the labor market study, or more specifically the comparative analysis of personnel structures and qualification requirements of different international organizations, helped us to identify similarities and differences in the educational and professional background of successful employees as well as in the required skills and qualification.

The methods used in the labor market study were a combination of quantitative and qualitative research techniques. In our view, this multi-method approach was the best means given the nature of the topic. As mentioned in the introduction to this report, there is very little empirical information available on the educational and professional backgrounds of employees at international organizations as well as the qualifications and skills they need for a successful application and job performance. In studies like that of PROFIO in which the subject matter under investigation is fairly undeveloped and requires basic and exploratory research, qualitative methods are essential to identify and define relevant terminology, variables, underlying concepts, and possible connections between phenomena which might be difficult to detect through other means. Exploring the complexity of individual educational and professional backgrounds as well as employees' perceptions and evaluations requires a focus on the individual. Qualitative interviews are a unique tool for detailed investigation of people's personal perspectives and for detailed subject coverage, as the exploratory and interactive nature of qualitative inquiry gives the research subjects the possibility to "describe their experiences in their own terms" in interaction with the researcher.[24]

Furthermore, qualitative methods were applied because interviews are seen as a particularly good means for the preparation of surveys: "The in-depth knowledge of social context acquired through qualitative research can be used to inform the design of survey questions for structured interviewing and self-completion questionnaires."[25] Here, the qualitative

---

[24] Ritchie, J. & Lewis, J. (2004). *Qualitative research practice: A guide for social science students and researchers*. London: Sage, p. 34.
[25] Bryman, A. (2004). *Social research methods* (2nd ed.). Oxford: University Press, p. 457.

Table 2.1. International Organizations examined in PROFIO study

Time frame	International organization	Research methods
Oct 2004 –Jan 2005	Organization for Security and Co-operation in Europe (OSCE), Vienna, Austria	exploratory interviews with HR managers Online survey with all contracted employees in the professional category – Population: 268 – Response rate: 43.4%
Apr 2005 – Jan 2006	European Union, Brussels, Belgium: – General Secretariat of the Council of the European Union – European Commission – European Parliament – Committee of the Regions	30 semi-structured interviews with: – employees of the EU Council Secretariat in the professional category; – employees of the European Commission, the European Parliament, and the Committee of the Regions in the professional category; and – successful candidates of the competition. Online survey with all employees of the EU Council Secretariat in the professional category – Population: 1376 – Response rate: 39.4%
Jul 2005	UN agencies and programs in Bishkek, Kyrgyzstan: UNDP, UNFPA, UNICEF, UNAIDS, and UNODC	12 semi-structured interviews with employees in the professional category
Jul – Dec 2005	European Space Agency (ESA)	22 semi-structured interviews with employees in the professional category at the European Space Operations Centre (ESOC) in Darmstadt, Germany, as well as at the European Space Research and Technology Centre (ESTEC) in Noordwijk, the Netherlands
Aug 2005 – Feb 2006	United Nations Environment Programme (UNEP), Nairobi, Kenya	20 semi-structured interviews with employees in the professional category
Jan – Apr 2006	World Bank, Washington, D.C., U.S.	27 semi-structured interviews with employees in the professional category

Source: Authors

method of interviewing was helpful for exploring and identifying terminology, concepts, or subjects for investigation before relevant questions
were constructed accordingly. Central themes that cut across the variety
of answers obtained through the open interview questions were used to
design the survey questions and categories of reply. Quantitative online
surveys were carried out to test if the results obtained through qualitative
interviewing apply to a larger group of employees.

The selection of the research population was done on the basis of the research questions. At almost all of the chosen organizations, we carried
out semi-structured, face-to-face interviews with human resource directors and/or staff members who are somehow involved in the selection
process of their organization, for example as part of an interview panel.
This particular category of staff was able to contribute relevant information on how the selection process functions and the decisions on the suitability of candidates are made, as well as which qualifications are required in the respective organization. Furthermore, to learn more about
the educational and professional backgrounds of staff in international organizations, we carried out interviews with successful employees working in the professional category in various sections or units of the organizations.[26]

Our interview participants came from a number of different countries
and regions. Such a diverse composition of the research population with
respect to national backgrounds helped us to compare different professional outlooks and experiences. As German citizens must compete with
applicants from other countries, it is not sufficient to examine the professional and educational backgrounds of successful German employees at
international organizations. Therefore, the education and professional experience of their colleagues from other countries was analyzed in detail
as well to determine whether there are patterns and/or differences in the
education of successful employees at international organizations. Our interviewees had an advanced university degree and professional work experience the in international public service. Finally, the interview participants differed in terms of sex and age.

The interviews were completed either in English or German. The quotes
made by German interviewees and used in this study were translated
into English. The number of interviews conducted was between ten and
thirty per organization.

---

[26] The selection of the interview participants was mainly done by the organizations examined according to our selection criteria. They provided the PROFIO research team with a
list of contact information.

Topic guides setting out the key topics and issues to be covered during the interview were created to ensure that all results can be combined and compared. The interview questions, or "topics", were derived from the research questions and stated objectives of the PROFIO study. However, the structure of the interviews was sufficiently flexible to permit topics to be covered in the order most suitable to the interviewee and to allow the researcher to be responsive to relevant issues raised spontaneously by the interviewee.

In each study, all interviews were recorded in order to be analyzed in detail at a later time. Each interview was transcribed in full length. This procedure was important for detailed analysis and to ensure that the interviewees' answers are captured in their own terms. When reviewing the interview transcripts, the research team identified main themes or categories under which the qualitative data was labeled and sorted. This process included a combination of multiple readings by more than one researcher and continual returning to the data until no further dimensions of the categories emerged. By applying these methods of data management, internal reliability was ensured as more than one member of the research team agreed about the main themes identified. The researchers tended to identify similar themes independently of each other. Once the categories within the data were identified, an index or "thematic framework" was developed describing both the recurrent categories and issues introduced into the interviews through the topic guide.[27] Following this method, the raw data was organized according to this index. Finally, in some studies, the qualitative data was compared, related, and contrasted to the quantitative data collected.

At the OSCE and the General Secretariat of the Council of the European Union, the qualitative data collected from the interviews was used to design large-scale online surveys.[28] For this purpose, the qualitative method of interviewing was helpful to cover a wide range of viewpoints and determine the ideal design of the survey. Although the survey design varied slightly among the organizations examined, the main focus was on the employees' educational backgrounds and the evaluation of the university

---

[27] The content of the index varied slightly depending on the international organization examined.

[28] The research team only obtained the permission to carry out an online survey from these two organizations. The online surveys were carried out using professional, field-tested software developed by the German company Rogator (http://www.rogator.de). During the period of time in which the surveys were available online, hosting and data storage was provided by the software company. The company does not relay any information to third parties and guarantees data security on its server system that is up to date with the latest developments in the IT sector.

education concerning the acquisition of competencies necessary for a successful job performance and selection processes. Therefore, the online questionnaires mainly contained questions about the educational and professional background, internships, experience abroad, and skills and qualifications needed to work at the organization. In each study, all interview and survey participants were assured of the complete confidentiality of their responses in keeping with professional research standards.[29] Table 2.5gives an overview of the research methods applied at the international organizations selected.

Following the analysis of the quantitative and qualitative data and other information gathered in each sub-project of the labor market study the research team prepared reports from its findings.[30] The reports were submitted to the study participants for comment.

In this report, the main findings of all studies carried out are summarized and compared to each other to identify patterns in the education and skills of successful employees at the international organization chosen and map the diversity thereof. Furthermore, recommendations given by professionals for educational institutions for curriculum development are summarized. The statements by interview participants used throughout the report were selected because they exemplify the opinions held by the majority of our interview participants.

2.2. The curricular study

In the second part of the project, the curricular study, a comparative analysis of study programs in Germany and abroad that prepare people for careers at international organizations was carried out to identify "best practices" concerning professional education for international public service. Here, the content and composition of the study programs' curricula, curricular development and evaluation processes, teaching methods, extracurricular and career development activities, the faculty composition, and cooperation agreements were the focus of the comparative analysis.

---

[29] The PROFIO research team guaranteed data protection of standards under the terms of European and German law. Protection of the privacy of all participants was ensured through anonymous data collection, data aggregation, and analysis on an aggregated data level. No connection was made between the persons taking part in the study and the answers they have given. No third party had access to the data set. It was further guaranteed that the collected data will be used only for the purpose of the research project PROFIO.

[30] All reports can be found online at http://www.db-thueringen.de. For titles and specific URLs see Preface, p. 6.

This part of the project was divided into the following sub-projects:
- a study on educational programs at professional schools in the United States;
- a study on educational programs at higher education institutions in German speaking countries;
- a study on educational programs at higher education institutions in France, Belgium, and in the parts of Switzerland not covered in the other study.

The selection of the educational institutions and study programs was primarily done on the basis of the research findings of the labor market study. The studies carried out at the international organizations showed that higher education institutions provided professionals – regardless of their nationality – with the knowledge, relevant research methods, and techniques specific to the subject area/discipline studied. However, the acquisition of all other professional competencies required for a success-ful application and work performance at international organizations (in particular social-communicative, implementation-related, and personal competencies) mainly took place outside the higher education institu-tions. Therefore, according to employees at international organizations, universities could do much better in preparing young academics for the workplace.[31] The necessity for a practice- and internationally oriented as well an interdisciplinary degree program which focuses on the develop-ment of professional competencies for the international public service and that thus prepares students effectively for work in international organiza-tions was identified.

With regard to this result, we decided to examine on the one hand graduate degree programs with a strong practice-based curriculum for professional education at professional schools in the United States in more detail. The selected programs focus on professional competency de-velopment targeted to students' employability in the national and inter-national public service. Moreover, they have strong reputations in train-ing students for this professional field. They received the highest ranks for their excellence in this field in the U.S. News and World Report rank-ings.[32] Table 2.2 gives an overview of the programs examined in the U.S.

Furthermore, these schools and programs have existed for many years and thus have a solid foundation of training students for this professional

[31] For more details on the research finding of the labor market study, please refer to Chap-ter 3.
[32] Hartigan Shea, R. (Ed.). (2004). *America's Best Graduate Schools* (2005 ed.). Washington, D.C.: U.S. News and World Report.

field, whereas in other countries they are still in the process of being developed, as in the case of in Germany. Although the higher education sector in Germany is currently undergoing major transformations as a result of the Bologna Process, it is clear that degree programs with a strong focus on professional education for the field of international relations, international public affairs, public policy, or even public administration rarely exist.[33] German universities have tended to develop curricula with a strong theoretical content and minimum reference to practicability and employability. The concept of professional schools in the field of public policy has not yet become fully rooted in Germany and other European countries. In Germany, for instance, only two professional schools which provide programs for professional education in the field of public policy exist: the Hertie School of Governance and the Erfurt School of Public Policy.[34] Education for professions (or at least for the "higher" ones) still remains within the university and does not really focus on practicability and employability.

Therefore, for the purpose of this study, it is essential to learn more about professional education for international or national public service as it is done at many professional schools in the U.S. Attention is focused on the measures that professional schools use to deal with a problem similar to the Germans'. When drawing on current experience in other countries to improve the German higher education system, it is important to take into account differences in the higher education system. Higher education institutions in the countries examined represent very different stages of institutional development. In general, higher education systems in the U.S and Germany are influenced by different cultural, social, political, and economic value systems, assumptions, and thought patterns.[35] Therefore, assuming that the "best practices" identified in the U.S. are smart in some contexts, the process of application of these practices in the German higher education system should not be left out.

In addition and with regard to the employees' selection processes at international organizations, it is apparent that German young professionals

---

[33] Robert Bosch Stiftung. (1999). *Stuttgarter Appell an Bund und Länder, Wissenschaft und Wirtschaft: Für mehr Internationalität in Bildung, Ausbildung und Personalpolitik.* Retrieved July 5, 2007 from www.berlinerinitiative.de/materialien/1999_stuttgarter_appell.pdf
This is a joint declaration of the German Council on Foreign Relations, German Institute for International and Security Affairs, and the Robert Bosch Foundation with recommendations on how to improve the international focus of schools and universities as well as the German presence in international organizations.
[34] This was accurate at the time when we carried out the research project. In the meantime, some more schools have been started at public as well as private universities.
[35] See introduction for more information on differences in higher education systems.

Table 2.2. Examined Programs at U.S. Professional Schools

Educational institution	Study program(s)
Maxwell School (Syracuse University) [Ranked #1 in 2005 in the U.S. News & World Report ranking of Top Public Affairs Schools]	– Master of Public Administration – M.A. in International Relations – Master of Public Administration & M.A. In International Relations (joint degree)
John F. Kennedy School of Government (Harvard University) [Ranked #2]	– Master of Public Policy – Master of Public Policy/Urban Planning – Master of Public Administration – Master in Public Administration/International Development – Mid-Career Master in Public Administration
School of Public Affairs and Environmental Sciences (Indiana University – Bloomington) [Ranked #3]	– Master of Public Affairs
H. John Heinz III School of Public Policy & Management (Carnegie Mellon University) [Ranked #8]	– Master of Public Policy and Management – Master of Information Security Policy and Management – Master of Public Management
Gerald R. Ford School of Public Policy (University of Michigan) [Ranked #8]	– Master of Public Policy – Master of Public Administration
School of Public Affairs and School of International Service (American University) [Ranked #10]	– MAIA Comparative and Regional Studies – MAIA International Economic Relations – MAIA International Politics – MAIA U.S. Foreign Policy – M.A. International Communication – M.A. International Development – M.S. Development Management – M.A. International Peace and Conflict Resolution – M.A. Global Environmental Politics
Edmund A. Walsh School of Foreign Service and BMW Center for German & European Studies (Georgetown University) [Ranked #17]	– Master of Science in Foreign Service – Master of Arab Studies – Master of Eurasian, Asian, and East European Studies – Master of German and European Studies – Master of Latin American Studies – Master of Security Studies
Rockefeller College of Public Affairs & Policy (State University of New York at Albany) [Ranked #10]	– Master of Public Administration – Master in Public Affairs and Public Policy

Educational institution	Study program(s)
Graduate School of Public and International Affairs (University of Pittsburgh) [Ranked #21]	– Master of Public Administration – Master of Public and International Affairs – Master of International Development – Master of Public Policy and Management
School of Public Policy and Management (The Ohio State University) [Ranked #42]	– Master of Public Administration – Master of Arts in Public Policy and Management – Master of Art in Arts Policy and Administration
Irving B. Harris Graduate School of Public Policy Studies (University of Chicago) [Ranked #17]	– Master of Public Policy – Master of Science in Environmental Science and Policy – One-year Master of Arts (A.M.)
Robert F. Wagner Graduate School of Public Service (New York University) [Ranked #17]	– Master of Public Administration – Master of Urban Planning – Master of Science in Management
Paul A. Nitze School of Advanced International Studies (Johns Hopkins University) [Ranked #26]	– M.A. in International Relations – Master of International Public Policy
Elliott School of International Affairs and School of Public Policy and Public Administration (George Washington University) [Ranked #10]	Elliott: – M.A. in International Affairs; Asian Studies; European and Eurasian Studies; Latin American and Hemispheric Studies; International Development Studies; International Trade and Investment Policy; International Science and Technology Policy; Security Policy Studies – Master in International Policy and Practice SPPPA: – Master of Public Administration – Master of Public Policy
Fletcher School of Law and Diplomacy (Tufts University) [Not ranked]	– Master of Arts and Diplomacy – Master of Arts – Global Master of Arts

Source: Authors

compete against highly qualified students from other countries. Therefore, it was essential not only to examine German universities and their
study programs, but also to compare them with the training and education students obtain at higher education institutions in other countries, in
particular in industrialized countries.

Finally, some of the programs chosen to be examined in the U.S. were
mentioned in the labor market study as being very good means to prepare oneself for work in international organizations. Generally, it is important to underline that in the scope of this study, we analyzed a highly
selected number of study programs available in the field of interest. As
Derick and Jennifer Brinkerhoff indicated in their book *Making a Career in
International Public Service*, there are various graduate degree options in
the U.S. which provide different kinds of professional education for international work. In general, they described three types of degree programs:
area studies (e.g., Latin American, African, Asian, Middle Eastern, and
European Studies), technical sectors (e.g., health, education, environment,
agriculture, economics), and generalist degrees (e.g., international affairs,
public administration, public policy, and business administration).[36] In
this study, the emphasis was placed on generalist degree programs in the
fields of international affairs, public administration and public policy.

In addition to the study on degree programs at professional schools in
the U.S., studies on educational programs in Germany and other European countries that aim to prepare students for international work were
performed to identify "best practices" concerning education for international public service and compare them with the results obtained through
the study in the U.S. As mentioned before, in European countries the concept of professional education for national or international public service
has not yet become fully rooted, although a small number of degree program in the fields of public policy and governance have been developed
recently. Furthermore, there are no rankings available in Germany or
other European countries that list study programs and higher education
institutions with regard to professional competency development for the
field of international relations, international public affairs, public policy,
or public administration.[37] Therefore, in the scope of this study we ana-

---

[36] Brinkerhoff, D. W., & Brinkerhoff, J. M. (2005). *Working for change: Making a career in international public service*. Bloomfield: Kumarian Press, p. 96.
[37] For Germany, the Berliner Initiative has created an overview of study programs with an
international orientation. As there is no information on the practical orientation and competency development provided, this list was not sufficient for the purpose of this study.
Meanwhile, the German Academic Exchange Service has published a "Top 10 of international master-programs at German universities" (www.daad.de/presse/de/2006/8.1.1_

lyzed a highly selected number of heterogeneous educational programs in the field of international and European affairs, public administration and public policy and public or global governance which provide to some sort of professional education for international public service. However, although we examined a wide variety of study programs, we tried to ensure that the selection of study programs was done on the basis of the research findings of the labor market study.

All graduate degree programs examined have some sort of practice-based and internationally oriented curriculum and focus on professional competency development targeted to students' employability. Fundamentally, although we examined a heterogeneous selection of educational programs, most of the crucial categories (e.g. practicability, international orientation, and interdisciplinarity) are relevant to all programs so that a systematic analysis of best practices was possible even if not all programs aim similarly to qualify students for the international public service. Furthermore, some of the programs were mentioned by many professionals as very good means to prepare students for international work. Table 2.3 shows the study programs analyzed in German-speaking countries. Table 2.4 gives an overview of the educational programs examined in Switzerland, France, and Belgium.

The comparative approach of the curricular study served as an important tool for establishing best practices concerning professional education for international organizations. Through cross-national comparison, we not only identified best practices in the German higher education system, but we also examined and explained similarities, differences, and features of a selected number of Western European and American study programs which aim to prepare students for international work. In doing so, we hoped to address at least the second part of the deficit identified by Ulrich Bopp in his foreword to the report of the work of the Berliner Initiative in the year 2004:

"An exhaustive discussion between high-profile representatives of the current administrative practice and the higher-education institutions ready to reform concerning the demands placed on future administrative leaders has not yet taken place in Germany. The experiences of the excellent American, British, and French professional schools are hardly taken note of and reflected upon."[38]

4106_liste.pdf, retrieved July 25, 2007). Furthermore, the Center for Higher Education Development (CHE) develops a general university ranking every year.
[38] Berliner Initiative. 2004. Ergebnisbericht 2003. Berlin, p. 6.

Table 2.3. Educational Programs examined in German-speaking Countries

Educational institution	Study program(s)
European School of Governance (EUSG), Berlin	Advanced Training for Public Servants
Free University of Berlin, Humboldt-Universität zu Berlin, and Technische Universität Berlin	Postgraduate Program in European Studies
Hertie School of Governance, Berlin	Master of Public Policy
Humboldt University of Berlin, Free University of Berlin, University of Potsdam	Master of Arts in International Relations
Center for European Integration Studies, University of Bonn	Master of European Studies
German Development Institute, Bonn	Postgraduate Program
University of Bremen and the International University of Bremen	Master of Arts in International Relations: Global Governance and Social Theory
Erfurt School of Public Policy, University of Erfurt	Master of Public Policy
Zeppelin University, Friedrichshafen	M.A. Public Management and Governance
University of Hamburg (Erasmus Mundus Program)	Master of European Law and Economics
University of Konstanz	Master of Public Policy and Management
University of Potsdam	– Master of Public Management – Master of Global Public Policy
Europa-Institut of Saarland University, Saarbrücken	Master of European Law
German University of Administrative Sciences, Speyer	Master of Public Administration
Eberhard Karls University of Tübingen	– Master of Advanced International Studies – Master of Peace Research and International Politics
Diplomatic Academy of Vienna, Austria	– Special Program in International Studies – Diploma Program – Master of Advanced International Studies
University of Vienna, Austria	Master in European Studies
University of St. Gallen, Switzerland	Master of Arts in International Relations and Governance

Source: Authors

Following the selection of the degree programs to be examined in the U.S. and Western Europe, detailed information on the programs and educational institutions was collected by reviewing the internet sites and brochures received from the institutions. In a second stage, semi-structured, face-to-face, and/or telephone interviews were carried out with program directors, faculty members, and directors of career services at the educational institutions. In all studies performed, we used the same method of data collection to ensure the quality and comparability of the data collected during the interviews. As with the labor market study interview guidelines setting out the key topics and issues to be covered during the interview were created. The design of degree programs' curricula and how they educate their students for careers at international organizations was focus of the analysis. Best practices concerning professional education for international organizations in the U.S. were identified and later related and compared to the best practices in study programs at higher education institutions in Germany, Austria, Switzerland, France, and Belgium.

All interviews were conducted in English or German. The interviews were recorded in order to be analyzed in detail at a later time. Each interview was transcribed in full length. Concerning data management and analysis, the same methods were applied as we used in the labor market study.[39] Main themes or categories were identified into which the qualitative data was subsequently placed. From the studies in Germany, Austria, Switzerland, France and Belgium, reports on the findings were prepared.[40]

In addition to these large-scale studies, smaller-scale studies were done to provide a general overview of the degree programs available in three other Anglo-Saxon countries: Great Britain, Australia, and New Zealand. Here, information provided by all public and private universities in Great Britain, Australia, and New Zealand on the World Wide Web was reviewed, and all relevant degree programs that aim to train students for careers in international organizations were listed. Databases with basic information on the selected programs (e.g., objective, duration, contact

---

[39] The content of the index varied depending on the study carried out.
[40] Hoelscher, P., Herz, D., Dortants & Linke, K. (2005). *Studie zu Studiengängen und Bildungsangeboten Frankreichs, Belgiens und der Schweiz, die für eine Karriere in internationalen Organisationen ausbilden.* Retrieved from http://nbn-resolving.de/urn/resolver.pl?urn=urn:nbn:de:gbv: 547-200601430; Krause, C., Tschirschwitz, C., Herz, D., Dortants, S. L. & Linke, K. (2006). *Bericht über Studiengänge und Bildungsangebote im deutschsprachigen Raum, die für eine Karriere in internationalen Organisationen ausbilden.* Retrieved from http://nbn-resolving.de/urn/resolver.pl?urn= urn:nbn:de:gbv:547-200601418

person) were created. Furthermore, a small-scale study on educational programs in Russia was conducted. Here, interviews with program coordinators at the Moscow State Institute of International Relations (MGIMO University) and the Diplomatic Academy of the Ministry of Foreign Affairs of the Russian Federation were conducted to obtain information on how these institutions prepare students for international work. Table 2.5 gives an overview of the research methods applied in each project of the curricular study.

In addition to analyzing the study programs, we also examined one of the most renowned and ambitious German scholarship programs that aims to qualify students for international work. The objective of the "Carlo Schmid Program for Internships in International Organizations and EU institutions" is to improve the German representation of personnel in international organizations as well as the general job prospects of interested and highly qualified young scholars in the field of international politics and administration. Within the context of an internship program, it aims to familiarize the students with the work and the problems in the field of international administration and also to enhance their intercultural competence. Furthermore, accompanying measures such as preparation and post-processing seminars should improve the opportunities of qualified young people for a future career in the international field.

Table 2.4. Educational Programs examined in Switzerland, France, and Belgium

Educational institution	Study program(s)
Collège d'Europe, Bruges, Belgium	– Master of European Economic Studies – Master of European Legal Studies – Master of European Political and Administrative Studies – Master of EU External Relations and Diplomacy
Institut Universitaire de Hautes Etudes Internationales, Geneva, Switzerland	– Master in International Affairs – Master in International Studies
L'école des Hautes Etudes Commerciales – IOMBA, Geneva, Switzerland	International Organizations M.B.A.
Institut des Sciences Politiques, Paris, France	Master of Public Administration

Source: Authors

Table 2.5. Research methods of the curricular study

Time frame	Project	Research methods
January 2005 – September 2005	Study on educational programs at higher educational programs in Great Britain, Australia, New Zealand, and Russia	– Some semi-structured, face-to-face interviews were carried out with program directors and faculty members. – Internet research, document review, and correspondence with program coordinators.
December 2005 – February 2006	Study on educational programs at higher education institutions in Switzerland, France, and Belgium	– 10 semi-structured, face-to-face and telephone interviews were carried out with program directors and faculty members. – Internet research, document review, and correspondence with program coordinators.
December 2005 – June 2006	Study on educational programs at professional schools in the United States	– 23 semi-structured, face-to-face interviews were carried out with program directors, faculty members, and directors of career services. – Internet research, document review, and correspondence with program coordinators.
December 2005 – June 2006	Study on educational programs at higher education institutions in German-speaking countries	– 19 semi-structured, face-to-face interviews were carried out with program directors and faculty members. – Internet research, document review, and correspondence with program coordinators.

Source: Authors

The reason why we chose to examine the "Carlo Schmid Program" (CSP for short) in this study is that we were first of all interested in the extent to which it prepares young scholars for functions in international organizations or provides an entry opportunity to these. Through the analysis of this scholarship program we were able to obtain information to what extent internship programs are entry-level opportunities for young German scholars and whether they are an important component in the process of professional competency development. Second, we wanted to know more about the educational backgrounds and further career paths of current scholarship recipients and alumni, as well as the application and selection process for such a scholarship. As another renowned German scholarship program, the "Stiftungskolleg für internationale Auf-

50

gaben", has already been evaluated concerning how it prepares and supports young German scholars for a career at international organizations, we decided to examine the "Carlo Schmid Program" in more detail instead. A multi-method approach – a combination of qualitative and quantitative research methods – was applied to achieve the stated objectives. In the first stage of the study, semi-structured interviews were conducted with members of the selection committee and with applicants.

Topic guides were developed to ensure that the results could be combined and compared. The data were collected during the selection interviews for the CSP 2005/06 program in Bonn. In a second stage, an online survey with program alumni and scholarship recipients of the year 2004/05 was carried out. A questionnaire was created that contained questions covering the following topics: experiences of those participating in the CSP, educational background, current state of employment, future career plans, basic data about one's participation in the CSP, sociodemographic information, and work and future development of the CSP Network. A report on the results of the study was prepared.[41] Table 2.6 summarizes the research methods applied.

Table 2.6. Research methods of study on Carlo Schmid Program

Scholarship program	Research methods
Carlo Schmid Program for Internships in International Organizations and EU Institutions	Semi-structured interviews with: 42 applicants, CSP program year 2005/06 7 members of the selection committee Online survey with all with program alumni and scholarship recipients of the year 2004/05 Population: about 240 Response rate: 71.6%

Source: Authors

In the following chapters of this final report, the results of both the labor market study and curricular study are summarized and compared with the objective of highlighting best practices in preparing young scholars for international work and to thus develop policy proposals for future reforms in the higher education system in Germany.

[41] Studzinski, J., Herz, D., Schattenmann, M., Dortants, S. L. & Linke, K. (2005). *Evaluation of the "Carlo-Schmid-Program for internships in international organizations and EU institutions"*. http://nbn-resolving.de/urn/resolver.pl?urn=urn:nbn:de:gbv:547-200601395

3. Results of the labor market study

In this section the results of the labor market study are presented. As mentioned previously, in this sub-project of the PROFIO study, we took a closer look at the recruiting techniques of international organizations as well as the qualification profiles and determinants for the success of their applicants and employees. This involved gathering, describing, and analyzing empirical data on recruitment processes and success factors for being hired and promoted at international organizations. Here, we not only explored how the recruitment and promotion process is supposed to work according to human resource directors or the general recruiting policies of the international organizations examined. As some interview partners were either program (hiring) managers or staff members involved in selecting personnel, for example as a member of an interview panel, we were able to gain more insight into the selection process in general and gather more detailed information on the evaluation criteria and tools used for selecting candidates in particular. Therefore, the comments presented in this section provide a perspective on how recruitment actually functions at the international organizations examined rather than recapitulate the "official" picture of how it should be in the "ideal case" or according to human resources policies.

In addition, we collected qualitative and quantitative data on the employees' educational and professional backgrounds. We were mainly interested in the subjects they studied, from which educational institutions they earned their degrees, how they evaluate their education, and where they worked prior to their current place of employment. The data collected was compared, related, and contrasted to identify patterns in the educational or professional backgrounds of successful employees and map the diversity thereof. Here, we not only determined what type of education and professional experience is required by international organizations. This further allowed us to identify competencies necessary for successful application and job performance. Moreover, using the employees' evaluation of their university education, we were able to identify whether or not educational programs actually provided the employees with the necessary qualifications. In this context, we collected suggestions for educational institutions on how to best prepare students for work in the international arena.

52

3.1.   Educational background

One formal and substantive requirement for positions in the professional category at the international organizations examined in this study is an advanced university degree (master's degree or equivalent).[42] Therefore, it is not a surprise that almost all employees who participated in our study earned at least a master's degree. The following comments show that staff members responsible for selecting suitable candidates regard a graduate university education, leading up to either a master's degree or Ph.D. as a "very important" qualification for professional posts in their organizations:

"Secondly, which is also a very important criterion is the diploma that people bring in. There it is very important for us that they have a Master's degree or higher. The Master's degree or Ph.D. in science, for instance, in the science directorate we are specifically looking for Ph.D.s for instance. So they look for very highly educated specialists. (Human Resources staff member at ESA)

"And that is, I think, a Master's level degree the minimum level required if you want to advance to any level in the U.N. Maybe officials who are civil servants from the UN who are slightly older would be able to progress for the BA only but I think at present it is almost impossible to expect to have a career with no sort of limitation and not have a Master's. That is for sure." (Human Resources staff member at UNEP)

Generally, for the OSCE, ESA, UNEP, and the institutions of the European Union, a master's degree is regarded as completely sufficient for a successful application and career development in the respective organization. However, our study conducted at the World Bank has shown that a Ph.D. appears to give candidates and higher-level staff a comparative advantage in recruitment and promotion processes, although it is not regarded as a formal requirement specified in human resource policies. According to the professionals interviewed at the World Bank, a Ph.D. demonstrates the ability to conduct quality research and publish, which are considered important qualities given the World Bank's emphasis on generating and disseminating its own research to client countries as well as the development community. When compared to people with a master's degree, candidates who earned a Ph.D. are said to be able to pursue quality research and thus go beyond the World Bank's day-to-day operational business:

"A Ph.D. in anything is helpful for being recruited, because there is something, maybe you know this yourself, the person who has stopped at the master's stage has not jumped over the barrel. There is something about the person who commit them-

[42] Some international organizations may accept candidates with a first degree (e.g., B.A.) with a combination of relevant academic qualifications and extensive experience as well.

selves to going all the way, getting the analytical skills, writing the dissertation. It is just a sign of discipline and a structured mind. Somebody who can actually jump over barrel after barrel after barrel and get to the end of the education system. That is number one, a Ph.D. That does not mean that there are not good master's people in the world. There are, but they cannot have that extra edge that is needed."(Human Resources staff member at the World Bank)

"I think I was hired because I have all the degrees that you have to have. A Ph.D. is very well liked here."(Staff member at the World Bank)

"A Ph.D. is certainly useful for entry." (Human Resources staff member at the World Bank)

Aside from the advantage that candidates with a Ph.D. might have in higher-level staff recruitment, professionals at the World Bank also addressed the importance of a Ph.D. with respect to promotions within the organization. They suggested that a Ph.D. is helpful in moving up the career ladder. The following comments refer to the positive relationship between a Ph.D. and the probability of getting promoted or "moving upwards" within the World Bank:

"In the mid term, if you want to apply for a managerial position, I probably think that it [Ph.D.] is also useful again when you present yourself." (Staff member at the World Bank)

"I do have lot of operational experience, but for management positions, that is not enough. Because here at the World Bank the analytical work is very important. So there is something probably missing that will keep me. Here I could probably move up one more. But I wonder if I could be a manager, because inside the bank it is very important to have publications and it helps to have a Ph.D." (Staff member at the World Bank)

"Without a Ph.D. you can get in as a consultant. But if you don't have a Ph.D., I do not think you can move upwards." [...] Right now to get in the Bank, you need to have a Ph.D. if you want to make a career" (Human Resources staff member at the World Bank)

In the PROFIO study, we were further interested in whether international organizations tend to hire staff from specific schools and universities. Our study at the World Bank largely supported the assumption that the organization exhibits an institutional bias toward degree programs at American and British universities. In the view of several professionals at this organization, an Anglo-Saxon degree can be helpful for being hired, as the following comment shows:

"So they [applicants] might not be US citizens, but they have studied in the US. They have this academic background that we are attracted to. They come from a multicultural environment and they had some exposure and their thesis, their work is focused, because they have a certain degree of advice from their professors. [...] In a

54

certain way that can only give more chances to the students, more exposure to what they are trying to do."(Human Resources staff member at the World Bank)

There might be different reasons for this bias toward Anglo-Saxon higher education institutions at the World Bank. One reason that was mentioned by interviewees was that American and British institutions, in particular the U.S. professionals schools in the field of public policy, tend to better prepare students for the professional world. In comparison, the German system lacks or is perceived to be lacking degree programs that provide students with professional competency development. (A more detailed evaluation of the German higher education system will be given in section 3.8.)

Another reason might be reputation. Several professionals as well as hiring managers suggested that staff is often recruited from prestigious universities, especially Ivy League schools and reputable British universities. However, in spite of the World Bank's suggested tendency to hire from specific Anglo-Saxon universities, there appears to be willingness to diversify along this dimension; that is, to increase staff coming from other educational traditions.[43] A shared rationale among several professionals points to diversity as an important objective to recruit across a variety of universities:

"We do try to avoid recruiting only from certain universities, because we know that this is not healthy for the organization. And we are doing better than we used to, because at least we are aware of it. But it is not easy, because sometimes we find the best people in the best schools. But we try to give space to schools which have more recent master's in development, economics, or other issues that are relevant for us. So we try to diversify this and not to recruit only from certain U.S schools or the London School of Economics."(Staff member at the World Bank)

"When we recruit people, they very often come from certain schools that are in the top positions in the different rankings, but we do try to diversify through outreach activities. [...] We do not have any objectives that we recruit anybody form Yale or Columbia. That is not our goal. It is not easy, because at the senior level, decision makers in an organization, maybe they do not come from a diverse background, so we try to push for a diverse academic background, but the top is not as diverse as we would like." (Staff member at the World Bank)

Despite these attempts to diversify, the World Bank still seems to exhibit a certain institutional bias toward particular higher education systems and universities with regard to recruitment and promotion decisions, something that was not identified at the other international organizations examined. At the OSCE, ESA, UNEP, and the institutions of the European

---

[43] The World Bank recently created an internal Task Force on Diversity and Inclusion to address this issue, among many others.

Union, staff is recruited from a range of different universities all over the world. However, there too some hiring managers mentioned the professional schools in the U.S. as very good means to prepare oneself for a career in their organizations, as they provide practically and internationally oriented postgraduate education.

Although an advanced university degree is regarded by all hiring managers or staff members who are involved in the selection process of their organization as a substantive requirement for any professional position, some of them stressed that it should not be overestimated, as it does not tell much about the candidates' personality and professional competencies necessary for a successful performance on the job. Here, the importance of professional experience as another substantive qualification requirement besides university education was mentioned at all international organizations examined in this study. Extensive professional work experience contributes to the candidates' professional development and expertise needed for a successful performance on the job. According to many professionals involved in recruiting staff, the longer the professional record, the less important the university education is for selection decisions. Some of them also said that extensive relevant work experience could "replace" not only a master's degree but also a Ph.D. Therefore, a university degree is often regarded as a more "formal" requirement than a criterion that really affects selection decision for higher professional positions, as the following statements made by staff responsible for recruiting personnel show in an exemplary manner:

"Of course, one of the criteria – in fact, what they call a professional background – is a master's degree. I'm not sure if that is a very good criterion, because a master's degree doesn't make you qualified in itself. But at the end of the day, on the paper, they have to put some minimum standard in terms of what is required, and that is just a requirement."(Human Resources staff member at UNEP)

"I think one of the things that is unfair is that in recent recruitment processes that I have seen that the emphasis is on education, you must have a certain level of education, you must have a master's degree, which I think is counterproductive, because there are a lot of useless master's degree out there, which are completely theoretical, which focus on macroeconomics issues like trade issues. They are important in explaining poverty, but they are not important in enabling people to have the tools to manage and design projects which can get people out of poverty."(Human Resources staff member at UNDP, Kyrgyzstan)

"It's not a Ph.D. that's going to equip you for the workplace, and I've seen a lot of people who have a fantastic academic education, but they don't have the cap on in the workplace." (Human Resources staff member at the GSC)

"Also a lot of developing country experience could replace a Ph.D. It is not necessary that everyone has a Ph.D., but if you have a lot of relevant developing country experience a Ph.D. is not necessarily needed. There are a lot of people who have a master's degree." (Human Resources staff member at the World Bank)

However, regardless of the importance of work experience for professional positions, a graduate degree remains an important qualification requirement at the international organizations examined, in particular for entry-level positions.

When looking now at the educational background of professionals in international organizations, it is apparent that most of them have studied and hold a master's degree, as Table 3.1 shows. Out of the 26 interview participants at the World Bank, ten hold Ph.D.s, 15 have Master's degrees and one has a Bachelor's degree.[44]

Table 3.1. Highest university degree of employees at GSC and OSCE

Highest degree obtained	GSC	OSCE
	n=506	n=109
Ph.D. (or comparable degree)	11.5 %	13.8 %
Master (or comparable degree)	68.8 %	61.5 %
Bachelor (or comparable degree)	12.4 %	16.5 %
Other	6.1 %	2.7 %
None	1.2 %	5.5 %
Total	100 %	100 %

Source: Authors' survey data
Notes: Professional categories only

In the PROFIO study we further hoped to determine which fields of study are required by the international organizations. As the organizations have different goals, tasks, and instruments, it can be assumed that their staff is recruited from a variety of different academic fields. UNEP and ESA are technical organizations with specific activities: UNEP serves as a focal point for environmental action within the UN System, and ESA is Europe's leading space science and technology organization. With regard to their core activities, these organizations recruit staff with expertise in the disciplines of environmental and natural sciences and engi-

---

[44] Two respondents have postgraduate degrees in addition to their Master's degree. The staff with a Bachelor's degree holds a non-network positions and has additional years of postgraduate schooling, with a focus on technical skills

neering.[45] Therefore, hiring managers of these organizations stressed that expertise in a subject area or discipline related to the organizations' core activities is regarded as a success factor for recruitment, as the following statements show in an exemplarily manner:

"Most of our jobs are rather specific. And we require recruiting somebody who has got expertise in fresh water in marine areas or we are recruiting somebody who has got expertise in publication processes. Whatever it happens to be, they are quite specific. [...] Those kinds of things are always considered in the process, but the type and range and in-depth expertise that they have developed is very important." (Human Resources staff member at UNEP)

"For some levels you do need very specific qualifications and very specific experience like if you are dealing with water, then you really need to have a background in water science and then the specific experience that you can adapt or replicate or transform into other environments, in other cultures, in other societies." (Human Resources staff member at UNEP)

"Approximately 70 percent of our employees are from the area of science and engineering. The majors we recruit are [...] mechanical engineers, electrical engineers, computer scientists, physicists, mathematicians, and in the area of space science, astronomers and astrophysicists." (Human Resources staff member at ESA)

However, at UNEP and ESA there are also professional posts in other sectors, such as project management, policy development and implementation, financial administration, technical services, communications, and human resources. For these sectors expertise in other subjects is needed as well. Professionals involved in recruiting staff at ESA and UNEP described it as follows:

"Nowadays [we would look for] a Master's in Business Administration, Financial Management, Management, those areas.... [...] So, in the administrative areas, that is more the driving force." (Human Resources staff member at UNEP)

"We would be looking for someone with that legal, because you know we have to look at the decisions of the governing, you know we have rules of procedure. Sometimes they require very legalistic interpretation. So, we would be looking for lawyers, we would be looking for this international cooperation experience, somebody who has studied international cooperation or international whatever."(Human Resources staff member at UNEP)

"Now, more and more, especially for some positions, also managerial knowledge is important. In fact, even accounting knowledge is now starting to be important in some positions" (Human Resources staff member at ESA)

---

[45] ESA. (2006). *Careers at ESA*. Retrieved July 5, 2006, from www.esa.int/SPECIALS/Careers_at_ESA/SEMV1TXO4HD_0.html and Secretariat, U.N. (2002). Secretary General's bulletin ST/A1/2002/4: Administrative Instructions. Staff Selection System, United Nations Secretariat.

Table 3.2. Subjects studied by professionals at UNEP

Frequency	Subjects
mentioned very often	– Business and economics (accounting, finance, marketing, management studies, etc.) – Engineering (electrical engineering, environmental engineering) – Natural sciences (biology, chemistry, geology, physics, geography, environmental science) – Humanities (history, literature, philosophy, religion, anthropology) – Education
mentioned often	– Communication studies (journalism, public relations, media) – Political science – Social and behavioral sciences (psychology, sociology, social work) – Law
mentioned less often	– International studies (international affairs, international relations) – Public affairs (public policy, public administration, public management) – Modern and classical languages

Source: Authors' survey data.
Notes: Some interviewees mentioned more than one subject.

Many hiring managers at UNEP and ESA stressed that regardless of the job to be carried out, expertise in economics and budgeting, management and policy analysis is becoming a more relevant criterion for any professional position at ESA and UNEP. Therefore, applicants who studied a technical sector degree program combined with a more general degree program (e.g., public administration, public policy) seem to be best prepared for a successful career at UNEP and ESA concerning their educational background.

When comparing the qualification requirements set for professional positions at UNEP and ESA with the empirical information gathered on the educational backgrounds of successful employees, it is apparent that they correspond with the areas of expertise required by both organizations. As Table 3.2 indicates, at UNEP the subjects most frequently studied among the professionals participated in our study were in a financial or management-related area (e.g., business administration, accounting, and finance), a technical area (e.g., engineering), in environmental and natural sciences (e.g., geography, biology, ecology), and humanities (e.g., history, anthropology). Many employees at UNEP combined a technical sector or environmental/natural science degree program with a more general degree program, mainly a management- or finance-oriented degree program.

At ESA most employees obtained their degree in engineering (e.g., electrical engineering) and/or natural science (e.g., physics, astronomy).

Table 3.3. Subjects studied by professionals at ESA

Field of study	Frequency
– Electrical engineering – Mechanical engineering / aeronautics and aerospace – Economics (incl. personnel management and MBA)	4
– Physics – Computer science	3
– Law	2
– Telecommunication/communication technology – Process engineering – Materials – Psychology – Political science	1
+ 2 Young Graduate Trainees (1x engineering, 1x social sciences)	

Source: Authors' survey data.
Notes: In total, 25 fields of study were mentioned (some interview partners mentioned more than one degree).

However, degrees in other disciplines like politics, economics, business administration, and social science were also studied among the employees, as Table 3.3 shows.

To draw conclusions from these results, it is apparent now that a degree in a technical area or in natural science and a broad understanding of management, financial, and political issues can be seen as success factors for recruitment at ESA and UNEP. A degree solely obtained in one specific academic field seems not to be sufficient to fulfill the tasks and responsibilities. These organizations need people who are able to work across different sectors and deal with multiple tasks associated with their job. Derick and Jennifer Brinkerhoff also concluded in their book *Making a Career in International Public Service* that in addition knowledge and skills specific to the organizations' task and activities, "[i]nternational public service requires a basic understanding of economics, budgeting, financial management, planning and evaluation, policy analysis, and performance measurement and management [...]."[46]

The OSCE and the institutions of the EU are organizations whose goals and activities differ from those of UNEP and ESA. Basic priorities of the OSCE are in the fields of early warning, conflict prevention, crisis management, and post-conflict rehabilitation. Therefore, the OSCE recruits for

---

[46] Brinkerhoff, D. W., & Brinkerhoff, J. M. (2005). *Working for change: Making a career in international public service.* Bloomfield: Kumarian Press, p. 90.

Figure 3.1. Main subjects studied by OSCE professionals

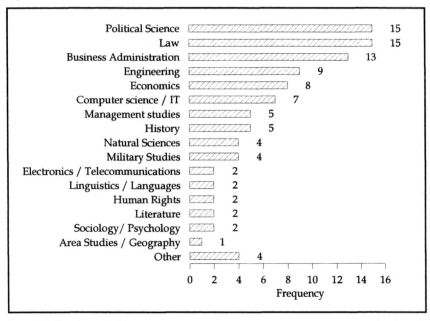

Source: Authors' survey data.
Notes: n= 100. The subject groups are based on recoding of open questions on the subjects studied.

a much broader range of activities than the other organizations examined do. The OSCE needs people with the following fields of expertise: administration and support, civilian police, democratization, economic and environmental affairs, education, elections, general staff/monitoring functions, human rights, media affairs, military affairs, political affairs, and rule of law.[47] As Figure 3.1 shows, the subjects studied most frequently in the highest degree among the employees at the OSCE were mainly in the fields of expertise required by the organization: law, political science, and business administration. The relatively high number of people who studied business administration can most likely be explained by the specific demands of some posts in administration and support. At this organization, the combination of political science and business administration was mentioned as being a very good means of preparing oneself for a contracted position in the OSCE.

[47] OSCE (2006). *Employment.* Retrieved July 5, 2007, from www.osce.org/employment/13109.html

Figure 3.2. Main subject of the highest degree professionals at the GSC

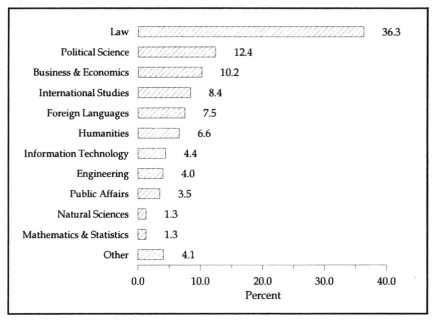

Source: Authors' survey data.
Notes: n= 476. Employees in the language service have been excluded as almost all of them have studied foreign languages.

The *institutions of the EU* have a wide range of activities and goals as well. Hence, in particular, the General Secretariat and the European Commission hire people with degrees in various fields. In general, employees in professional posts at these institutions should be highly competent and able to work flexibly in any one of the organizations' Directorates. Therefore, a combination of specialists and generalists are needed. As Westlake and Galloway described it, "there is no standard 'profile' of the typical Council official."[48] Their university degrees range from the classics to medicine and their prior work areas include education, research, computer programming, banking, and lobbying. Some observers argue that this great variety of experience in private companies, public service, and other EU institutions increases the effectiveness and impartiality of the Secretariat's work, which can "prove invaluable in times of protracted ne-

[48] Westlake, M., & Galloway, D. (2004). *The Council of the European Union* (3rd ed.). London: Harper, pp. 355-356.

gotiation" and "greatly assist not only the Council's internal operation, but the Council's inter-institutional relations in EU policy-making."[49]

When analyzing the data collected on the educational background of the employees at the EU institutions, it is apparent that they also reflect the qualification requirements set by the institutions: The subjects studied most often for their highest degrees were foreign languages, law, political science, business, economics, and international studies. Figure 3.2 gives an overview of the subjects most frequently studied at the GSC. From this, we can conclude that law, political science (including international affairs and public policy), business, economics, and foreign languages (or any combination thereof) would to be a good means of preparing oneself for a career at the GSC.

The *United Nations agencies and programs* cover a wide range of international development arenas, for example: socioeconomic development (UNDP), family planning (UNFPA), children and youth (UNICEF), education and science (UNESCO), drugs and international crime (UNODC), and HIV/AIDS (UNAIDS).[50] The employees interviewed at UN agencies and programs in Kyrgyzstan studied a variety of subjects such as international relations, social sciences, law, journalism, history, anthropology, conflict management, humanitarian aid, human rights, international development studies, and medicine. Most of them stressed that both generalists in terms of knowledge and skills and people with specific expertise in sectoral approaches and geographical regions are needed. Many UN agencies and programs have offices around the world and require people with country- or region-specific knowledge.

The World Bank serves as a financial intermediary, aid agency, development research institution, consulting company, and intergovernmental agency. Given this combination of multiple functions and activities, it can be assumed that the World Bank hires staff from a variety of different academic fields. In fact, our study exposed that the World Bank increasingly recruits people from outside its traditional hiring themes, which included for instance economists, engineers, and urban planners. One hiring manager, when asked about which fields of study would increase the likelihood of getting hired, associated fluctuating demands with these changing recruitment priorities:

> "That's a very difficult question because our business has been changing. It is a dynamic process. Years ago when Wolfensohn was in his second term he pushed very

[49] Sherrington, P. (2000). *The Council of Ministers: Political authority in the European Union.* London: Pinter, p. 52.
[50] For UNEP cf. our statements above.

Table 3.4. Main subjects studied by professionals at the World Bank

University Education – covering major and minor fields	N
Economics	12
Political Science / Development	8
Information Systems / Information Management	4
Business Administration	4
Public Policy / Public Administration	3
Legal Studies	2
Education	2
Engineering / Computer Science	2
Other	4

Source: Authors' survey data

Notes: n=26. Subjects were mentioned more than once.

hard for the World Bank to work on a set of very important social issues, like education, health, social protection -- issues which became very important for the institution. Mostly, social issues and safe-guard. Those issues are important to our institution, they will always be. But there is a shift in priority to infrastructure. A couple of
years ago infrastructure used to be very active, then we shifted more to social issues,
and now infrastructure is coming back because we realize that is very important for
the World Bank to come back to this area. So it's hard when the bank's business
keeps changing, which then has a direct impact on recruitment. Some time ago we
were trying to reduce our portfolio in infrastructure; we didn't need that many engineers. But with all the infrastructure coming back, we need more engineers now.
[...] So it is always a dynamic process. But even though there will always be a shift-
ing back and forth between priorities, there are certain areas where we will always be
needing people, like management, polity, public sector management, infrastructure.
We will always need people there, no matter how many. We need environmental people. There are so many areas." (Human Resources staff members at the World Bank)

However, a very strong sectoral and technical expertise that can be applied in the respective sectors of the organization is still seen as a crucial
success factor for recruitment. Here, as the following statement made by
a hiring manger shows, sectoral knowledge not only includes technical
skills with respect to one particular job but it refers mainly to a broader
knowledge that cover other sectors as well:

"If I look at a technical professional whom I hire then the sectoral knowledge within
that area for instance if I am hiring someone for water, I need someone that has this
sectoral knowledge, not just a water education. The sectoral knowledge whether they
had worked for rural water development or urban water development or whether they

have done sanitations or you know. I am looking for that, you need to have that sectoral expertise." (Human Resources staff member at the World Bank)

Here, it is apparent that the World Bank searches for people who are both generalist in terms of knowledge and skills and people with specific expertise in sectoral approaches. The variety of different fields studied among the interview participants indicated in Table 3.4 can be seen as a result of changing recruiting procedures and/or as a result of the breath and multitude of developmental aspects that the World Bank pursues.

What stands out here, of course, is the high frequency of economic studies across the professionals' educational backgrounds. This underlines a commonly held view that for professional positions in the World Bank, especially within the respective development networks, an educational background in economics is considered indispensable. This may come as no surprise given the World Bank's institutional profile as an international financial institution, aside from its development and knowledge functions. However, while some professionals identified a degree in economics as very important, an educational background in economics appears not to be *sine qua non* for working at World Bank. The professionals who have no formal education in economics bring in technical expertise and sector specialization relevant to the World Bank's operational areas. These include, for instance, knowledge management and education.

When drawing conclusions from the results presented here concerning qualification requirements and educational backgrounds of successful applicants and employees in the professional category, it can be determined that most of organizations examined tend to hire employees with a multidisciplinary academic background, combining, for instance, a degree program in natural science or economics with development studies or public policy. However, with regard to the subject areas or disciplines in which academic degrees were mainly obtained, they vary by the organization and depend on the job in question. But without variation, international organizations seek people with expertise in at least one area or sector relevant to the organization's tasks. Therefore, specialization of knowledge can be regarded as a crucial qualification requirement, as we have particularly seen at UNEP and ESA as well as at the World Bank to some extent. However, for a successful career development in the international public service, it seems that it is no longer sufficient to study a single discipline in isolation or obtain only one degree in a specific field of study. Goals and activities of international organizations are multidimensional, and they require staff members who are both generalists and specialists and able to deal with different and complex issues emerging in the workplace: A natural scientist at UNEP should also have an understanding of policy development and implementation, as well as be familiar with basic business and accounting skills. Someone who applies for a position as an election expert at UNDP regional office in Kyrgyzstan should possess specific knowledge about elections systems and the socioeconomic situation in Kyrgyzstan in addition to basic project management skills. Therefore, a multidisciplinary background – as opposed to a sole area of expertise – was mentioned to be very helpful for a successful application and job performance. Jennifer Brinkerhoff described it as follows: "International organizations demand a 'generalist' capable of understanding the work of specialists and able to synthesize knowledge from various fields. The perfect candidate should be prepared to wrestle with complex issues, sort them out, and produce logical and responsive conclusions."[51] A broad education makes one more flexible in dealing with the challenges that may emerge in the context of international work than a sole area of expertise. One professional explained it as follows:

"Any education is relevant because when you land somewhere you have to do everything yourself. The more education and broader education you have – the broader experience – the much better you will survive."(Human Resources staff member at UNDP, Kyrgyzstan)

Finally, regardless of which organization we looked at in this study, it is apparent that many professionals continue their formal education after graduating from university by pursuing other postgraduate degrees or being involved in "life-long learning" activities. As tasks and responsibilities as well as organizational contexts are constantly changing, it was said that a commitment to "life-long learning" was essential for a successful career development.

3.2. Professional background

Besides university education, another important qualification requirement for working at international organizations is likely to be the professional experience that employees gained in employment prior to their current position. As outlined in most vacancy announcements and job descriptions posted, professional positions in international public service typically require several of years of work experience.[52] The organizations examined in this study do not hire people with less than one year of work

---

[51] Brinkerhoff, D. W., & Brinkerhoff, J. M. (2005). *Working for change: Making a career in international public service*. Bloomfield: Kumarian Press.

[52] Here, according to human resources polices, internships do usually not count as professional work experience, although they are regarded as very beneficial for gaining practical experience.

experience. This applies to entry-level positions in the professional category as well; for instance, a Junior Professional Officer at UN agencies and programs as well as at the World Bank's headquarters in Washington D.C. is required to demonstrate that he or she has gathered one to two years of professional work experience.

Most hiring managers at the international organizations examined stressed that professional work experience gained at the national and/or international level in a relevant field of expertise is a crucial factor for recruitment. As mentioned before, some of them even place greater emphasis on work experience than on the applicants' university education. A professional at UNDP described it as follows:

"Practical experience is very important. [...] The longer ago it was that an applicant finished his or her studies, the more practical experience dominates his or her application. If someone has worked for international NGOs for ten years, no one will pay attention to what he or she studied. We always look for the person with the most possible experience in that particular area." (Human Resources staff member at UNDP)

Since careers in the international public service are so dynamic, most hiring managers stressed that candidates need a broad range of competencies and a high degree of flexibility to respond to challenges emerging in the workplace. Furthermore, they need to adapt quickly to living and working conditions in other countries. Therefore, professional work experience gathered abroad and in different sectors and positions (as opposed to one's home country and in one sector) was said to be useful for successful career development. Static career paths which consist of work experience gained solely in one sector and country were rated as not very helpful, since one would not gain insight into other sectors and organizational structures and thus acquire the necessary amount of flexibility. On the other hand, as some of the hiring managers at UNEP highlighted, it is always important to find the right balance: Too many short-term assignments are not always seen as an advantage. Therefore, they recommended that graduates be careful and more strategic in choosing their jobs.

"And I think working internationally, it helps to be well-rounded in the work that you do because the work is defined almost daily in the UN. It is not something that is static and you are doing the same thing every day. You have a different challenge because something new has come up or there is a new emerging environmental threat that you have to deal with or there is a new rift between two countries that you have to work out or that kind of thing. So it is not a static thing. So different experiences in different ways are helpful." (Human Resources staff member at UNEP)

"That is another piece of advice, I would say. Because when we look at people's CVs, if they have changed their job every six months and they have done three months at

*this and four months of that, it looks like they are not able to hold down a job and stick with something. And I think you have to try and strike a good balance, you know, go into something for a few years but when you are young, do not stay there too long because it is better to get a bit broader experience in a number of areas."
(Human Resources staff member at UNEP)*

As the following comments made by staff members responsible for re-cruiting personnel for international organizations show, candidates – par-ticularly those who apply for higher professional positions – should be able to demonstrate that they have gained significant work experience abroad and in different sectors:

*"We would rather have somebody who has been all over the world, been through the system, been through ranks, maybe has a little private sector experience. But we would like someone who has worked in different parts of the UN System and cer-tainly different countries, in a variety of administrative roles, managing HR, etc."
(Human Resources staff member at UNEP)*

"I do not know many people who have a career like a laser beam. It does not exist. Or if it exists, it is not good for an employer. Today, in the position I am now, I do not favor people who have been in the UN for 20 years. Why? Because we are not work-ing behind closed doors. We are part of the real world here. So it is better to know the real world."(hiring manager at UNEP)

"You look at education, you look at skills, and you look at where they might have been, if someone has a broad international experience. It is positive because they have actually survived somewhere. It is often very difficult to take a person out of their environment and say you should work in a developing country." (Human Resources staff member at UNODC)

"What matters is the depth of technical experience and the breadth of experience, the ability to work across boundaries, to collaborate with people from their own profes-sion and people from other professions or across sectors or across countries or across disciplines that go beyond operations. To successfully manage a project they have to have that knowledge." (Human Resources staff member at the World Bank)

As internships or volunteer work are not defined as formal qualifica-tion requirements at the international organizations examined, they were not rated as being very important for being hired by the staff members re-sponsible for selecting suitable candidates. For professional positions at international organizations, paid work experience is required. However, many hiring managers said that internships, traineeships, and volunteer work are very good learning experiences and opportunities for profes-sional competency development. But they recommended that people should make sure that their internships provide real involvement in the actual work of the organizations and thus an opportunity to develop pro-fessional skills. One professional at UNEP described it as follows: "It is important to find an employer that offers a substantive assignment that is going to keep you busy, because this is really what helps to prepare you to join an international organization." The following statements made by hiring managers at the international organizations examined illustrate that internships and volunteer work abroad are rated as a good means to prepare oneself for a career in international public service:

> *"I think [students] should do lots of internships and find small jobs and things like that, travel. I think it is important that you show that you are interested in working in different countries, and if you want to work in an international environment that you are not afraid of going to a developing country." (Human Resources staff member at UNEP)*

> *"Just go and work somewhere – any kind of an office just to understand how to interact with people. At the end of the day, people don't ask you, 'What's your degree?' But you have to know how to function in the workplace." (Human Resources staff member at the GSC)*

> *"Do not be scared to take one or two years to do volunteerism in third world countries or to do an internship at an international organization for one year. It is not waste of time. You learn a lot. It is a great experience. You should not be scared to diversify your background. You can always use these kinds of things. You should not pursue a straight career." (Human Resources staff member at UNICEF)*

> *"And try to get an internship with an international organization. Even if maybe the work might not be very interesting. But you get a lot of contacts. And that will help you later when you actually look for a job." (Human Resources staff member at the World Bank)*

Although hiring managers at international organizations regard work experience as a crucial factor for recruitment, it should be mentioned that this qualification is often counterbalanced by an assessment of the candidates' competencies. At some international organizations, a shift in recruiting techniques is reflected by the use of competency-based interviews.[53] By enhancing the use of this selection tool, hiring managers attempt to put more emphasis on the assessment of the candidates' competencies than on the assessment of formal qualifications (e.g., years of work experience, education).

Concerning individual interview questions, at UNEP, for instance, candidates are required to show how they would react in specific team situations by applying the experience they gained on the job or in other life situations. The candidates should demonstrate that they have the skills and ability to work effectively on an intercultural team, solve conflicts, set

---

[53] At UNEP, all other UN agencies, and ESA competency-based interviews are part of the recruitment process. Competency-based interviews are structured with questions that relate directly to the essential competencies (like management competencies, personal competencies) required for the position.

up work plans, and communicate effectively with their coworkers. The Human Resource Management Service at UNEP provides hiring managers with a set of questions for the assessment of the candidates' organizational competencies and core values. The following comments made by the interview partners illustrate what kind of competency-based questions they might ask during interviews:

"Normally, what we do is we start out with a kind of a general question, like in teamwork 'Can you please describe a case when you worked as part of a team?' And then they answer that part of the question. And then you have a series of sub-questions that go with that, like, 'Were you a team leader or were you a member of the team?' That is a simple question, but then depending on what the answer is, you can say, 'As a team leader, was there ever a case where you had to make a decision that was contrary to what the rest of the team wanted? How did they react? How did you persuade them to go your way? Or if you were a member of the team and you had what you thought was the best idea, how did you persuade the rest of the members of the team?' This is kind of the same thing but from a different angle. What we do is we ask for specific examples. So do not give us a theoretical thing that maybe you learned at school or you read but you say, 'Give me a specific example!'" (hiring manager at UNEP)

"We would interview the candidate, we try to find out whether those skills are there in that person. For example, we would ask him about teamwork and when he has worked in a team before and asking, 'What if the team fails and there is blame to be shared? How do you deal with it, and how do you deal with a conflict situation in a team?" (hiring manager at UNEP)

"When we do the interview, we are focusing on the attributes and the competencies. [...] So they will be asked a number of questions and follow-up questions about them being a member of the team, what they feel are good leadership skills, whether they have them, and where they have their weaknesses, and those kinds of things. So in the interview, we try to focus on those things which you cannot put down on paper." (Human Resources staff member at UNEP)

Most professionals at UNEP and ESA rated the method of competency-based interviewing as a "valuable" and "important" selection tool. As interviews allow them to assess the personality of the candidate as well as technical, professional, and organizational competencies required for the particular job vacancy, they ensure that the most qualified candidates can be selected. A professional at UNEP described it as follows:

"I can tell you that the interviews are an invaluable part of the process. And it very often happens that when we look through the application we draw up on the short list, we have a sort of idea of who we think is going to come out best. And then when we do the interview, we totally change our opinion because even if it is a telephone interview, you learn so much by the interview. That gives you a totally different perspective on that person, and they even put things down on paper, when you investigate and you really look for the qualities and skills, it is amazing what you can tell

from the interview. So the interview is very, very important, and it often changes our opinion totally of who we think is most suitable." (Human Resources staff member at UNEP)

Although at the World Bank interviews are not conducted on the basis of a specific set of questions, questions addressing motivations and behavior skills are asked as well during selection interviews, as the followings statement made by a hiring manager highlights:

"Then we always spend a lot of time to figure out whether the candidate is a culture fit, whether there is any behavior that says that the person can do team work, which is of fundamental importance to function here. Without the ability to work in a team, without communication skills, without good behavioral attitude... No matter how good you are technically. They always spend a good amount of time to find out how the candidate can work in a team, how he resolves conflict, how he works hard to get the job done, how he communicates with the clients. So behavioral aspects are very important in the process of interviewing." (Human Resources staff member at the World Bank)

In our study we were not only interested in the formal requirements regarding work experience, but also in the professional background of applicants and employees. Our data shows that all professionals who participated in the labor market study had previously gathered professional work experience. Since international organizations require a number of years of work experience for professional posts, this result is no surprise.

The sectors in which professionals worked prior to the current job were primarily in the international or national public sector, the private sector, and academia. Many employees have a mixed professional background. However, most employees at UNEP, the OSCE and the World Bank gained their professional experience in the international or national public sector, as Tables 3.5, 3.6, and 3.7 indicate. (In our understanding, the public sector comprises the sub-sectors of general government – mainly supranational, national/federal, regional/state, and local government units – as well as public corporations, i.e., corporations that are subject to control by government units.)

Table 3.5. Fields of professional experience before working at UNEP

Field of previous professional experience	Times mentioned
Public sector	Mentioned very often
Private sector	Mentioned often
Academia	Mentioned often

Source: Authors' data survey
Notes: Interviewees had the opportunity to mention more than one previous place of employment.

Table 3.6. Fields of professional experience before working at the OSCE

Field of previous professional experience	Times mentioned
Public sector	105
Private sector	48
Education & Research	21
Non-profit sector	17

Source: Authors' data survey
Notes: n=100 with 191 responses

At the OSCE, the area in which most employees gained professional experience was the public sector as well, as Table 3.6 shows. Here, the OSCE employees who gained their professional experience in the public sector mainly dealt with the following issues: political/ strategic matters, administrative activities, technical matters, legal affairs, cultural and social affairs, and elections.

At the OSCE, we further examined the length of time they were employed before working with the organization (cf. Figure 3.3): 35.6% had worked for about six to ten years and about 40% have working experience for more than 11 years. The average was approximately eleven years of professional experience. According to this result, the OSCE does not seem to be an organization which hires many entry-level employers.

Figure 3.3. Years of professional experience before working at the OSCE

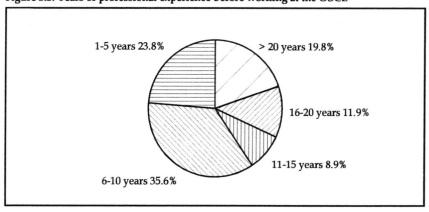

Source: Authors' survey data
Notes: n=101. Mean = 11.36 years.

As Table 3.7 indicates, the *World Bank* draws its employees from academia as well as the private and public sectors. Many of professionals have experience in both the private and public sectors. Others were directly hired from private sector jobs, and some came straight out of other international organizations or academia.

When asked to evaluate their previous work experience, many professionals at the organizations examined said that it contributed to their professional development in a positive way. Previous international work experience was viewed as particularly relevant for entering the organization and for their performance at their current job. Their work experience helped them accumulate relevant knowledge and skills, which gave them a competitive edge over other candidates in their respective hiring processes. The following comments underscore the usefulness of work experience:

"It was not that new to me to be in an international company also, I do not think the UN wants to take somebody who comes directly from a school, maybe it is good to have a few years' experience from somewhere else to kind of bring something new also to the organization." (Staff member at UNEP)

"It was my strong background in volunteering, some knowledge of Russian and my relevant experience in Moldavia. This was possibly the strongest reason. Basically, I tried to work in a very similar way in Moldavia on different projects but without resources. So I got a lot of ideas and I lived through some tough situations previously." (Staff member at UNDP)

"In fact I had more experience than many people who were here. [...] This accumulated knowledge, I think, was fundamental at the time when I got the position at ESA." (Staff member at ESA)

Table 3.7. Fields of professional experience before working at the World Bank

Field of previous professional experience	Times mentioned
Public Sector (e.g., multilateral international agencies, non-profit organizations, non-governmental organizations, government, public foundations, public administration)	17
Private sector (e.g., private companies, organizations, agencies, foundations, private consulting firms)	13
Academia (e.g., universities, research centers)	8

Source: Authors' survey data
Notes: n=26. Interview participants had the opportunity to mention more than one previous place of employment.

"I had experience at the IMF. Given the close relationship between the IMF and the World Bank in the African Region or, in general, working in developing countries, it is a highly valuable asset to have somebody who knows how the IMF works precisely and therefore seems to be up to the standards of an economist and secondly the knowledge of the institutional side, which is definitely an asset." (Staff member at the World Bank)

Professionals at the World Bank, UNEP, and ESA also referred to *young professional programs* offered by their organizations when asked about previous work experience in the international public service and its importance for being hired. The Young Graduate Trainee-Program at ESA, the Young Professionals (YP) Program at the World Bank and the Junior Professional Officer (JPO) Program at UNEP and the World Bank are regarded by many professionals as vehicles for career development in the respective organizations, as the comments below underscore:

"The JPO program basically allowed me to get in the operational part of the Bank, which would have been difficult without it. So that was a big step for me and then it was very clear that they would put me on the path for task manager and that is what happened. [...] I guess it is a matter of using your JPO time to establish yourself, so that people rely on you and need you in their work program and take on as many responsibilities as you can. So by the time the hiring comes up you are already doing all the work, you have been demonstrating for two years that you can do it, making yourself indispensable." (Staff member at the World Bank)

"That I got into the system... I am sure because I was a JPO. That is clear. I mean, JPO is one of the ways to get in. [...]. It is for sure an entry-point into the organization. And you see many of the JPOs remain in the UN, which is the whole objective of the government." (Staff member at UNEP)

"Although they say you should never expect an employment based on JPO, I think it is worth it for the one who is being the JPO. You get a glimpse of what it is like to work there, and in those years, you learn to know if you want to continue with the organization. And the organization also sees how you work and if you fit in." (Staff member at UNEP)

"Really, the Young Graduate Trainee Program is one way to get in because you have the opportunity to work here and you have the opportunity to show how good you are." (Staff member at ESA)

Figure 3.4 and Figure 3.5 give an overview of entry-level opportunities for graduates at UNEP and the World Bank.

The professionals who worked as Junior Professional Officers at UNEP and the World Bank rated the Junior Professional Officer Program (JPO) as a good means of preparing oneself for a career. This is because Junior Professional Officers can be directly involved in the development and management of support programs. They said that the expertise and insight they gained through the experience on the job was highly valuable

74

Figure 3.4. Entry-level opportunities at UNEP

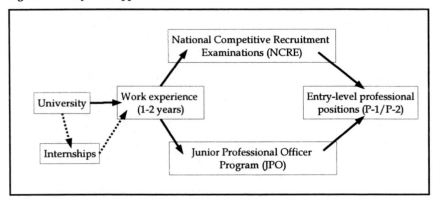

Source: Authors

for their careers, as they developed a profile and a reputation for themselves.

In addition to young professional programs, professionals at the World Bank mentioned that consultancies are also a good way to begin a World Bank career path. Some professionals interviewed were consultants before being hired as higher-level staff. They viewed consultancies as first-rate opportunities to get into the organization, get established in a certain field, and start developing a reputation that others know you for:

> *"And all during this time, the whole time I was at university, I was working as a consultant for the World Bank. So I was constantly doing projects and activities for the Bank and traveling. And the reason why I got this call for a one-year job was because that person had read something that I had produced for Uganda." (Staff member at the World Bank)*

> *"So I got a consultancy and I had to write a paper. People read the paper, I was asked to write another paper. And then things went well and I was in. Actually, there was a lot of demand for my work and I started working with many different people. So I got a lot of exposure. Then this position that I have now was open and I applied. You have to go through a completely new process. You have to do interviews with a panel, etc. But you have an advantage if you are already inside, because then the information comes from the inside whether you are good or not." (Staff member at the World Bank)*

In our study, we also asked professionals about internships, volunteer work, and any other preparatory experience they did prior to their employment, and whether they thought these were relevant either for starting a career at the organization or, more generally, for pursuing a career in international organizations. As the statements below show, particu-

Figure 3.5. Entry-level opportunities at the World Bank

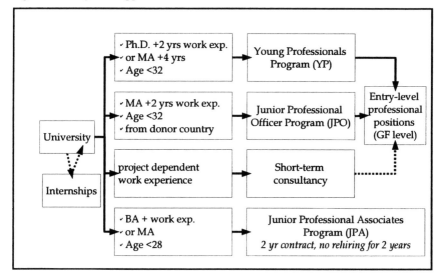

Source: *Chart by authors, based on interviews and www.worldbank.org*

larly professionals at UN agencies and programs and the World Bank had done one or more internships in the international or national public sector, for instance at UN funds, agencies, and programs, the World Trade Organization, and government agencies, and/or they were involved in volunteer work (e.g., United States Peace Corps or United Nations Volunteers) during or after their university studies. Most of them gained their practical experience abroad.

Most professionals rated *internships* and *volunteer work* – all of which can be performed either independent from or in the context of graduate programs – as very good learning experiences and opportunities for professional skills building. In particular, with regard to learning how to work and live with people from different backgrounds, they stressed the importance of doing internships abroad instead of or in addition to in one's home country. Moreover, internships and any other kind of preparatory experience are a good way to meet people and build relationships, which can be helpful for career development as they can provide one with professional support and information on the field of work one is interested in. Besides the networking aspect, some professionals mentioned that internships and volunteer work are essential tools to deter-

76

mine whether you are interested in and capable of working in international public service.

*"Of course, I did a number of internships. For two years I was a volunteer for the
United Nations Association. I worked there once a week. I taught classes on human
rights and human rights violation. I was teaching children at junior high and ele-
mentary school. And then I did a six-month internship at the European Parliament.
Those are the most relevant ones." (Staff member at UNAIDS)*

*"I have done several internships as a graduate, in my working career I did three
months in France, three months in Washington D. C., and South America. I did
some internships or consultancy work on a free basis in Guatemala, Nicaragua, and
all those experiences really provided me with insight on my field of specialization".
(Staff member at UNEP)*

*"They [internships] were very relevant. Very much so. It was working in the field,
especially the Peace Corps was an opportunity to live in a small village and see how
people perceived their own issues, how they analyzed them, how they saw development programs impact them. It is a special opportunity to get a lens on, what development looks like for the people you are trying to help. And get a feel for what its like
to live on one dollar a day and go through dramas that people go through in their
daily lives. So I think that experience carried me as much as my education did."
(Staff member at the World Bank)*

*"My internship at the European Central Bank was important because it always part
of a family of institutions. When I applied to work here, I started as a consultant.
And the fact that I had done some work at the European Central Bank - I had written
papers there. It gave the World Bank some kind of idea of me. And I think these kinds
of institutions, it is important to get in one of them. And then it is easier to move
around. Because there is this same culture in international organizations." (Staff
member at the World Bank)*

A relatively small number of employees at the OSCE, EU and ESA did internships or voluntary work during or after their studies.[54]

To sum up, the research findings underscore that paid professional
work experience is an important qualification requirement for professional posts at international organizations. It is not only a frequent formal
requirement. As our research has shown, staff members involved in a hiring process place great emphasis on work experience. The importance
and relevance of diverse work experience for career development is also
stressed by most professionals. Candidates for professional positions
should have gained their experience in different sectors and countries, as

[54] At the OSCE, only 35% of the employees who participated in our survey had done one or
more internships at all. Here, 10.9% of the internships were done at the OSCE and 16.4% at
other international organizations – so altogether, 27.3% of the internships were done at international organizations. For the other fields, the categories in the survey were less detailed: Another 27.3% of the internships were done in the public sector and 25.5% in the
private sector.

it shows that they acquired sufficient flexibility and the competencies needed for a successful job performance in dynamic and intercultural workplaces.

3.3. Competencies for successful application and job performance

Another important issue in the context of the labor market study was to identify competencies necessary for being hired and working in international organizations. We asked both staff members responsible for recruiting personnel and employees in other departments about the knowledge, skills, attitudes, and character traits required for a successful application and job performance. Based on the fact that all professionals who participated in our study had several years of work experience either in the international public sector or in other areas, it can be assumed that the question about required competencies was answered in terms of those experiences. Therefore, the statements given by them can be seen as a subjective evaluation in light of their professional experience rather than an "objective" picture of what skills and qualifications are needed to perform the various tasks at the workplace.

Because all interviewees brought their own understanding of terms such as "competency", "knowledge", and "skills" with them, there is not much use in engaging in a detailed discussion of the various definitions of these terms one finds in the literature.[55] In both professional and academic circles, these terms are defined differently, if at all. Quite frequently, they are treated as being interchangeable.

Since there is a variety of jobs and position available at international organizations, it can be assumed that the tasks professionals have to perform are diverse and require a variety of competencies. One professional described it as follows:

"It is important to realize that a variety of job types exist at international organizations and that these require a variety of abilities. One must have quite different physical abilities when working for UNHCR in a crisis area, for example, than when

[55] See for example Erpenbeck, J. (2005). *How new are the new types of competency development really?* Retrieved July 5, 2007, from www.scil.ch/congress-2005/programme-10-12/docs/workshop-6-erpenbeck-text.pdf.; Erpenbeck, J., & Heyse, V. (2004). *Kompetenztraining. 64 Informations- und Trainingsprogramme.* Stuttgart: Schäffer-Poeschl Verlag; Evers, F. T., & Rush, J.C. (1998). *The bases of competence: Skills for lifelong learning and employability.* San Francisco: Jossey-Bass Inc.; Rychen, D. S., & Salganik, L. H. (2003). A holistic model of competence. In D. S. Rychen & L. H. Salganik (Eds.), *Key competencies for a successful life and well-functioning society.* Göttingen: Hogrefe & Huber Publishers, pp. 41-62; Voncken, M. (2004). *Being competent or having competences. Social competences in vocational and continuing education.* In A. Lindgren, & A. Heikkinen. *Studies in vocational and continuing education.* Bern: Peter Lang AG.

working as a legal practitioner in Geneva. There are positions in which one must re-act incredibly quickly; the person must therefore be a go-getter. There are other posi-tions that are more cyclical: they require people who are very familiar with rules, regulations, and planning, and who are therefore specialists and analysts. A person must therefore be able to develop a multitude of abilities." (Staff member at UNDP)

Indeed, a range of knowledge, skills, and attitudes acquired through professional experience and university education was mentioned by the professionals when asked about the "perfect profile" of a candidate. Some competencies were said to be specific to the organization and/or the job that has to be performed. Yet when analyzing the empirical data collected in more detail, we were able to identify a range of basic compe-tencies needed for a successful job performance regardless of the job that has to be carried out. To create a better overview of the job-specific and basic competencies which apply to each post in the organizations, we de-fined groups of competencies. The classification used in this report, based partly on the differentiation made by Erpenbeck: personal, activity-ori-ented, task-oriented, and methodical and social-communicative compe-tencies.[56]

Before describing the competencies and their components identified, it is important to mention that some of the international organizations have already developed organizational competencies. As mentioned previ-ously, within the UN System and at ESA, organizational competencies are used for human resources processes such as recruitment, placement, development, and performance appraisal. Hiring managers at both or-ganizations are required to include these competencies in generic job de-scriptions and vacancy announcements so that they can be used as evaluation criteria for individual posts. Moreover, interview frameworks and other assessment tools are developed to incorporate competencies into recruitment and placement decisions.[57] The UN competency model (cf. Table 3.8) was developed through an intensive participatory process involving staff and managers of the UN.

The extent to which of these competencies and values apply to each post in the organization depends on the nature and characteristics of the post in question. However, staff members responsible for recruiting per-sonnel must select some competencies to assess the applicants' suitability.

---

[56] Erpenbeck, J. (2005). *How new are the new types of competency development really?* Retrieved July 5, 2007, from www.scil.ch/congress-2005/programme-10-12/docs/workshop-6-er-penbeck-text.pdf.
[57] ESA (2006). *Core skills. ESA's Generic Competency Model.* Retrieved July 5, 2007, from www.esa.int/SPECIALS/Careers_at_ESA/SEMYRSXO4HD_0.html.

Table 3.8. The UN Competency Model

Core Values	Core Competencies	Managerial Competencies
– integrity – professionalism – respect for diversity	– communication – teamwork – planning and organizing – accountability – creativity – client orientation – commitment to continuous learning – technological awareness	– leadership – vision – empowering others – building trust – managing performance – judgment / decision-making

Source: United Nations Department of Economic and Social Affairs (2005). *A Guide to a Career with the United Nations.* Retrieved July 26, 2007, from http://unpan1.un.org/intradoc/groups/public/documents/un/unpan000153.pdf.

Competency-based interviews are used to evaluate whether or not the candidates possess the organizational competencies.

3.3.1. Professional-methodical competencies

The first group of competencies we identified as essential for successful work performance is professional-methodological competencies. These refer to knowledge, skills and experience specific to the organizations tasks and the job. Methodical competencies can be described as problem-solving skills, as an analytical and systematic approach to work tasks, as the ability of structuring and classifying new information and as the ability of developing and realizing work and thought processes.

For all professional positions at the international organizations examined, professionals mentioned that specific expertise – knowledge and skills specific to areas and sectors in which the organization operates – is needed to perform and achieve the organizations' objectives. According to them, they must have the competency to carry out work in a specific field, as an expert and without supervision. For instance, specific knowledge about aerospace technology and the skills to be able to develop and implement a project on space technologies is demanded for a professional position at ESA. Or a professional position at UNDP regional office in Kyrgyzstan requires specific knowledge on election systems as well as the skills to run a project which implements an election system for upcoming elections.

Professionals at ESA, UNEP and the World Bank in particular stressed that they need knowledge and skills specific to the technical sectors of their organization. At UNEP, technical expertise is required in the following areas: Environmental Policy and Law; Environmental Technology, Industry and Economics; Environmental Early Warning Systems; Biodiversity, Land Degradation, Marine and Coastal Waters Expertise; Ozone Issues; Conventions and Law; Communications and Public Information.[58] Hiring managers at ESA mentioned that applicants should be able to demonstrate that they possess technical expertise; otherwise they will not be selected for any professional post at ESA. Three professionals at ESA described it as follows:

"No one without the technical or administrative competencies will get in here." (Human Resources staff member at ESA)

"We first of all require a background in the according discipline, along with the soft skills and foreign language skills." (Human Resources staff member at ESA)

"First of all you really have to target your knowledge on what the Agency needs. And in, this house this is an engineering background." (Human Resources staff member at ESA)

Our study at the World Bank has shown that strong technical knowledge is indispensable due to the consistent application of economics across all sectors of development; many respondents viewed at least some basic knowledge of economics as helpful, while several respondents attributed particular relevance to economic expertise for a career within the World Bank, as the following comment shows:

"But of course, my master and my Ph.D. were in international macroeconomics. So I was familiar with the topic the World Bank deals with. I was familiar with [...] the monetary policy, exchange rate policy because all my research was on that. So it really gave me a good theoretical background. So when I came here I was familiar with all these issues in the theoretical point of view. And that is very important. So this helped me." (Staff member at the World Bank)

As for the EU institutions, we identified that specific, or at least basic knowledge of the following can be very helpful for successful job performance: EU politics, law, and economics; the function, role and power of EU Institutions; EU administration; European history, culture, and religion; constitutional, international, and national law; international politics and economics. One professional at the GSC described it as follows:

"Of course it's good to have some knowledge in certain areas. They do need some generalists here in a certain sense, but I learned about EU law on my own in the first few years, so a little bit of law and a little bit of economics in order to feel more confident in matters I often have to deal with." (Staff member of the GSC)

---

[58] United Nations Secretariat (2002). *Administrative Instructions. Staff Selection System.* Retrieved July 5, 2007, from http://www.un.org/staff/panelofcounsel/pocimages/stai024. pdf.

Basic knowledge of international human rights standards, the history and activities of the OSCE and other international organizations, political and electoral systems, as well as civil society development techniques was said to be required to handle the various tasks and responsibilities in the OSCE field missions, as Table 3.9 indicates.

Table 3.9. Knowledge required for OSCE fieldwork

Knowledge in this field required	Percent
International human rights standards	72.5
History and activities of the OSCE	71.6
OSCE commitments in the human dimension sphere	70.6
Examples of OSCE activities in the human dimension	66.7
Civil-society development techniques	65.7
Introduction to political and electoral systems	57.8
Examples of OSCE activities in the politico-military dimension	57.4
Examples of OSCE activities in the economic and environmental dimension	53.7
Gender issues in peace building operations	48.6
Mine awareness	45.3
History and activity of other international organizations	41.3

Source: OSCE (2005). *Are we identifying and preparing mission members correctly? Managers talk back. The 2nd OSCE Meeting on Training and Recruitment.* Vienna: OSCE.

Notes: The survey was conducted by the OSCE Secretary in 2005 with all program managers in order to identify the skills and knowledge most needed for fieldwork in the current OSCE context. The survey was send to 240 program mangers at OSCE field missions. 144 people answered the questionnaire. The response rate was 60%.

Many of our interview partners mentioned that in addition to the knowledge specific to the organizations' activities they need a basic understanding of economics, budgeting, financial management, program planning and evaluation, as well as policy analysis, development, and implementation.

Furthermore, professionals at the OSCE and the UN agencies and programs examined indicated that knowledge specific to a country and a particular region of the world – including knowledge of the history, culture, society and economics – is important for working at their organizations. As described in the OSCE survey results:

"OSCE managers have indicated that new mission members often lack a sufficient level of awareness about the specificities of the region in which they will be operating. Mangers strongly recommended better preparation in this regard. Being familiar with the history, geography and demographic composition, politics, cultural particularities, etc., is important to develop and implement sustainable programmes."[59]

Most professionals at the UN agencies and programs, the EU institutions, the World Bank, and the OSCE said that basic knowledge of the organization and other international organizations is crucial to successful performance on the job. Gaining knowledge on the various international organizations during one's university education, was rated as particularly valuable in the early stages of professional development. With regard to the UN agencies and programs, it is helpful to understand the history and structure of the UN System and how the UN agencies and programs operate. They said in particular that one should possess basic knowledge of the development, structure, and functions of the UN agencies and programs; an understanding of the role the UN plays in the development of international law and policy; and the ability to think critically about the significance of the UN to contemporary world affairs. Furthermore, as the statements below, illustrate knowing the rules and guidelines as well as the terminology and the vocabulary of the organization is very helpful for carrying out the job:

"Knowing about the committees of the UN General Assembly, how the budget works, how things get done at the senior levels in New York are things that, unless you are really keyed into those, I would say most people who work here do not have a clue. Maybe you do not need to know, but it would be [...] very helpful if you did know." (Staff member at UNEP)

"So without knowing the rules and guidelines of the organization, especially in my line of work where there are so many administrative instructions and guidelines on how to administer those instructions... and there are also the master rules and regulations on finances that we have to know for dealing with the UN and outside. So I would think that if you do not have a grasp of this, it will be difficult to be successful." (Staff member at UNEP)

"One important thing is to know the UN bureaucracy and to know how to use the UN bureaucracy to achieve your goals." (Staff member at UNODC)

Furthermore, to accomplish the tasks at the workplace successfully, most professionals at all international organizations indicated that knowl-

[59] OSCE (2005). *Guiding principles and recommendations for the revision of the training standards for preparation of future members of the OSCE field operations. The 2nd OSCE Meeting on Training and Recruitment.* Vienna: OSCE.

edge and skills on how to organize and plan their daily work are very beneficial for their job. *Basic management skills*, including administrative abilities, organization and planning skills, time management skills, office management skills, staff and team management skills, leadership skills, and project management skills were mentioned, as the following statements made by professionals at UNEP, ESA, the GSC, and UNODC show:

"Good organizational skills are also essential. So that the person knows when you are asking them to do something the kind of systematic approach to the problem in order to go through it with the maximum impact in terms of getting the right thing at the right time." (Staff member at UNEP)

"Appropriate skills in planning, so that when you give people an assignment, they know how to organize themselves and plan how to do it, so that they do not spend too much time [on it]." (hiring manager at UNEP)

"You know, so, if you have management skills, let's say the UN system is just now waking up to the need for management expertise, managing people, resources. Personally, I think that is a big gap." (Staff member at UNEP)

"The ability to find people, structures, and programs is very important. Where is equipment, where is supply, where is support, where are my people?" (Staff member at UNODC)

"Planning and organizing is very important." (Staff member at ESA)

"On the other hand, it would not hurt to have some general management experience in order to be flexible within the organization and to do something other than just translating and sitting in your office, if you want to do more. So it would not be bad at all to have communication and organizational skills." (Staff member at the GSC)

A survey conducted by the OSCE Secretary in 2005 with all program managers in order to identify the most important skills and knowledge required for fieldwork in the current OSCE context, highlighted as well that management-related skills such as staff and team management, office management, strategic planning, programming and budgeting are necessary to perform the tasks at OSCE field missions.

In addition to basic management skills, many professionals at the international organizations examined stressed that project management skills, such as planning, design, monitoring, evaluation, report writing, and budgeting, are very crucial to their daily work, as project development and implementation are part of most activities in professional positions. Therefore, it is a highly valuable capacity to manage any kind of project efficiently.

As the statements below illustrate, most employees at the international organizations stressed that a successful career requires *analytical and criti-*

cal thinking skills. To accomplish one's tasks at the workplace successfully, one must have the ability to ask questions and collect information, identify a concept or problem, dissect or isolate its components, organize information for decision making, establish criteria for evaluation, draw appropriate conclusions, and develop solutions. Most professionals further added the importance of strategic thinking, including setting priorities, developing goals and strategies.

"The best way is not the straight line because here we have the big mine field. Why do you want to go there? What do you want to achieve? So, you have to have good analysis skills. I want to achieve lead-free gasoline in Africa. Then you have to have a good analysis of the situation. Why is there lead in gasoline now? Of course, there are scientific reasons, but also there are political reasons. Who is doing that? What refineries? If we do make it without lead, who is capable of investing in it? Why is this government in favor of it? So, you have to have good analytical skills." (Staff member at UNEP)

"I would say kind of a strategic approach to things, thinking through things to make sure that they make sense, to make sure that they are coherent, that you are able to get from a policy concept to getting something done and all the steps in between. And then you can see what needs to be done. Because we have, I say, some brilliant minds that can think about policy, can think about concepts, but they cannot get things done." (Staff member at UNEP)

"You also need the ability to quickly grasp and structure situations and to set priorities in order to quickly transfer these into operational political decisions." (Staff member at UNDP)

"But I suppose the sorts of skills that everyone is supposed to get at university are analytical and I think the situation, thinking up options, thinking up a logical conclusion are very important." (Staff member at the GSC)

Furthermore, some professionals mentioned that methodological expertise – the experience and know-how to select and apply the most appropriate research methods (qualitative and quantitative research techniques, econometrics and the use of software packages), and to design, coordinate, and carry out data collection and analysis activities – is important for professional positions at international organizations.

To accomplish the tasks at the workplace successfully does not only requires analytical or management skills, but also *IT or computer skills*. Professionals must at least be proficient in the most common software programs (e.g., Microsoft Word, Excel and Power Point), as most work is done on the computer. Three professionals explained it as follows:

"It is important to be quite familiar with computers. It may have been possible to be 'computer-illiterate' ten years ago, but you can't get by that way today." (Staff member at UNDP)

"IT tends to be something which is helpful. It tends to make you spend less time on a process so that it frees you to be able to deal with bigger issue." (Staff member at UNEP)

"I believe that people must be able to deal with communications technology today. It is taken for granted so much that it does not even need to be mentioned." (Staff member at the GSC)

Summarizing the results, we conclude that knowledge specific to the organizations' tasks, administrative and organizational skills, and project management skills as well as capacity to collect, organize and apply knowledge, in short professional-methodical competencies are very crucial for a successful job performance in international public service.

3.3.2. Social-communicative competencies

The group of social-communicative competencies includes knowledge and skills with which communication and cooperation at the workplace are made possible. These competencies are sometimes subsumed under "social skills", "soft skills", or "people skills". Regardless at which international organizations one works, adequate and effective skills related to working with people are of vital importance. One skill related to working with people and mentioned by many employees is the *ability to work in a team*, as most of the work at international organizations is done in teams. Teams can change very often and thus require frequent team formation processes across issues and sectors of the organization. Knowing how to form a team, work collaboratively and productively with colleagues – including encouraging their ideas and expertise and sharing the workload with them – as well as fostering team spirit, was identified as a very important skills set. The following statements made by employees at international organizations emphasize how important teamwork skills are:

"You have got to really be a team player, because you are working as part of a big team – whether it is in your section or your division of UNEP or the UN." (Staff member at UNEP)

"You want somebody who relates well, works well as a team member, because there is no work which you can do alone. In any unit or organization, you will be required to work with other members. So how your work cooperates with the others in order to complete the full set of tasks which either a unit or a department or a division is doing is a good qualification to have – working with teams." (hiring manager at UNEP)

"Teamwork is very important; it is becoming even more important." (Staff member at ESA)

"Among soft skills, the ability to work in a team is very, very important, so that one can get used to working with different teams. My team was completely Kirgisian at first but now I work with international employees, and you must always find a way to work with them and not to view your own ideas as the be all and end all, even if you do not understand certain things or it all seems to be moving very slowly. You must show patience and a certain tolerance threshold. That is certainly important and can be a source of frustration... I can say that in my own case." (Staff member at UNDP)

Furthermore, most professionals at the international organizations pointed out that communication skills – including presentation, rhetoric, negotiation, listening, drafting, and writing skills – are some of the main skills contributing to one's professional success. Communication skills are needed in some of the most decisive situations that occur in the work-place – with colleagues, at meetings, during disagreements, and at nego-tiations. Therefore, it is important to speak and write clearly and effec-tively as well as listen to others. One should be able to communicate one's thoughts and ideas effectively, whether in a verbal or written format. If one wants to succeed at an international organization, one must know how to write clear, succinct, and grammatically correct business commu-nications (e.g., letters or e-mails) for an international audience. Moreover, professionals stressed that the ability to write good project proposals, memos, or reports is an essential skill both for program managers and for many of those who report to them. Professionals at international organi-zations described the necessity of communications skills as follows:

"But I guess communication is something that you do not learn in the university. Well, you do... people are always assuming it is something that comes naturally, which it does, but then especially in this organization, it is very important." (Staff member at UNEP)

"It is very good if you are a good writer. I think not very many people are very good writers. [...] I mean obviously writing different languages, but you can write clearly and logically, can tell a story, and that is very much what we do here. You are doing evaluations. You basically tell a story. You say this is the story about this project, what worked, what did not work, and how it would have been better." (Hiring man-ager at UNEP)

"I suppose it comes to communication. I think you need to be able to write well, you need to be able to communicate well with the people you work with and with the delegations." (Staff member at the GSC)

"Communication is a necessity the ability to make an appointment and to express yourself in a good way." (Staff member at ESA)

"You need to be an effective and efficient communicator. Most of the time you have to listen. You are listening to the development officials. You are listening to the ex-ternal media, you are listening to your clients, and you are constantly listening all

*the time. So you should be an effective listener [within the area of communication] ."
(Staff member at the World Bank)*

To effectively work and communicate in an international organization that brings together people from different countries with different interests, goals, and opinions requires intercultural skills. Many professionals mentioned the importance of being a competent intercultural communicator. They said that candidates for professional posts should possess the ability to take into account aspects such as political ideology, religious affiliations, demography, and economic, social, cultural, and geographic realities. They should be able to tolerate the different interpretations others make about different facts and happenings. The professionals we interviewed described it as follows:

"I think if you want to work in the international context, you have to be very, very conscious of national differences. You have to be much more geographically conscious, sensitive to cultures and all the cultural diversity [...]. You need to be much more culturally conscious of these diverse backgrounds in terms of culture." (Staff member at UNEP)

"You have to be extremely flexible and accommodating in many ways. You have to be able to adapt to new situations and to working in a multicultural environment. And you have to understand that nothing is right and nothing is wrong when it comes to culture and ways of doing things. Because our way of doing it, or the European way of doing it, is not more right than the Asian way of doing it. It is just different. And when you mix all these cultures, you have different ways of approaching all issues and all problems." (Staff member at UNEP)

"And you have to have the cultural awareness to be able to work around it and to know that if you're with an Italian, he needs to explore all the different options, and he needs to talk and talk and talk and talk, whereas you, as an Anglo-Saxon or something, you've already thought about all this and you just want to get to the point. And everybody gets frustrated. So you have to have a huge amount of tolerance for this." (Staff member at the GSC)

"Any questions with regard to multicultural awareness or ability to adopt in a different country were a piece of cake for me to answer." (Staff member at ESA)

"I am the only German in my department of the UN. That is an interesting professional experience, because I don't think it happens to many Germans. It is associated with a certain amount of stress, in that you have to deal with and learn to interpret intercultural differences, and that you have to express yourself differently so the others will understand you. It is important to speak the language well and to have intercultural experience, to be able to remove yourself from the situation and see what the others mean and try to understand where they are coming from. What is their style of communication and what message are they trying to get across?" (Staff member at UNDP)

With regard to effective communication skills in cross-cultural and cross-sectoral contexts, professionals mentioned the necessity of diplomatic skills. This skill also includes the ability to communicate and negotiate effectively with people from different business, organizational and national cultures, as the following statements show:

"Then you have to have certain diplomatic skills. Again, we do things in one way, and you mean one thing by doing it. We can't be ironic, we can't be straight to the point, you can't use the same way of talking to people. At the end of the day, one thing in the UN you have to avoid is making enemies, unfortunately." (Staff member at UNEP)

"I talk with people in foreign ministries. I deal with them one-on-one, you know. I deal with foreign ministry representatives, the Ministry of Foreign Affairs, in the thirteen governments with which we have agreements; I deal with government officials. So some diplomatic skills would, I think, be very beneficial." (Staff member at UNEP)

"You have to be an international diplomat – otherwise, you just rub people the wrong way. And you cannot work on that basis. So, I think one of the very important things is to be tolerant, to be respectful, to value other people's viewpoints [...], because we all come from different places, we all have different experiences, but we have got to somehow work together to make it work, especially in the UN. So I think that is number one." (Staff member at UNEP)

"You have the top-level communication, diplomatic consultations. But in an international organization, you really have be able to communicate in a much, much more advanced way than you have to do in a uni-national – you know, if you're back in Sweden or whatever – you really have to be able to communicate with people. I see such a lot of misunderstandings of things just because of the culture problems." (Staff member at the GSC)

"It is how to deal with authorities. We have meetings with the ministers. It is communication skills that you need and that are required for this kind of dialogue. You have to learn, you have a meeting with the minister today, it goes well and thinks what was good, and what was not good. And then next time you try to improve. How can I reach the government? It is very important in our position to have the trust of the government. They need to trust us; they need to trust the institution." (Staff member at the World Bank)

Working and communicating effectively with people from different backgrounds requires not only cultural awareness, but also foreign language skills. The ability to speak one or two foreign languages can help to strengthen each person's communication abilities and intercultural skills, as relationships can then be built up more easily. Professionals at the international organizations examined mentioned that proficiency in English is a requirement for any position at their organization, as most written and spoken communication is done in that language. However, they further emphasized that speaking a second (or third) language is crucial. The following statements underline the importance of foreign languages skills:

"I think a solid foreign language education is very important to gain access to jobs at international organizations. English is a must, plus either French, Russian, or Spanish, and ideally one other language that qualifies you to deal with a special region, such as Persian or a Southeast Asian language. That's how you can set yourself apart from the others." (Hiring manager at UNDP)

"Language skills are a very deciding factor, very necessary for my current field of work".(Staff member at the GSC)

"Knowing 36 languages is not what is required, but certainly knowing English plus one or two very well and mastering English is a must. You cannot function in this organization if you do not master English. You will have too many obstacles, and at this stage one has to recognize that French comes far behind, far behind." (Staff member at UNEP)

"English is very important. But English is not all of it. If you really want to be successful, you need a second language, a second pillar. That depends on where you are, what area you come from. It can be Spanish, can be French as a classic, it can be Portuguese or whatever. Normally it is at least English and Spanish." (Staff member at the World Bank)

Within the group of social-communicative competencies, the results obtained from our study have shown that communication skills, including presentation, rhetoric, negotiation, listening, drafting, and writing skills, teamwork skills, intercultural skills, and foreign languages skills are very important for any post at international organizations.

3.3.3. Activity and implementation-related competencies

In addition to professional-methodical and social-communicative competencies, many professionals emphasized the importance of activity and implementation-related competencies which are very useful for their current field of work. The group of activity and implementation-related competencies includes skills, attitudes, and behaviors that enable a person to act in a proactive and overall self-organized manner.

First of all, working in international organizations implies a need for a *high degree of flexibility and mobility* to respond to the changing job responsibilities, organizational contexts, and other challenges that might arise in the workplace. Professionals said that candidates for professional posts at international organizations should possess the ability to adjust their behavior to the demands of a changing work and living environment in order to remain productive through periods of transition, ambiguity, or uncertainty. Behavioral flexibility and mobility would further allow one to function effectively with a broad range of people and groups and to adapt to a broad range of situations. Professionals at international organizations described this as follows:

"You must be willing to accept physical discomfort: heat, cold, filth, lack of warm water, noise, problems with the food. If you want to have a career later, you have to work in regions that don't have a central European climate. You have to react very flexibly. You have to be able to quickly learn the ropes in new work areas. You must be able to do everything for the first time on every mission. Your opportunities on the job market are much better if you're able to react flexibly and quickly become acquainted with new areas of responsibility." (Staff member at UNDP)

"I think if you do not have this flexibility or this cultural sensitiveness, you will have constant headaches and get very frustrated." (Staff member at UNFPA)

"I think also being flexible, being able to diagnose the environment when things are changing and knowing how to diversify yourself are important skills." (Staff member at ESA)

"I feel that things move more and more quickly, so you would need to be able to adapt to new tasks. You can not be afraid of taking on new responsibilities and should be prepared to take on more responsibilities." (Staff member at the GSC)

Furthermore, candidates for professional posts should possess the ability to work independently and be organized. *Self-management* is a crucial skill for successful job performance, as the following statement made by a professional at ESA shows:

"We are really looking for people who have the ability to run things independently. [...] You really have to be able to look after yourself. You need to be able, as simple as it sounds, to manage this huge amount of e-mails that comes through, figure out of these five different paths where to go along with your project. And be able to get hold of information and things they will make your job easier and use the people who might have some knowledge." (Human Resources staff member at ESA)

Moreover, professionals are required to be assertive and proactive if they want to achieve their objectives in the workplace. Furthermore, showing initiative and interest contribute to job success as well, as the following statements show:

"You need to be proactive. You should know how to do things quickly and by yourself." (Staff member at UNICEF)

"You have to be assertive and independent, in terms of being able to work independently. You have to be assertive, because people do not tell you what to do. You have to ask the questions. You need to have lots of willingness to be initiative and creative. You have to ask people; you have to bug people; you have to research; you have to be independent; and you have to have a very strong character." (Staff member at UN-AIDS)

"I think you need to have a bit of initiative. Because it's not an institution where your rule is very clearly defined, so it is up to you, and I think you can create your own initiative and your own credibility with the delegations." (Staff member at the GSC)

"One needs a lot of initiative to get into the right networks, and to learn to work the UN System. You have to be flexible. There will be issues, which you didn't expect. People can come and ask you questions like 'What are you doing here? How did you get this position? Why did you get this position'" (Staff member at UNEP)

3.3.4. Personal competencies

Professionals at international organizations mentioned that personal competencies are needed to do their work. These competencies involve demonstrating objectivity, *integrity*, and *ethical behavior*. The professionals interviewed said that one should be able to treat others fairly and in this way contribute to a climate of trust, acceptance, and respect for others' principles, values, and beliefs. Values such as integrity, respect for diversity, and honesty help one to a successful career. Professionals at international organizations described it as follows:

"You have to be, I would say, very much open, very much tolerant. You have to learn languages and you should always respect people from foreign countries. [...] There is still the mentality to behave as a colonisator and this is not correct. You should mix with local people and try to build up relationships. You should forget that you are coming from outside and you have power here. You should try to communicate and respect the culture." (Staff member at UNICEF)

"So I think one of the very important things is to be tolerant, to be respectful, to value other people's viewpoints and respect it at work and on things in general because we all come from different places, we all have different experiences but we have got to somehow work together to make it work, especially in the UN." (Staff member at UNEP)

"The other behavioral thing is somebody who really has the capability of respecting clients who are much poorer and have come from more difficult circumstances than any of us can imagine. I have seen people with the other characteristics, who do not have the respectfulness of another human being. They are not of any use here." (Staff member at the World Bank)

"What I would see as the sort of universal competencies for this organization would be integrity [...]. You have to be able to stand on your own, free from pressure." [staff member at the GSC]

"I think also that integrity is very important for the international civil servant. Qualities of honesty, integrity; I think that is also very, very important." [staff member at UNEP]

"I think you also need to be very gender conscious. You need to have the ability to be able to treat women and men equally. Despite all the conventions and decisions and policies, we still have a lot of differences in terms of in practice. So in other words, you need to come up with a very open attitude and be adaptable to all kinds of circumstances." [staff member at UNEP]

Furthermore, professionals mentioned that the *commitment to a stable work performance* as well as the *commitment to continuously acquire new skills and knowledge* is required for a successful work performance. One professional at ESA explained it as follows:

"I need people who can still learn. [...] Nothing stands still here. You have to be willing to learn new things constantly."

Working in international organizations includes facing difficult demands. Therefore, many professionals mentioned that one should be *able to resist stress* and remain energized. It is important to be realistic and work within one's own limits. Professionals further said that it is also important to be aware of personal preferences, potential strengths, and weaknesses. As the following statements show, employees tend to link enthusiasm for and effectiveness at their work:

"You really need to like this job, because if you do not like it, go do something else. If you want to stay here, you need to survive on your own and be independent." (Staff member at UNAIDS)

"I think in terms of personal skills, it is very important to be motivated and to want to work in development. This is something very important to me, and I try to remember my motivation in difficult times. I try to make a difference somehow, though it just is a small one." (Staff member at UNFPA)

"You have to be strong mentally, quite strong in order to be able to manage. You have to be very insistent and persistent and strong, because you can get a lot of criticism and a lot of hassle and harassment and everything. [...] You have to know how to protect yourself against a big organization like this, because it's difficult and you're abroad. You're in a foreign climate. And you're very much more a victim of the culture and what's going on inside the organization than you would be if you had all your networks outside. You don't. You're alone." (Staff member at the GSC)

"You have to have passion to work in an environment like this one. [...] You cannot leave your country and come here to do business as usual. It does not work back home either. So you really need passion. You must love what you want to do. So people who are determined, I am sure they will get the work here because they have taken the right steps before, not only in the academic background but also with hands-on work and some kind of voluntary skills could be part of the curriculum, like you have to go and serve six months or one year away, or you have to do one year in a Latin American, Asian, or African country as part of the curriculum to promote that within the university." (Staff member at UNEP)

Table 3.10 Competencies for successful application and job performance

Social-communicative competencies	– Communication skills
	   – Presentation skills
	   – Rhetoric skills
	   – Drafting skills
	   – Writing skills
	– Intercultural skills
	– Diplomatic skills
	– Foreign language skills
	– Negotiation skills

Personal competencies	– Integrity – Respect for diversity – Self-awareness – Tolerance – Motivation – Stress resistance

Professional-methodical competencies	– Job-specific knowledge and skills
	– Basic knowledge of the organization
	– Basic knowledge of other international organizations
	– Basic knowledge of economics and politics
	– Basic knowledge of policy analysis, development, and implementation
	– Knowledge specific to a country or region
	– Basic management skills
	   – Organization and planning skills
	   – Office management skills
	   – Time management skills
	   – Staff and team management skills
	   – Leadership skills
	   – Project management skills
	– Analytical and critical thinking skills
	– IT/computer skills

Activity and implementation-related competencies	– Flexibility – Mobility – Assertiveness – Initiative – Self-management

Source: Authors

To sum up the results obtained concerning the knowledge, skills, and personal attitudes needed for a career in international organizations, Table 3.10 gives an overview of the competencies required for a successful application and job performance at the international organizations examined in this study. Here, it is important to mention that these competencies do not operate independently. It is their successful interaction which enables professionals to work effectively. At the same time, their list of competencies is rather long and somewhat idealistic. It would be unrealistic to expect a candidate to fulfill all of these requirements one hundred percent. Furthermore one must keep in mind that employees have a tendency to overstate the qualifications needed to do their work.

3.4. Competency development at higher education institutions

In the last section of this report, we described the competencies needed for successful job performance at the international organizations examined. As mentioned in the introduction to the labor market study, this research project goes beyond the questions about required competencies. It also focuses on the development or acquisition of these competencies, in particular during one's university education. Therefore, another very important issue in this study was the employees' evaluation of their university education with regard to the development of the competencies needed for their current field of work. This allowed us to identify which of the competencies required were acquired and developed during their university education.

When analyzing and drawing conclusions from the empirical data collected concerning university education and competency development, one must keep in mind that the professionals who participated in our study already had several years of professional experience in the international public service and that their answers to the retrospective question about their university education and level of job preparedness can thus only be answered in view of these experiences. This is, however, precisely what we hoped to obtain: a subjective evaluation in light of professional experience rather than an "objective" picture of what universities do.[60] Furthermore, as the interview and survey participants obtained their degrees in different countries and at different times, the following evaluations do not refer to specific higher-education institutions. The professionals' experiences provide too much variation to draw precise conclusions concerning a specific higher-education system, such as the German or Anglo-Saxon one. However, we sought to detect possible patterns among the professionals' answers.

3.4.1. Successes in competency development

Generally, when reviewing the data, it is apparent that the professionals' answers covered a wide range of possible replies, ranging from 'not

---

[60] This latter aspect was examined in the curricular study.

important/completely useless' to 'very important/very helpful', only to name the extreme ends of the continuum. The majority, however, rated their university education as useful for their current field of work, in particular with regard to the development of some skills within the group of professional-methodical and social-communicative competencies. Most professionals mentioned that the analytical and critical thinking skills needed for a successful career at international organizations were provided by their university education, regardless of the area in which they earned their academic degrees.

For example, in the survey conducted at the OSCE, the professionals were asked to rate how significant their university education was for developing certain skills.[61] Here, as Table 3.11 indicates, the OSCE employees rated analytical skills and communications as being taught quite well in their university education, while management, social, and leadership skills are rated lower but are still in the upper area between less important and important. With a mean of nearly 3, the professional expertise needed for working with the OSCE was said to have been provided by one's university education, yet this still leaves room for improvement.

The results of the survey conducted with employees at the GSC show a similar picture regarding skills and knowledge provided by university education (cf. Table 3.12). While language and analytical skills were rated as being taught very well in higher education programs, communication and social skills, professional expertise, and intercultural competence are rated lower but are still in the upper area between "less important" and "important". With a mean of nearly two and less, detailed knowledge on EU institutions and processes, management skills, leadership skills, and IT/computer skills needed for working at the GSC were said to have been provided in one's university education, yet this certainly leaves room for improvement.[62]

---

[61] The skills were defined as follows: Communication skills (presentation skills, rhetoric, writing skills); Leadership skills (Assertiveness, Task delegation, ability to motivate others); Analytical skills (ability to identify and solve a problem, critical thinking); Management skills (administrative abilities; organization skills, time management); Social skills (intercultural competence, ability to deal with conflicts, interpersonal skills); Professional expertise (Background knowledge for their current occupation).

[62] Here, when drawing conclusions, one must keep in mind the educational backgrounds of the GSC employees: Most of the employees (72.8%) who work in the Language Service studied foreign languages as their major subject and, as our study has shown, they rated their university education highly in providing them with language skills, while detailed EU knowledge could have been taught better. In contrast, employees of all other DGs, who have their majors mainly in law, political science, business and economics, evaluated their university education as "less important" in developing language skills but as "important" in providing detailed knowledge on EU institutions and processes.

Table 3.11. Evaluation of university education by OSCE professionals

Skills	University education was ...
	|4 = very important
Analytical skills	|3.51
Communication skills	|3.09
Professional expertise	|2.97
Management skills	|2.77
Social skills	|2.76
Language skills	|2.74
Leadership skills	|2.54
IT / computer skills	|2.36
	|1 = not important

Source: Authors' survey data
Notes: Values in table are means of a 4 point scale. n=96-98 (number of answers for each skill).

Summarizing the results obtained from the surveys at the OSCE and GSC, it is apparent that analytical and critical thinking skills were mainly developed at higher education institutions, whereas the acquisition of all other competencies, in particular management skills, leadership skills, as well as IT/computer skills did not take place at university.

A more detailed picture can be shown when interpreting the data collected through qualitative interviewing. Firstly, as the statements below illustrate in an exemplary manner, professionals at ESA, UNEP, the World Bank and the UN agencies and programs also said that the academic training they received at university did well in developing analytical, critical thinking, and problem solving skills. These skills were gained primarily through hands-on problem-solving exercises and situational projects or more specifically in situations where they had to apply their knowledge:

"I think what we get from university is a lot of tools. It is a way of doing things. It is a way of analyzing. It is a way of approaching a certain problem in a structured way. You know, that is what we very often get. It is not how to develop a budget. It is more as a tool. But the tool can be applied to a certain extent." (Staff member at UNEP)

"I think what I got from my degree mainly is how to solve problems, how to tackle a new area, how to approach it and how to gain information about that area." (Staff member at UNEP)

Table 3.12. Evaluation of university education by GSC professionals

Skills	University education was ...
	|4 = very important
Language skills	|3.2
Analytical skills	|3.1
Communication skills	|2.8
Professional expertise	|2.8
Intercultural competence	|2.5
Social skills	|2.2
Detailed EU knowledge	|1.9
Management skills	|1.9
Leadership skills	|1.8
IT / computer skills	|1.7
	|1 = not important

Source: Authors' survey data
Notes: Values in table are means of a 4 point scale. n=493-501 (number of answers for each skill).

"The methods of learning things and acquiring new knowledge – that's what it was good for." (Staff member at ESA)

"My history degree developed my ability to assimilate large amounts of information, to prioritize them, to summarize them effectively, and to be economical with my written and spoken work." (Staff member at UNDP)

"In terms of the master's, I think that gave me theoretical structures with which I can particular analyze development issues. I learned strategic analyzing skills, which help in the developing sector. The most relevant course, which I first thought would be least relevant, was strategy. That really forced me to be much more objective about what I do... To think about link aims, objectives, inputs, resources and everything and to look at everything I do in a much more logical way. So I can combine the objective with the subjective side. My decisions are much better now and I am much more effective now, when it comes to spending money." (Staff member at UNDP)

"I learned how to solve problems and how to investigate solutions and policy options. It [problem solving] trains your mind. It specifically trains you to do things. I think that education gives you the skills of thinking, learning, searching for solutions." (Staff member at the World Bank)

"In terms of skills, I would not say that any of the hard skills that were taught there are being used in my current job. But in terms of being able to think analytically and solve problems it helped a lot." (Staff member at the World Bank)

Furthermore, in particular, the employees at ESA, UNEP, and the World Bank pointed out that their university education provided them with sound theoretical and substantive knowledge, relevant methods and techniques specific to the subject area studied, as the following statements indicate:

"I would say it was pretty good in terms of the substance. I mean, I did geography and ecology for coursework. I did physical geography, biogeography, and those kinds of things which are very closely related to (a lot of) environmental issues. It gave me a very good understanding of basic ways that things work in the natural world. [...] Things to do with soil biology and plant ecology and physical events, all these kinds of things; I have a basic understanding... So it was pretty good." (Staff member at UNEP)

"So, yes, my university prepared me for my technical expertise, prepared me also in a way that I was trained to question technical issues or facts or just to make sure that we have a sound base, or that whatever decision we take is based on correct information. But that is probably something that is probably not specific to any university; it could be developed generally when you go to university." (Staff member at ESA)

"My master's and my Ph.D. were in international macroeconomics. So I was familiar with the topic the World Bank deals with. [...] I was familiar with monetary policy, exchange rate policy, because all my research was on that. So it really gave me a good theoretical background." (Staff member at the World Bank)

As highlighted by professionals at the OSCE and GSC, interview participants at the World Bank also said that social-communicative competencies were acquired in their education. At the World Bank professionals mentioned that, in particular, intercultural and communications skills were mostly gained through either attending educational programs with an international student body or studies with an international and/or development perspective, as the following statements show:

"I think the intercultural communication came from Russian studies and studying at SAIS, where there are people from 60 different countries. So that's where I think I picked up the intercultural skills." (Staff member at the World Bank)

"I would say I didn't have any special training. But the environment of the schools is multicultural. I had to teach at Stanford so I just got thrown into it [...] That required me to communicate well." (Staff member at the World Bank)

3.4.2. Shortcomings of competency development

As previously mentioned, we were not only interested in the skills and knowledge provided by educational programs. Another objective of this study was to identify which competencies needed in the workplace were not imparted at higher education institutions.

99

Figure 3.6. Skills missing from university education of GSC professionals

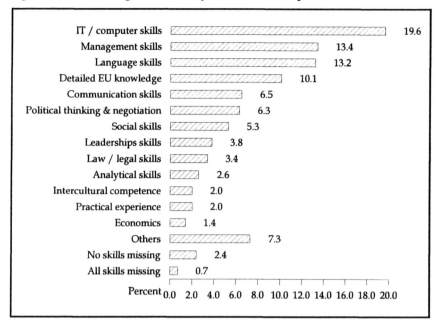

Source: Authors' data survey
Notes: n=289. *Answers to open question on missing skills and qualifications were recoded into categories.*

The survey conducted at the GSC showed that IT/computer skills (19.6% of all answers), followed by management skills (13.4% of all answers), language skills (13.2% of all answers), and detailed knowledge on EU institutions and processes (10.1% of all answers) were lacking from university education, as Figure 3.6 shows.

As Figure 3.7 shows, the OSCE employees said that management, social, and leadership skills, and the professional expertise required for working with the OSCE were not imparted at higher education institutions.

Professionals at ESA referred as well to basic management skills, project management skills, leadership skills, communications skills, and also personal competencies such as flexibility and adaptability. At UNEP many professionals mentioned that knowledge of the UN System was not provided by their university education. One professional at UNEP described it as follows:

Figure 3.7. Skills missing from university education of OSCE professionals

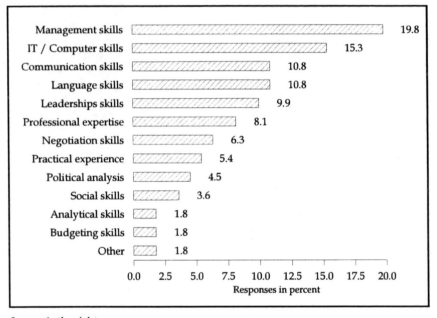

Source: Authors' data survey
Notes: Answers to open question on missing skills and qualifications were recoded into categories.
The 0.1 percentage points missing to are due to rounding errors.

"From my experience, something that I never received and either in my studies or within the UN is really a lesson on the UN. What is the UN System all about? And there are many things that I cannot answer today even though I have been in the UN now for eight years and will probably stay, and there are certain things I will probably never know which would be helpful if I did know and it would take some time now for me to figure them out if I wanted to."(Staff member at UNEP)

Furthermore, some of the employees interviewed at UNEP mentioned a lack of flexibility in educational programs. They said that it would have been beneficial to their career development if their university education had offered them the opportunity to choose between a greater variety of courses and combine degree programs in different disciplines, as the following comments show:

"If I look back, I think that the current system is much better, where you can do a bachelor in economics and a master in political science. Now you have a much better possibility of combining different fields in order to fit your future career perspectives much better."(Staff member at UNEP)

In general, when asked what was lacking from their university education, professionals at all international organizations examined in this
study said that practical training or workplace learning needed for developing basic competencies was not provided. Here, professionals stressed
the importance of work-related competency development through traineeships, internships, and volunteer work that can be done during university education. As mentioned in section 3.2 when describing the professional background of employees in international organizations, work experience was viewed as particularly relevant for entering the
organization and for the accumulation of relevant knowledge and skills.
The following statements illustrate again that professionals developed
most skills needed for their current field of work on the job:

*"I think what allowed me to come here to ESOC is more what I did after university.
And probably looking back now, my university education lacked practical knowledge
in the industry." (Staff member at ESA)*

*"I would not say that I could have arrived at this position straight after coming out
of the university. You need to have experience, especially when you manage people
and projects." (Staff member at ESA)*

*"I cannot overstress the importance of internships. I have done several internships as
a graduate. [...] And in all those experiences, they really provided me with insight in
my field of specialization but also in the difficulties to convey a message, to transmit
information, to teach people, or to learn from them. So not only cultural boundaries
are obstacles but [also] language barriers, social barriers, and cultural barriers in
general; food could be a problem." (Staff member at UNEP)*

*"I learned a lot when I was in volunteer work by my sole objective when I went to
work with this program in order to see how effectively it could be used to promote the
engagement of African consultancy in development projects. It gave me an opportunity of looking at things without having a motivation of money per se at the beginning. So that gave me a very good opportunity to just concentrate on doing best in
the course which I was working for. And then this opens up your mind of being able
to understand the problem, [and] how to have some solutions, too." (Staff member at
UNEP)*

Drawing conclusions from the results presented in this section, it is apparent that professionals at the international organizations examined acquired the competencies needed for their current field of work in dualistic terms: university learning and workplace learning. Analytical and
critical thinking skills as well as subject-related competencies were
mainly developed during university education. Professionals further
mentioned that their university education provided them with knowledge, relevant methods, and techniques specific to the subject area studied. But the acquisition of all other competencies and expertise required

by international organizations, in particular social-communicative, activity and implementation-related, and personal competencies, took place at the workplace. The results of this study show that basic competencies required, for instance IT/computer skills, basic management skills, project management skills, and knowledge specific to the organization, are not sufficiently developed during university. Besides the lack of competency development, the professionals identified further weaknesses of their university education: (1) lack of internationalization of the curriculum, (2) focus on theory rather than practicability, (3) lack of interdisciplinarity, (4) lack of international comparative topics, (5) lack of courses on international organizations, (6) lack of workplace learning. Although the order and entries slightly differ with regard to the organizations examined in this study, it is apparent that higher education institutions must make some investment if they want to prepare their students better for international work.

3.5. Evaluation of the German educational system

At the World Bank, we conducted a separate analysis of German staff's perceptions of their university education in Germany.[63] We also added to this analysis comments made by a few German professionals at other international organizations examined in this study. Thus, we were able to specifically address weaknesses of the German education system that potentially hinder a professional career at international organizations in general and the World Bank in particular.

Many German professionals at the World Bank rated their German education as flawed and of little use for their current job. What is noteworthy here is that the criticism is backed by experience they had in their Anglo-Saxon graduate education, which adds a comparative component to their evaluations.

When asked to identify weaknesses in their education, professionals referred to the theoretical focus of the German education system as being "too much" and of little use to their current work. For one, the heavy emphasis on "reading books" inhibited knowledge application and the acquisition of important skills needed for their job at the World Bank; these include, for instance, communication skills exemplified in debating and public speaking skills, as well as analytical skills and strategic thinking skills, which require a more applied approach to teaching and learning.

---

[63] The sub-sample analysis included eight German professionals working at the World Bank. Most of them earned degrees in the German higher education system and in the Anglo-Saxon higher education systems.

Here, references were frequently made to Anglo-Saxon educational experiences as "best practice" examples.

"Honestly, I think the German system is very much reading books. It is not very relevant to what we are doing here, I think. I never studied here [in the U.S], but I noticed with my colleagues that they have many more analytical skills, and they are also much more into debating different concepts. [...] I think that is really something that is lacking." (Staff member at the World Bank)

"The German approach is very much one where you have to learn everything, the theories, mathematics. [...] Today, a lot of German economics at the university level is really not very relevant and regarded as opposed to having a practical and pragmatic approach, while economics in Britain is taught in a way where you are asked to think to question the system, to analyze yourself. You learn to assess whether a system is really realistic and what you can use it for. What we could do to make it better. It gives you more courage to question things. It's a more pragmatic approach. [...] Universities [in Germany] are so far and often remote from what really matters to our daily lives." (Staff member at the World Bank)

"And it [hands-on problem solving] really throws you in a very different world, and also psychologically...all of a sudden you start realizing, you start seeing yourself in these kinds of positions, which is the exact opposite of what you learn in German universities. I am just talking about the underlying messages that you get at the Kennedy School like 'you can do it' , 'you'll be in an interesting position of responsibility' later on and how would you deal with it, they prepare you for that." (Staff member the World Bank)

The issue of knowledge application as a weakness of the German higher education system with regard to preparing students for careers in international organizations was also raised by a German professional at UNDP:

"It now seems that my two years at [a leading U.S. university] were much more beneficial, precisely because they were very, very practically oriented and practical. Still, however, I wouldn't want to be without the basics. These were taught to me very, very well at [a big German university] – basics in the sense of the instruments needed in the social sciences and basic knowledge about Eastern Europe, the EU, and all the other things I studied while I was there. I don't think it would make much sense to exercise one's practical skills without having these basics. Both sides are important. Unfortunately, though, the conditions for studying are very different, even when the students and professors at each institution are equally good. This also goes for how well the libraries are stocked and how big the classes are." (Staff member at UNDP)

Other professionals at the World Bank shared a concern related to the relevance of the materials covered at university. As some professionals suggested, the selection of topics simply did not reflect what "really matters to our daily lives." In terms of breadth, one said that German curricula are "too narrow" and insufficiently integrated across multidisciplinary boundaries to allow for the type of generalist background, in addition to a specialized one, that is of high value for working at the World Bank. Again, as "best practice examples", professionals referred to their education outside of Germany. The following comments exemplify some of their concerns:

"One of the things that happens in Germany's education, going back to the earlier topic, is, it is too narrow, it is too much in silo terms, insufficiently integrated across multidisciplinary boundaries. This is one of the things that happens much more in Anglo-Saxon education in general than in Germany." (Staff member at the World Bank)

Concerning the selection of topics and teaching environment, they claimed, in a broad sense, that the German education system lacks an international outlook. In terms of the materials covered, one professional described the German curriculum as very specific to the German market and is often remote to what was happening on the international agenda during one interviewee's education. Hence, such lack of exposure to internationally-oriented topics either encouraged German professionals to pursue a graduate degree at an Anglo-Saxon institution or demanded a great deal of initiative to learn about topics of interest, as one professional suggested whose education took place in Germany only. When addressing specifically valuable topics for a career in international organizations, one professional said that substantive knowledge on international organizations was lacking in German education, while it appears to figure prominently in the curriculum of some U.S. graduate programs. The following comments exemplify the points mentioned above:

"What matters is the integration of the stuff, of the curriculum with what is on the international agenda. The important things in economics are, or when I studied, were defined by what is happening in the U.S. labor marked primarily, the academic labor market in America, the UK, and a few other countries, but Germany is not among them." (Staff member at the World Bank)

"At German universities, you do not even know what kinds of organizations exist. Sometimes you learn about the United Nations, but that is it. There [in the U.S.], I learned about what the World Bank is and what the World Bank does and the IMF and something that was useful." (Staff member at the World Bank)

In addition, several professionals criticized the teaching profession at German universities. While the education system was described in more general terms as "introverted" or "top-down" in its approach to teaching the student body, another described the quality of teaching as "second- and third-rate," compared to international standards. The fact that German faculty teaches and publishes largely in German exacerbates the disconnect of German universities for mainly English-driven market trends, as one professional suggested.

"I think in Germany you have one professor and he just teaches what he believes in. And that is pretty much about it. It is very much top-down. [...]I also believe that the university system really needs to change in Germany and needs to open up. It is all so surprising to me how introverted they are. They have no clue what we are doing here. So the university should also try to link up with international organizations so that they know what is required." (Staff member at the World Bank)

"In essence, the stuff that I got in Germany was useless. I am sure that you have heard that now many times. It is both the selection of topics, meaning the matrix choices in the curriculum, but it is also purely the quality of the teaching and [...], it is quite frankly by international standards, a lot of it is second and third-rate. It is just not first-rate." (Staff member at the World Bank)

"Also, I think that I only gained the elements that I needed through a lot of self-initiative. So I think if I had studied, you know Germany gives you a lot of freedom in terms of education, and particularly when it comes to economics, many students actually use it to choose the simplest way possible and if they do so they might have good grades, but they face deficits in their education itself and I see that very often. Let us put it in other words; a German education in economics allows you to finish a degree in economics and at the end of the day not even be an economist." (Staff member at the World Bank)

Aside from concerns with the curricula or teaching methods in the German education system, professionals raised one more issues that they see as directly affecting recent graduates' chances for pursuing a successful career at international organizations: Professionals at the World Bank and UNDP stated that the length and structure of the German education translates into a comparative disadvantage for Germans vis-à-vis, for instance, graduates from Anglo-Saxon universities. Germans are typically "older" and bring less work experience to the job than others:

"Definitely older once they [German graduates] are done. They arrive and have less work experience, which is a downside, and that really has nothing to do with the quality of the people or anything, but it is disadvantage, because at age 33, other people will have had ten years of work experience, whereas you have six and that matters because your CV is shorter." (Staff member at the World Bank)

"And then there is the structure of study programs, where people in Anglo-Saxon countries gain some work experience after their B.A. and then go back to university. That means that my colleagues from New York have excellent applications with their degree plus work experience. I can't compete with them then." (Staff member at UNDP)

Moreover, two German professionals voiced the opinion that the German educational system does not reward competitive behavior – a behavior they regard as positive and also critical for succeeding in the competitive environment of international organizations. Finally, respondents addressed the advantage associated with networking among universities as well as entertaining and fostering direct ties to the World Bank. Here, some U.S. and British schools were mentioned as having strong network ties and research cooperation with the World Bank in particular. Such networking appears to be lacking from German universities. The subsequent comments exemplify German's concerns:

"The education system in Germany is not oriented to provide us with a sense of competitive behavior. Competition is totally lacking at all universities, and I would say if you want to succeed in IOs, particularly if you go to the IMF or the World Bank or even the United Nations, I think you have to be very competitive in your behavior. I mean that in an American positive sense." (Staff member at the World Bank)

"I do not see it [networking between German universities and the World Bank]. If it really does happen, it would be an exception. I do not know why that is- if it is an issue on the university side, or..." (Staff member at the World Bank)

Summarizing the concerns shared by German professionals at the World Bank and other international organizations with respect to their education, we conclude that, in general, respondents are dissatisfied with the education they received in Germany. The following listing briefly identifies some suggested weaknesses and disadvantages of the German education system when linked to usefulness and job-preparedness: (1) lack of international outlook, (2) focus on theory rather than practicability, (3) curricula with emphasis on outdated rather than cutting-edge topics, (4) lack of cross-country comparative topics, (5) lack of development perspective, (6) lack of methodological training. Such concerns lead some German professionals to acquire relevant skills through additional education abroad. Germans in the sample who did not pursue a graduate education abroad stressed the need for "a lot of self-initiative" to acquire the competencies necessary for a job in the international public service. Based on such evidence, it appears that the German education system is ill-suited to prepare its students for a career in international organizations.

3.6.   Recommendations to higher education institutions

In this section, recommendations given by professionals at the international organizations on how to best prepare students for careers in international organizations are summarized.

3.6.1. Enhance competency development

As mentioned before, universities provided the professionals in our study with analytical and critical thinking skills as well as subject-related knowledge and competencies. However, with regard to the development of all other competencies needed for a successful job performance, professionals said that universities could do much better. Curricula in university education were often criticized for being overloaded with a specified and theoretical perspective on certain subject elements, which reduces flexibility and reference to practical issues. Professionals said the strong theoretical focus and the heavy emphasis on knowledge acquisition inhibited the learning of the competencies needed for a successful career at international organizations. By focusing too much on factual knowledge, there remained too little time for knowledge application and competency development. One professional at the GSC described it as follows: "Universities should focus more on practical aspects instead of theoretical issues – the importance of 'skills' instead of 'pure knowledge'." To compensate the lack of competency development, they suggested for one thing that universities should incorporate specific courses on competency development in the curricula of their educational programs to adequately prepare students for working in the international public service. Course design must address the specific nature of the competencies of a particular profession. First of all, they stressed that universities should ensure that students sufficiently develop the intellectual abilities of reasoning and critical thinking they need throughout their careers, as the following statement indicate:

"Universities should reward [students] more for critical thinking rather than learning by memorizing, foster presentations and class interventions, teach [them] how to write short documents and synthetic notes, and foster constructive criticism." (Staff member at the GSC)

To foster analytical and critical thinking skills, small classes in which interactive learning methods can be applied, rather than mass lectures which purely focus on the delivery of facts, should be integrated into curricula. Small classes are further venues where students can sharpen their communication skills, such as, for instance, debating skills, presentation skills, and how to make arguments in class. One professional at the World Bank described it as follows:

"I think it would be worth seeing how Oxford or Cambridge… It is a totally different system, where you work much more one on one, where you have debates about things, where it is outspoken, where it is not about handing in homework […] So, I think the mass university does not really help."

Furthermore, most professionals specifically indicated that universities could put more emphasis on training basic management-related skills, such as organizational and planning skills, staff and team management, and time management, as these skills are needed for any position in international organizations and careers in most other fields as well. In particular, courses developing project management skills should be a substantial part of educational programs. Students who are interested in pursuing a career in the international public service should know how to develop, implement, and evaluate a project. The following statements given by professionals underline the importance of developing and promoting certain competencies during one's university education:

"Universities should prepare students to fulfill management tasks." (Staff member at the GSC)

"And for a young person who is at the university today, they need to be taking leadership courses. They need to take management courses even if they are certificate courses." (Staff member at UNEP)

"For the universities, they should introduce what we call 'side courses' which prepare people in communication, public speaking, leadership, [and] programs that link them to international networks." (Staff member at UNEP)

"In addition to high-quality education from a substantive point of view, preparing the students from a managerial and leadership point of view, and dealing with them as partners and colleagues instead of subordinates." (Staff member at UNEP)

As mentioned before, not only "hard skills" should be sufficiently trained at universities, employees at international organizations also stressed that training courses developing social-communicative and personal competencies should be offered as well. As the following statements indicate, students should learn to work in intercultural teams, communicate effectively, and organize themselves:

"Focus on other things like teamwork and also really emphasize good writing and communication skills... some supplementary courses. I think if we start molding people early, then we will get a better result at the end... If we are talking about cultural diversity, the earlier you sensitize people to be culturally sensitive and to know how to integrate and communicate in diverse environments, then you definitely get a better effect than starting much later when they are set in their ways." (Staff member at UNEP)

"Universities should provide training in effective communication - written and oral - and good training in foreign languages. They should teach students to work in a team and in a hierarchical structure." (Staff member at the GSC)

"Teach them to manage themselves – how to cope in a highly politicized, uncertain environment. Teach diplomacy, tact, listening skills, negotiation skills.... Teach them

to write and to speak in public. Teach them the absolute need for a good work-life balance, the need to adapt culturally but not give up their identity." (Staff member at the GSC)

"They need to take diversity courses in intercultural differences. The more they can understand and appreciate the different cultures, the more suitable they are going to be for a UN position." (Staff member at UNEP)

Moreover, with regard to the development of social-communicative competencies, the analysis of the professionals' responses revealed that most of them recommended that universities should enable their students to work professionally in at least two foreign languages. Universities should not only offer languages courses, as this is not regarded as sufficient by professionals, but rather more they should be a substantive and mandatory component of each educational program aiming to prepare students for international work. One professional at UNDP described it as follows:

"Foreign language courses during one's studies should be encouraged, especially for the languages of international organizations: English, Russian, French, and Spanish. They should be required and not just take place occasionally, but rather a good amount of time should be reserved for them. Intensive courses and language courses abroad should be offered." (Staff member at UNDP)

3.6.2. Increase opportunities for workplace learning

Professionals at all the international organizations we examined strongly recommended increasing the number of opportunities for practical-oriented and workplace learning which contributes to the students' "preparedness for practice and professional life", as many competencies can only be developed at the workplace. To compensate the lack of learning in – and about – practical contexts, they suggested that universities should integrate extensive training periods, preferably on the international level, into their programs. Here, they rated internships, traineeships, and volunteer work as very good learning experiences and opportunities for competency development outside of academia. To ensure the quality of workplace learning, universities should make sure that internships or other programs provide real involvement in the actual work of an organization. Furthermore, it is important that the internship is academically integrated into program. Internships should be designed around a set of specific and sequenced tasks, activities, and experiences and closely related to other course elements through supervision, tutorials, seminars and written assignments. Students should share and discuss their experiences with academic staff and other students throughout the training period. If internships are not integral components of curricula, then universities should at least support their students in finding appropriate places, even simply regarding information on entry points.

With regard to workplace learning, professionals stressed the importance of gathering practical experience abroad. Working and living in another country is said to be important for the development of social-communicative and personal competencies. As our study and other studies have shown, work experience abroad is one main qualification hiring managers seek when assessing the suitability of their candidates. Therefore, integrating or increasing the number of opportunities for internships or other structured programs into the curriculum of educational programs would constitute the foundation for supporting the employability of students in the international public service, as the following statements illustrate:

"The universities should seek to prepare the people for the new challenges coming. And not just sitting in the classroom. Take up challenges in post-conflict areas. Where are post-conflict countries? Can we go there and practice our conflict-resolution skills? Yes, you need to be in the field where the action is much more than sitting and listening to the lecturer. If you are in Europe, challenge yourself by coming to the Sudan or Congo. [...] Those would really enhance the understanding and the broad scope that university students should have when they leave, because if it is too narrow, then they are thinking of only one direction. They are not even opening opportunities for employment for themselves because they are just narrowly thinking about one thing." (Staff member at UNEP)

"One thing that universities do not teach is how to work. So somehow, there has got to be a change, and there should be a hands-on work training, not only through internships, which I think are very valuable, but through doing one semester or one term in a multicultural international organization or resolving and addressing problems that some multicultural environmental organizations are having. Maybe the students could deal with them on a case-by-case-basis from the beginning. If the students are clear that that is what they want, that is the career they are looking for, they should be able to show a grasp of the different problems that you are facing in international organizations." (Staff member at UNEP)

"I think if the universities can do something in particular, it would definitely be to give the students the opportunity to have some placements as part of the course and not necessarily in the same country if possible, within industry or even exchanges with universities for three or six months." (Staff member at ESA)

"I think these universities have a great program, where they have integrated the practical experience with the classroom experience. So students spend some time in the classroom and a significant amount of time outside the classroom, getting something like an internship, but it is structured kind of differently. They come back with the experience, the practical experience, bring it back to the classroom and then you know have like a debate or common discussion about it and then evaluate the experience." (Staff member at the World Bank)

Professionals pointed out that internships and any other kind of preparatory experience are a good way to get to know people and build relationships, which can be helpful for career development as they can provide
one with professional support and information on the field of work one is
interested in. One professional at UNEP described it as follows:

*"Internships are a great way not only for you to get to know people [and] to get to
know the work but it gives you exposure to the type of work so you can decide what
area you might want to work in. So internships, of course, are very helpful." (Staff
member at UNEP)*

3.6.3. Balance theoretical and practical training

One issue in professional education is the relative importance of theory
and competency development. The question as to which of these two aspects of professional concern should be more strongly emphasized was
raised among the employees in international organizations who took part
in our research project. Although professionals highly stressed the importance of competency development, knowledge application, and workplace learning, they also said that universities as academic institutions
should not limit their curricular offerings to training courses on certain
key competencies needed for the workplace. On the contrary: they should
provide a solid combination of both academic courses *and* training
courses to equip students with thorough knowledge in a certain field of
study, the intellectual tools necessary to analyze situations and shape responses accordingly, as well as a wide range of useful competencies and
practical experiences. Ideally, students need some direct guidance as to
the nature of the field, some early practice in the field, and the opportunity to select for themselves a concentration and the mean to complete it.
Therefore, curricula should be fluid and comprehensive in nature by allowing students to take coursework that is focused on the delivery of
broader and/or specific knowledge while simultaneously offering
courses for knowledge application, competency development, and workplace learning. One professional at the World Bank described how the
balance between theory and practice was achieved at the university
where he or she studied:

*"I think the balance that was maintained there [respondent's graduate program] was
substantially due to the ability of the university to offer coursework which reflected a
number of different countries involved, focusing on East Asia or South Asia or Latin
America. Much exposure was given to the whole student body on that cause, which
is quite large, to a number of initiatives, to a number of events, activities... experiences, if you will, across the globe. And there was ample time for seminar and re-*

view. It was not just the concentration on university requirements, but the extension to seminar and review and the ability to read were very much in the British tradition of reading around a topic and then reviewing these regions." (Staff member at the World Bank)

3.6.4. Include applied policy seminars, case workshops, and team-based projects

To develop a well-balanced curriculum, one recommendation made by professionals was that universities should offer applied policy seminars, case workshops, situational coursework or team-based and hands-on projects. Here, professionals criticized, in particular, mass lectures that purely teach facts without any practical outlook or opportunity for knowledge application and competency development. Active learning/teaching methods which focus on real-world application in small classes instead of frontal modes of instruction were said to be very useful for preparing students to work in international organizations. By including case workshops, simulations, and team-based projects, students would be enabled to apply their knowledge and skills acquired in prior academic training. Moreover, while working on "real-world" projects for clients from the private or public service, students could experience kinds of problems they encounter in their future professional life. Hands-on projects would also provide an opportunity to learn the different phases of a project and thus experience a project life cycle – from the moment the project is conceived to its completion.

"In the US, there is a module called a 'workshop' that consists of a group of students that organizes an applied research project in cooperation with an international organization. I think that was one of the projects that prepared me best, as it combined all the elements of my current job in one single project. That means research, preparing specific topics, and finding literature. It also included time in the field. We were in Poland and Brussels and carried out a lot of interviews there. We carried out field research and then wrote a report, which we were able to present at the headquarters of the World Bank, among other places." (Staff member at UNDP)

"You choose a subject, work in a group, work on that almost throughout the whole year, and then you write a big report. It gives you a lot of freedom, but it is also very difficult sometimes to handle that freedom and you have from your normal education in high school these ideas that you have to have a teacher in front of you who will tell you what to do, and you do not have that there. But in the end, even though I was quite frustrated, I do think that it gave me some skills for acquiring knowledge of new problems, working with other people, writing reports, doing presentations, and things like that." (Staff member at UNEP)

"The curriculum should be very case-study based, because your students need to re-late to real situations. Concepts, formulas, models, yes, but supported by more case studies than anything else." (Staff member at the World Bank)

"Your entire class is built on this one situational project. And you are either playing a role or solving a problem, a complex problem, with different people playing differ-ent roles. [...] You really go in-depth into the scenario, and you are not just learning things on a very high level. [...] You are learning about one particular situation and applying your management principles or your hard skills. You are applying all of that to one particular situation. That was really good." (Staff member at the World Bank)

Project-oriented and team-based learning was rated as very beneficial for competency development by professionals, as students would acquire other skills in addition to project management skills such as client orien-tation, teamwork, and leadership skills that one needs in order to be suc-cessful in international public service. Employees at ESA, UNEP, and the World Bank described it as follows:

"In the universities, they should put more emphasis on building teams to work on projects. For example, in the last year before graduation, you designate several teams and they have to design a project. And they have to really sell the project and try to compete with any external company that is providing similar projects. [...] It helps you to start working in teams, because you always have weak points in the team, you have strong points in the team, and you have different people with different charac-ters. And the entire environment forces you to [...] create a product at the end of that. [...] In fact I would suggest [...] that the teachers sometimes should be acting as directors of a company, and try to evaluate the work not so much academically but in terms of value, other value." (Staff member at ESA)

"One thing that I liked about my school is that you work in teams all the time, solve problems, case studies, and they always put teams together that maximize diversity and to also set potential for conflict. I remember many times was very frustrated, be-cause you were dealing with people from four different countries, age groups, and gender and it was just so complicated to first of all draw out the same understanding of the problem at hand. But what we also learned is that if you were actually able to work through this frustration, the output would be much better than if you had ho-mogenous group." (Staff member at the World Bank)

3.6.5. Enhance extracurricular activities

Another recommendation made by professionals to enhance practicality in curricula was that universities should offer a sufficient amount of ex-tracurricular activities. They should organize study trips to international organizations or speakers' series, meetings, and conferences with practi-tioners to inform students about the functioning of international organi-zations, work conditions, recruitment strategies, and selection procedures. The following statements made by professionals at the GSC, ESA, and World Bank underline the usefulness of learning from practitioners:

"Universities should inform students about the internal functioning of the institutions, and organize visits to EU institutions in order for them to get a closer and more concrete insight into the way the institutions operate." (Staff member at the GSC)

"Universities should teach how they actually work, organize excursions to institutions, have simulations of meetings/procedures, etc., give more information about possibilities for internships. In short: be more in contact with real life." (Staff member at the GSC)

"Universities should bring the students more in contact with EU practitioners through the headquarters and field level, frequent visits to EU institutions or EU field offices, frequent lectures by practitioners in universities." (Staff member at the GSC)

"It would be good to get more guest speakers from ESA in. Just to encourage ESA to come and make presentations." (Staff member at ESA)

"We had presidents and foreign ministers visit the school, which opens the mind tremendously. And they come for brown bag lunches, some of them. And you can actually have a discussion with global players." (Staff member at the World Bank)

3.6.6. Increase cooperation with IOs, governments, and NGOs

In addition to extra-curricular activities, professionals suggested that universities should encourage close academic and other kinds of cooperation between faculty, students, and international organizations, governments, and non-governmental agencies. Practitioners from the private and public sector can be involved in the actual teaching process, in the curricular development and evaluation, as well as in career development activities. In the opinion of many professionals, teaching staff and students should maintain and update their skills and knowledge through a constant involvement of practitioners. There should even be a systematic evaluation of educational programs by practitioners to ensure the appropriateness in providing students with the most necessary knowledge and skills. Professionals said that academic programs should demonstrate responsiveness to new developments in the field of study by incorporating and building on practical and professional experiences. When interacting with and learning from leading professionals, students gain a good sense of the "real world" and about potential career paths. Furthermore, employees also stressed the link between theory and application: taking classes instructed by leading professionals introduced them to the applied dimension of what they had learned in their respective programs. The following statements underline the importance of such cooperation:

"It's crucial that the universities take into account the real tasks and challenges a specific career field includes and, in cooperation with the institutions, develop adequate curricula to prepare students to live up to those tasks and challenges."(Staff member at the GSC)

"I think the better way to prepare students is really to try to have more projects combined with ESA, so that you have really integrated them, and that is motivating for the student and also for the people of ESA."(Staff member at ESA)

"If you have a master's program like that, you should have firm agreements with international organizations concerning internships. Several American universities in particular have agreements with the UN. If you start up a program like that, you definitely need someone who will not only create an internship pool, but also make actual contracts or solid connections with international organizations. I believe this is very important." (Staff member at UNDP)

"It [education] was very relevant because of where we were located. I don't know if it is unique to this area but the university I was at, the professors were generally working in the profession that I am in. So I was not in pure academia, I was actually taking classes from professors who worked in the federal contract area or worked for MIT and all that stuff. So for whatever reason all the education I got, when I got out and started working I was able to apply a lot of what I had learned." (Staff member at the World Bank)

"The emphasis within the curriculum should encourage people to go on these traineeships and this whole issue of partnerships between universities, with private, public, NGOs, industries. We have for example here, when you study in the States or in the UK, you have a career office there. They are there to help you to get work, even during your curriculum or when you have Christmas holidays or summer holidays." (Staff member at the World Bank)

3.6.7.   Provide knowledge on IOs

As for the actual content of academic programs, most professionals strongly recommended that universities provide students with basic knowledge of the development, structure, and functions of international organizations; an understanding of the role they play in the development of in international law and policy; and the ability to think critically about their significance to contemporary global affairs. Furthermore, they suggested that those administering educational programs should create detailed modules on the instruments of international law and international economic development. Professionals at international organizations described it as follows:

"A master's Degree by coursework on international organizations and peacekeeping, something like that, I would outline a very long and detailed module on structure and function of various international organizations including their constitution, the various instruments of international law such as the various international conventions and other things like this. Many people do not know the impact of international organizations." (Staff member at UNIDO)

"Things like: What are the real mandates of each of the UN organizations? Where does one stop and one start? It is not really that clear cut, but it is something that would be helpful to know. What is the difference between being part of the UN Secretariat and not being part of the UN Secretariat? For example, in UNEP we are not part of the UN Secretariat. Why not? What does that mean? Why do I care as a staff member? What difference does it make to me? What is the difference between an organization and a program? The UNEP and UNDP are pro-grams. You have the World Trade Organization as an organization. What is the difference? Why should I care? There is a lot of talk now about the UN Environment Organization and transforming UNEP into that. Why? What does it mean?" (Staff member at UNEP)

"A basic course in how international organizations operate. It is pretty useful even if you have not been in one to understand the way that they have governing bodies and those give man-dates to the programs and you are there to deliver a program, work with governments, and all these kinds of things. And how the whole thing is structured, it is a valuable experience. It is something that I have never had that I just learned by being in it. But it would give people a head start to understand that." (Staff member at UNEP)

"They could provide detailed courses on the institutional structure and legislative procedures, and they could encourage contact with the institutions." (Staff member at the GSC)

"Provide something like a general course on the EU institutions (role, functioning, powers, etc)." (Staff member at the GSC)

3.6.8. Enhance the internationalization of higher education

Another suggestion made by professionals is that educational programs should be significantly internationalized in substance and structure to ensure international orientation in learning. Structurally, several professionals suggested that programs should be open to a diverse and international student body, which sets the context for helping students to develop a cross-cultural understanding of people and different perspectives. Essentially, such exposure would help students adjust to the international environment of international organizations, if they choose to pursue this particular career path. Two professionals described it as follows:

"I think it is important for the students to be able to get the opportunity to study with people from other countries, and remove all these stereotypes that the Spanish

are like that and the Germans are like that and the British are like that." (Staff member at ESA)

"When you are preparing a course, you should think about putting people in different countries so that they get the cultural and the language backgrounds that they need. That is what I would suggest."(Staff member at ESA)

"The education should be open to other nationalities. If only Germans take part, it doesn't do any good. It should also incorporate a great deal of experience abroad, both as a prerequisite for the study program and during the master's program, if possible." (Staff member at UNDP)

Similarly, the exchange of foreign students and scholars across cultural and geographical boundaries as well as partnerships and cooperative programs with universities in other countries could provide an international enrichment. International exchange programs can serve as an important measure to help students to acquire important international experience. Moreover, universities should not only offer and support such exchange programs; rather, it is more important for them to encourage their students to use these opportunities, as it would provide them with essential intercultural and language skills.

"I think they should try to either study or work abroad. I think it is important not to be too fresh in a sense – that they should try to practice, go to another country, and try to live there [...]. You can try to get the international experience which looks good on your CV and you also learn a lot. How it is to be the only representative of your culture in another culture." (Staff member at UNEP)

"Universities should motivate their students to spend some time studying abroad to improve their language and intercultural skills." (Staff member at the GSC]

"If you come just from your own country, always lived in your own country, never lived abroad, never looked across your own border, it just sends the wrong signals and so people who have studied or lived abroad are just a more natural fit and people who recruit for the World Bank know this and they are also able to articulate their experiences in a different way from people who lived the entire time in Germany." (Staff member at the World Bank)

"It is important to weave in the global cultures into the curriculum through exchange programs. Many students who study in isolated cultures fail when the come into international organizations." (Staff member at the World Bank)

Aside from providing students with the opportunity to study abroad, another recommendation was that English should the medium of instruction and research, as the following statement indicates:

"The university can offer a curriculum that's based in English and have an international diversified student body. Having an international student body makes it easier. It creates an environment that you encounter in international organizations." (Staff member at the World Bank)

Finally, the curriculum of the university should reflect the preparation of international citizens, through facilitating language competency and understanding of global, international, and regional issues. Every program aiming to prepare students for international work should have some global affairs content in its curriculum. The internationalization of higher education can be achieved by diversification through a thematically broader range of subjects covered and often an interdisciplinary orientation, as professionals suggested. Here, the importance of the integration of an international and intercultural dimension into the curriculum was mentioned to be a key stimulus of internationalization.

3.6.9. Enhance interdisciplinary aspects

In the opinion of many professionals, educational programs should include and combine coursework from various disciplines. This helps to develop an early understanding of different concepts, for instance. To experience multidisciplinary and interdisciplinary coursework would allow students to increase the breadth of their knowledge. This would help them to be successful in a cross-disciplinary and collaborative workplace such as at international organizations where employees have to work effectively across different fields and sectors. Professionals at international organizations described it as follows:

"In general, give the possibility to combine studies from different departments like humanities, political science, law, and economics. A too narrow education field narrows the mind." (Staff member at the GSC)

"And it would certainly be a benefit to have had courses that give you a basic understanding right across the border if you could. In those days, I think, degree courses were much narrower. And you did not really have the opportunity to mix geography and economics and any other. But nowadays, I think, you can tailor it. You know, we were on a course [of study] and you did those courses and that was it to get your degree, whereas now, you can pick much more... That is a real advantage, because you can build up a set of things which, if you know where you are going, then it helps." (Staff member at UNEP)

3.6.10. Offer joint and dual degree programs

According to most professionals, universities should provide opportunities for students to supplement their education with joint and dual degree programs to increase the breadth of their knowledge. They said that it would have been beneficial for their career development if their university education had offered them the opportunity to choose between a greater variety of courses and combine degree programs in different disciplines. Employees at UNEP and the World Bank described it as follows:

"I think you need to start making more well-rounded people like I said. Even if it means offering dual course programs – I have seen that offered a lot in America and Australia where they offer you a dual package program in one thing and another, and you qualify in two degree programs and you acquire a lot more skills. You find sometimes that is not what you need in life – to just be an expert in one thing." (Staff member at UNEP)

"The other thing that I see is that the curriculum should be fluid, but within a framework. It should be fluent enough for students to make choices or selections that would prepare them for a career of their choice. For instance, if somebody wants to be a public sector management specialist, then they should have the core curriculum and the additional curriculum, unlike somebody who wants to be a transport specialist - they also need to have a core and an additional curriculum."(Staff member at the World Bank)

3.6.11. Enhance career development activities

Many professionals mentioned that universities should provide students with early support and involvement in the career-finding process by assisting them in developing a professional network, improving interviewing and résumé-writing skills, and offering career information sessions.

As the personal interview is seen as an important assessment mechanism within the selection process at most international organizations examined, professionals said that universities should help students to prepare themselves well for the interviews. It is important that they are able to highlight their strengths and qualifications, and relate them to the particular position for which they are applying. Professionals described it as follows:

"Interview techniques are another thing. There are definitely skills involved in doing a good interview. It comes with practice, but I think that is something that in preparing people to move from university to try and get jobs, it is quite a useful thing to do. That is again something they did not used to do but maybe they do now." (Staff member at UNEP)

"I think career counseling is very important in this regard. Career counseling in universities is very important." (Staff member at UNEP)

"Universities should regularly organize conferences with EU practitioners on substance matters such as on recruitment possibilities and application strategies." (Staff member at the GSC)

3.7.   Conclusions from the results of the labor market study

When drawing conclusions from the demonstrated results concerning qualifications requirements and educational backgrounds of successful applicants and employees in the professional category, it can be stated that most of the international organizations examined in this study tend to hire employees with a multidisciplinary academic background, who combined, for instance, a degree program in natural science or economics with a postgraduate program in development studies, international relations, or public policy and administration. However, with regard to the subject areas or disciplines in which employees primarily earned their academic degrees, these vary by the organization and depend on the job in question. Yet without variation, international organizations seek people with expertise in at least one area or sector relevant to the organization's tasks and objectives. Therefore, specialization of knowledge can be regarded as a crucial qualification requirement, as we have particularly seen at UNEP and ESA as well as at the World Bank to some extent. However, for a successful career in the international public service, it seems that it is no longer sufficient to study a single discipline in isolation or obtain only one degree in a specific field of study. Goals and activities of international organizations are multidimensional, and they require staff members who are both generalists and specialists and able to deal with the different and complex issues that emerge in the workplace: As stated before, a natural scientist at UNEP should also have an understanding of policy development and implementation, as well as be familiar with basic business and accounting skills. Someone who applies for a position as an election expert at the UNDP regional office in Kyrgyzstan should possess specific knowledge about elections systems and the socio-economic situation in Kyrgyzstan in addition to basic project management skills. Therefore, a multidisciplinary background – as opposed to a sole area of expertise – was mentioned as being very helpful for a successful application and job performance. International organizations demand a "generalist" capable of understanding the work of specialists and able to synthesize knowledge from various fields. The perfect candidate should be prepared to wrestle with complex issues, sort them out, and produce logical and responsive conclusions.

An institutional bias toward a certain higher education system and universities with regard to recruitment and promotion decisions was only identified at the World Bank. The organization exhibits an institutional bias toward degree programs at Anglo-Saxon universities. Hiring managers suggested that staff is often recruited from prestigious universities, especially U.S. Ivy League, U.S. professional schools, and reputable British universities. The lack of practically- and internationally-oriented degree programs that provide students with professional competency development was mentioned as a weakness of the German education system when compared to degree programs at Anglo-Saxon higher education institutions in the U.S. and Great Britain.

Besides university education, another important qualification requirement for working at international organizations is likely to be the professional experience that employees gained in employment prior to their current position. As outlined in most vacancy announcements and job descriptions posted, professional positions in international public service typically require several years of work experience. The importance and relevance of diverse work experience for career development is stressed by most professionals. Candidates for professional positions should have gained their experience in different sectors and countries, as it shows that they acquired sufficient flexibility and the competencies needed for a successful job performance in dynamic and intercultural workplaces.

Through the labor market study we were able to identify competencies required by the professional world and to determine which of these competencies were acquired through academic training. The study has shown that the following competencies are essential for a successful job performance in international organizations: professional-methodical, activity and implementation-related, social-communicative and personal competencies. The analysis of the empirical data revealed that these competencies were acquired in dualistic terms: university education and workplace learning. Professionals said that their university education provided with them with the knowledge and skills of a specialized field of study, analytical skills and techniques of independent research. But the acquisition of all other basic competencies required by international organizations took place outside the class room. Since all competencies are crucial for a successful application and job performance and have become important criteria for employability at international organizations, higher education institutions must to do much better concerning competency development.

If they wish to act strategically as institutions that prepare students for professional life, they should or must somehow influence students' activities in developing their professional competencies. The recommendations made by professionals have shown that higher education institutions could do more to help students develop certain competencies and thus prepare them more efficiently for the workplace. In particular, educational programs which aim to prepare students for working in the international public service should pay sufficient attention to developing professional competencies. Professionals stressed that all basic competencies described should be defined as learning objectives of educational systems. However, although universities should enhance competency development, they should not become vocational or training institutions. The curricula of educational programs should reflect a healthy balance between theory and practice or academic and non-academic training. Professionals said that the curriculum should provide a combination of modules which concentrate on specific knowledge-transfer and modules which aim for the development of certain competencies and focus on practicality.

Furthermore, many professionals indicated that the implementation of active and problem-based teaching methods is the best means of equipping students with the competencies needed. Case workshops and teamwork projects enable students to apply their knowledge and provide them with the opportunity to experience real-life situations that may occur in the workplace. Here, the use and enhancement of project-oriented methods were said to be an important recent development, as they promote the development of social-communicative as well as activity- and implementation-related competencies. In this context, professionals also stressed the importance of work-related competency development. Internships or other structured programs included in educational programs would offer a great opportunity for competency development. Besides developing competencies, universities should increase their international orientation, the opportunities for extracurricular activities, the interdisciplinarity of their study programs, the number of joint and dual degree programs, and the scope of their career development activities. Furthermore, any kind of cooperation between universities and international organizations was regarded as helpful and even necessary to ensure the practical and professional outlook of educational programs. Practitioners should be involved in the teaching process, curriculum design and evaluation, and career development activities.

In summary, the recommendations made by employees at international organizations for higher educational institutions on how to further develop their academic programs and thus better prepare students for international public service are as follows:
1. Enhance competency development;
2. Increase opportunities for workplace learning;
3. Ensure an appropriate balance between academic and non-academic training;

4. Include applied policy seminars, case workshops, and team-based projects;
5. Offer more extracurricular activities;
6. Increase cooperation with governments, non-governmental organizations, and international organizations;
7. Provide knowledge on the role and function of international organizations;
8. Increase the internationalization of higher education;
9. Enhance multidisciplinary and interdisciplinary aspects of educational programs;
10. Offer joint and dual degree programs;
11. Enhance career development activities.

When drawing conclusions from these proposals, an internationally- and practically-oriented as well as interdisciplinary postgraduate educational program that focuses on professional competency development seems to be the best measure to prepare students for working in the international public service. This may even (or especially) apply to the German higher system, as one professional whom we interviewed said:

"Germany seems to be on the same level as other countries concerning scholarship programs. What is lacking are specific graduate programs. One would probably have to investigate which [graduate] programs exist, which have the best concepts, and which should be systematically promoted. It is difficult, however, if there are too many institutions like this, as international organizations have a limited intake capacity, and they tend to look at the universities they know, such as the LSE in England and the well-known policy schools in America. My opinion is that Germany needs institutes that combine political science, law, and economics in one degree program and have a more practical orientation like some programs in France, the U.S., and England. Germany is at a disadvantage for not having such schools and should therefore work on the profile of programs like this." (Staff member at UNDP)

As described by the professional in order to give proposals for future reforms in higher education, it is necessary to examine which graduate degree programs exist in Germany and other countries and how they educate and train students for careers in international organizations as well as whether they have already put the proposals mentioned above into practice. A comprehensive analysis of different degree programs aiming to prepare students for work in international organizations was carried out in the curricular study (cf. Chapters 4 and 5).

3.8. Germans at international organizations

In the scope of this study, we further hoped to find out to what extent German candidates fulfill the qualifications requirements at international organizations and how they measure up to their competitors from other countries, meaning what strengths and weaknesses they might have. This should help to determine whether or not German degree programs prepare their students for careers in international organizations and how they could do better.

In advance, it should be pointed out that the assessments given in this section refer to the personal perceptions of individual staff members in human resources departments as well as staff from other departments at the international organizations examined in this study. Therefore, one cannot jump to the conclusion that *all* Germans have or lack certain qualifications or experiences. As one professional described it, when discussing differences between German professionals and staff member from other countries, the individuals' personalities should be considered as well:

> *"It is hard to separate individuals, because I think of people as individuals rather than nationalities. And I have had three Germans and they are all very different in terms of their approach. So, it would be very difficult for me to say, because I had one that was excellent, one that was very good, and I had one that was not so good. It does not have anything to do with nationality or maybe even their educational background but rather the type of person that they are. How do they see things? How do they work? How do they get things done? How do they talk to people or interact? How do they build consensus around things rather than just kind of acting on their own? Are they able to think on their own without constant instruction?" (Staff member at UNEP)*

The most conspicuous deficit of German candidates, however, seems to be their long period of education or study in comparison to candidates of other nationalities. It has been a well-known problem for quite some time now that has already been criticized as an obstacle for a successful German personnel policy in international organizations.[64] The long period of education at German universities is one reason why German applicants are often older than young professionals from other countries. This entails two disadvantages in particular: First, compared to competitors of the same age from other countries, Germans have less professional experience. Professional experience is a substantive qualification requirement for professional positions in international organizations, and staff mem-

[64] Robert Bosch Stiftung (ed.), (1999). *Stuttgarter Appell an Bund und Länder, Wissenschaft und Wirtschaft: Für mehr Internationalität in Bildung, Ausbildung und Personalpolitik.* Retrieved July 5, 2007, from www.berlinerinitiative.de/materialien/1999_stuttgarter_appell.pdf. This is a joint declaration of the German Council on Foreign Relations, German Institute for International and Security Affairs, and the Robert Bosch Foundation with recommendations on how to improve the international focus of schools and universities as well as the German presence in international organizations.

bers responsible for recruiting personnel place even more emphasis on it than on the candidates' educational background. Second, the lack of certain qualifications and competencies may result from their lack of professional experience because these qualifications cannot be or were not acquired by academic training. Professionals involved in the recruitment of staff at the ESA described it as follows:

"Generally speaking, trainees but also other German applicants, especially for junior positions, are usually much older than the average. This is due to the long education. It starts with their high-school education and continues with their studies at university." (Staff member at ESA)

"In general, the education system in Germany is old-fashioned. Old-fashioned because people get their degrees very late. [...] If you consider that we are looking for people with first experience, then already there we have got a problem. [...] It is a disadvantage for the Germans because they start later." (Staff member at ESA)

"I have made the experience that some – e. g., Germans – come here at 30 years of age and still have not worked at all. Here, they compete with French and British candidates who got their degree when they were 22 and are now prepared to take on more responsibilities. There, the Germans are at a disadvantage." (Staff member at ESA)

"In Germany, students have more freedom, but then you're 35 and sending in your applications with 29-year-old French people or Italians for the same position. And you often lose to them." (Staff member at UNDP)

Therefore, a long period of study and a higher age with comparably less professional experience are major obstacles for a successful recruitment of German candidates. (This will probably change due to the introduction of the consecutive B.A./M.A. system.)

Another deficit highlighted by some professionals was the Germans' lack of mobility. In some cases, this was mentioned to be the main reason for the low numbers of German applicants. Professionals at ESA described it as follows:

"Unfortunately, German applicants very often lack the willingness to go abroad or to go abroad with the organization." (Staff member at ESA)

"The mobility of the Germans is not as high as, for instance, that of the Italians." (Staff member at ESA)

The major results for this low mobility are well known (cf. page 17) and are affirmed by staff members:

One interview partner mentioned the comparably high salaries in the German private and public sector and the living standard as a reason for the Germans being "tied to their roots". Furthermore, the lack of attractive re-entry opportunities in the German public and private sector hinders highly qualified candidates to seek employment in the international public service.

The assessment of the Germans' technical knowledge is very positive across the organizations examined in this study. The majority considers them to be "well qualified", "very competent", "knowledgeable", and having a "strong technical experience". At the World Bank and to some extent at the ESA, Germans are particularly appreciated for their work in certain technical areas. At the World Bank, they are viewed as very qualified in technical fields such as engineering, agriculture, infrastructure, and the environment. There appears to be a general recognition of German expertise in these areas. In the field of human development, Germans bring mostly implementation experience, which does not prominently factor into the World Bank's development approach. The subsequent comments exemplify the technical strength of Germans in certain areas (e.g., engineering), as opposed to other fields (e.g., human development):

"Where the World Bank is looking for Germans is certain technical areas, like infrastructure, transportation, urban development. Those are areas where Germans apparently are good. So engineering fields in a way. I think agriculture is also one of them." (Staff member at the World Bank)

"They are known for technical skills in certain areas [...] agriculture, environmental stuff, certain sections of engineering, I think water and power engineers. [...] But those areas are areas that Germans are known for, engineering, agriculture; less human development skills, meaning education, health and social protection and probably less economics, and stuff like that." (Staff member at the World Bank)

"And my problem with the Germans that I have hired has been, maybe it is just because it is human development, but we get more practitioner types who have gone out and worked in poor countries or have worked at KfW or something, where they implement programs and then they expect they'll come to the World Bank and it is the same. But in the World Bank, we are a bank essentially, so the analytical skills are highly prized and the practitioner skills are not as highly prized: Because we do not actually implement things, we finance to implement things. [...] If I had to characterize any negatives of the German people I have hired and worked with, they tend to come from the implementation side rather than the analytical side." (Staff member at the World Bank)

A member of the human resources department at ESA also rated the technical expertise of Germans as "very good". However, at the same time, this evaluation is put into perspective when they point out the overall context:

"In terms of expertise [the Germans] are very good. But, nevertheless, you have to consider on the other hand that this is a competition. If other people can present themselves stronger than it is the case here, you can say as many times as you want

that the candidates from Germany are good. So, the others then have the better hand and that becomes apparent then." (Staff member at the ESA)

The quote above indicates a weakness of German applicants – presentation skills and the ability to "sell" oneself during job interviews. Some professionals said that the German university education could do better preparing students for interviews by enhancing the training in presentation skills. It was mentioned that career development is obviously a larger component of education at universities in other countries.

Aside from a largely positive evaluation of their German colleagues' technical skills, some professionals said that Germans have very good organizational and language skills. Furthermore, Germans are described as results-oriented, pragmatic, and straightforward. Such skills were viewed as strong assets by many professionals. Results orientation is very valued, as it cannot be taken for granted among staff. Finally, many professional described their German counterparts as "very respectful of other cultures", which is a key asset for working in a multicultural environment. In terms of language skills and intercultural skills, one professional at UNEP mentioned that Germans even have a comparative advantage, as they are forced to learn other languages and therefore must be more open towards other nationalities.

"Well, we are going to get a little bit into to clichés here but never mind. I think the first thing is that for the most part, since German is not an official language of the organization, Germans know from the start that they are not arriving in a conquered land, that they have to fight for their place. That helps, unlike British and Americans on the one hand and French who speak the two working languages of the UN, so there is an attitude there which is more open. I think that Germans are always frank, very high in their reliability index, and that is a well-known factor. I think in general, this is one of the nationalities that is very appreciated – not necessarily the most appreciated in some ways and the most efficient." (Staff member at UNEP)

However, another professional at UNDP mentioned that Germans seem to have difficulty integrating themselves in a multi-cultural working environment, as they are not used to being a minority group.

"I think Germans also have trouble fitting in at international organizations, because they're in the minority there, which they're not really used to. There are many Germans and Germany is a large area to work in. That causes the same phenomenon within Europe that the Americans have in their country. Because there are so many of them, it often results in a somewhat closed attitude. [...] The Germans are a bit closed-minded and have little perspective for anything beyond their own realm, with regard to both their own domestic policy and in their career prospects and orientation." (Staff member at UNDP)

The analysis of the professionals' evaluations suggests that Germans are, overall, well-appreciated, both in terms of professional and behavioral skills, albeit with some exceptions. However, what is noteworthy here is that many Germans working at the international organizations examined in this study very often have an international background, or more specifically, a degree from an Anglo-Saxon higher education institution. For instance, at the World Bank, among the eight Germans interviewed, five held at least a master's degree from an Anglo-Saxon university. One professional at the World Bank described it as follows: "I think the Germans who make it here generally have some kind of international educational background often times, or maybe they grew up abroad." Moreover, it is apparent that many German professionals at international organizations gained work experience abroad prior to their employment at the organization.

Therefore, one can draw the conclusion that many Germans who work at the international organizations examined in this study may not reflect the "typical" educational and professional background of German officials in general, as they obtained a university degree, also training and work experience abroad. As previously mentioned, German professionals who earned a degree both in Germany and the U.S. or Great Britain rated their German education in comparison to their Anglo-Saxon graduate education as being of little use for their current job. According to them, the German higher education system could do much better to prepare students for international work. Some suggested that the weaknesses of the German education system are, among others, an insufficient international outlook and the lack of practical training.

The question whether such deficits directly affect levels of German representation in international organizations is part of an ongoing discussion in Germany.[65] When we asked professionals (Germans as well as their colleagues from other countries) about the potential causes for the low representation of German citizens in international organizations, many of them stressed that there are several social and political factors that must to be taken into account. The weakness of the higher educational system in Germany was mentioned as one factor among several others. Although this study is not designed to examine factors leading to German underrepresentation, as this was already done by other studies, we will now briefly summarize potential causes leading to the low representation of German citizens in the staff of international organizations.

---

[65] Robert Bosch Stiftung (ed.), (1999). *Stuttgarter Appell an Bund und Länder, Wissenschaft und Wirtschaft: Für mehr Internationalität in Bildung, Ausbildung und Personalpolitik.* Retrieved July 5, 2007, from www.berlinerinitiative.de/materialien/1999_stuttgarter_appell.pdf.

According to one view, the monetary, financial, and social incentives inherent in German society are sufficiently strong to make an international career less desirable. Further, a lack of (attractive) re-entry opportunities in the German public and private sector hinders potential and highly qualified candidates to consider employment at an international organization abroad. Professionals at the Word Bank described it as follows:

"It simply has to do with the way the German society is organized and all the other monetary, financial, and social incentives that Germans have to stay in German. That is a long-term issue that really has to do with German society structure and it is similar to Japan and it will not change any time soon. It is much more ingrained in the fabric of German society." (Staff member at the World Bank)

"Those people we are trying to target, who have experience in development, let us say people from Kreditanstalt, BMZ. There are a lot of them who are not interested in working for the World Bank. They think the World Bank is arrogant or abroad and they don't want to go abroad. They are afraid of when they come back, what is going to happen? Are they going to find a job again in Germany? I have seen that kind of behavior." (Staff member at the World Bank)

According to another view, Germany needs to change its personnel policies. It was said that German governmental representatives fail to identify suitable candidates for certain professional posts. According to one professional at the World Bank, the German government does not offer help in the targeted candidate searches in the World Bank, as the following comment suggests:

"On the managerial level, what we see is that Germany is unable to identify candidates for posts: [...] France sends us, within two or three weeks, 15 CVs from the top people in the country. [...] And from Germany we got two applications. If Germany was more practical, if those institutions were in charge of this, and that is the Ministry of Foreign Affairs, I guess the BMZ. [...] If those people would be able to lead us quicker to potential candidates, whom you can actually take serious, that would help a lot. Some countries are really active in that, and others are not." (Staff member at the World Bank)

Furthermore, as some professionals suggested, Germany should bring in younger people rather than middle-aged officials. Other countries do much better in this regard. Young people would have the opportunity to grow within the organization and develop their own professional network which might be helpful for their future career in international organizations. Programs such as the *Junior Professional Program*, the *Carlo Schmid Programm* and the *Stiftungskolleg für internationale Aufgaben* were mentioned as being very important means to bring more young talents into the organizations. More structural programs to support young professionals in their professional development should be created:

> "But then I think the German government needs to look at its policy and priorities in terms what they finance, because my experience is that they often finance a lot of middle-aged gentlemen, a lot of money flows in this direction. I met very few young people working for them. Maybe they have to think about the professional opportunities they are giving their young people who are interested in that. Maybe if you are going to sponsor a master, they should have a commitment to this German organization."' (Staff member at UNDP)

A perusal of the three hypotheses suggested that the weaknesses attributed to the German education system appear to be one factor among a number of others that influence levels of German representation. Therefore, raising the number of German personnel in international organizations will depend on how well universities and research institutions, the German government, and German professionals at international organizations work together to achieve the common goal.

4.   Results of the curricular study – United States

This and the next chapter will describe the results of the curricular study of the PROFIO project. As mentioned in the section about our research design, we selected a number of study programs that show in an exemplary manner what sorts of educational offerings exist for students who wish to become qualified for careers in international organizations. These programs primarily comprise master's degrees in fields that traditionally prepared students for careers in their national administration (e.g., public policy, public administration, public affairs) as well as those that educate students on global affairs (e.g., international relations, international affairs, diplomacy studies, regional affairs). The list of programs examined in this study is certainly not exhaustive. Far more degree programs are available to students interested in working for international organizations. As we saw in the labor market study, there is no one specific educational track that guarantees one will be properly qualified for such careers, but rather many possibilities exist. For the purpose of our research, however, it was necessary to generate a sample of programs to examine more closely.

First of all, we were forced to limit our investigation to programs in one general field for the sake of comparability. It would be impossible to directly compare the curricula of engineering, medicine, law, architecture, and political science study programs. Public policy, public administration, and diplomacy studies are the traditional offerings for students hoping to work in the national or international public service graduation. Also, according to Derick and Jennifer Brinkerhoff,

"International public service requires a good working knowledge of governments, political systems, and how they operate. [...] These degrees have much to offer in terms of effective public service, flexibility, and reward. A master's of public administration or public policy can enable you to acquire necessary analytic and management skills, expertise in governance [...] including agenda setting, constituency building, and managing policy reform."[66]

Furthermore, we had to narrow down the degrees to be examined: we chose master's degrees[67] as they are offered in many countries around the

[66] Brinkerhoff, D. W., & Brinkerhoff, J. M. (2005). *Working for Change: Making a Career in International Public Service.* Bloomfield: Kumarian Press, pp. 98-99.
[67] In doing so, however, we eliminated mid-career master's degrees, because they are designed to be much more intensive and to have a different balance of theoretical and practical elements than master's programs open to students with only a B.A. and perhaps a few years of work experience.

world and all function under the assumption that students have completed their general education elsewhere.[68] Wherever possible, we used rankings to ensure our selection of the best programs available. We furthermore selected study programs at regular universities and chose not to include small colleges or universities of applied science (*Fachhochschulen*), also to increase the level of comparability. Finally, the countries in which we investigated programs of study had to be limited due to lack of time and financial resources. From the outset, it was clear that German and U.S. programs were to be incorporated in this study in order to compare the opportunities in these two countries with each other. In the labor market study, many mentions were made of elite programs in western European countries: Sciences Po and the ENA in France, the Collège d'Europe in Belgium, the Diplomatic Academy of Vienna, and others.

These are the reasons why the programs were included in our curricular study. However, this does not mean that programs not listed here are not equally capable of qualifying their graduates for careers in this field. It is important to keep this in mind when reading. Also, the 'best practices' highlighted here work well in the context of the program in which they are offered, but we do not claim that they are the absolute best options in any given educational setting.

4.1. Programs for careers in international organizations

Approximately 250 professional schools of public policy, public administration, or public affairs exist in the U.S. today. In addition, many institutes or departments offer degrees in related areas such as government, international relations, or diplomacy. Some programs are well-known for their strong international focus, whereas others have defined their area of comparative advantage in different fields (for example, urban planning, information technology, econometrics, or environmental science). They were all founded on different principles and in various time periods, yet they are all well-established by now (the youngest institution in this study, the Harris School at the University of Chicago, was created 18 years ago).

One can currently observe several trends at the institutions in our study. There is, for example, a great deal of movement toward international programs, and since 9/11, security has also become a major topic of interest. Domestically-oriented programs are grappling with the thought

---

[68] "We believe that the master's level is where you should focus on gaining practical skills targeted to employment, unless you know in advance that you will pursue a PhD or a research-oriented career." Brinkerhoff/Brinkerhoff (2005), p. 99.

of incorporating more global elements into their curricula, even if this means dealing with global issues on the local level. Some programs have also experienced a huge amount of growth in the past five to ten years, which means they are now able to hire more faculty members and expand their course offerings (e.g., the Ford School of Public Policy at the University of Michigan and the Harris Graduate School of Public Policy at the University of Chicago). The teaching of new skills is being incorporated into many programs, especially communication and leadership or management skills. This is primarily based on feedback from alumni. Some of these skills-based courses are required in the curriculum, and others are offered in addition to the program but not for credit. Another interesting development is the movement away from traditional research papers and toward projects students must do outside of the university in their last semester or quarters before graduation (often called "capstone courses").[69]

The majority of the institutions in our study offer two-year master's degrees in public policy, public administration, international relations, and/or international affairs. Some have further branched out to offer more specific degrees (e.g., International Development, International Peace and Conflict Resolution) or also offer degrees in their 'niche area' (e.g., Urban Planning, Environmental Science). However, most programs offer a general MPP, MPA, or MA-IR and allow their students to specialize through their concentration. Many of these degrees are said to prepare students for work in the public sector, though they define this quite broadly and do not expect their students to work in one sector their whole lives.[70] Interestingly, some of the programs claim to prepare for both a professional and academic career (e.g., Georgetown University and Ohio State University). Many interview partners said their students plan to take on professional and non-academic careers, yet it is clear from the career placement statistics that at least a small percentage of graduates from most programs do go on to earn a Ph.D.

The interview partners gave a wide variety of answers when asked about the comparative advantage of their degree program or programs. Some of them responded with one particular subject within the MPA or MPP, such as economics, analytical skills, or legislative development.

---

[69] Section 4.5 will deal with teaching methods and types of examinations in greater detail.

[70] This seems to be a fundamental difference between the expectations of American and European program directors with regard to their view of their graduates' career prospects. The general assumption in various European countries – including Germany – is that careers tend to stay in one general area (academia, government, or private industry) and not include any lateral movements into the other fields.

Others spoke of specific features within the context of their program that were not directly related to an area of study: international focus of the curriculum, the ability to design one's own concentration, or the dialog between students and faculty. A third group mentioned advantages their students have because of offerings of the university at large (foreign languages, area studies, business programs, etc.). However, the advantage most often named was interdisciplinarity -- in a broad sense of the word. This means that many faculty members consider breadth to be an important factor for students' future professional success.

We will now discuss the findings of the study of U.S. professional schools in detail. They shall be divided into the core or academic components of the curricula, the additional components such as foreign language requirements, the teaching methods used in the programs, the composition of the faculty and student body, career services, and cooperation agreements with other institutions. The results of the studies in Western Europe will be presented in Chapter 5.

4.2. Core components of the curriculum

When examining academic programs, the first and foremost aspect is the academic core: Which courses must all students take? Upon what principles or decisions is this based? What is the main focus of the program in general, and which areas of specialization are available? These are therefore the aspects we will discuss first.

4.2.1. Curricular development and evaluation

Only about half of those interviewed in this study made specific statements on how their curricula are developed or evaluated. However, the majority of them mentioned that input typically comes from three main sources: (1) students, (2) faculty, and (3) practitioners in the field. The last group can and often does include a combination of alumni, employers, or adjunct faculty members working in fields considered to be target professions for the program graduates. Some programs have special committees specifically for the purpose of reviewing the curriculum on an ongoing or intermittent basis:

"The only direct influences [on our curriculum] are from our Advisory Council. The rest is purely indirect, through our students working somewhere and us having contact with our alumni and thus hearing about whatever is appreciated, but we have an Advisory Council for our specific Center, and I know the School as a whole has an advisory board as well. These boards consist mainly of academics from Europe and

Germany in particular but also a lot of people from the business world." (George-town University, BMW Center)

"The School has a Board of Visitors who act as an advisory board to the Dean and the Associate Deans. And we are continually asking for their advice on the curriculum. [...] When we review the curriculum on a systematic basis every five years or so, we will ask professionals as well as academics from other schools to look and evaluate our program in a candid way. [...] We send questionnaires to our graduates. [...] And those have been very constructive. [...] Our employers -- our 'external customers', if you will -- are pleased with our graduates and have had great success and that they are well-prepared once they arrive there." (SPEA)

Our interview partners at American University mentioned having undertaken an actual process of benchmarking its "sister schools". Such formal decision-making processes on curricular affairs were the exception rather than the rule, though. Other specific methods of program evaluation mentioned in the interviews were alumni surveys, written feedback from the students' internship supervisors, and the results of the Presidential Management Fellowship application rounds[71].

The actual decision-making process varies among the professional schools and cannot be summarized here. However, it can be stated that all seem to be open to suggestions from people inside or outside of the program and that those recommendations that make sense will be realized. One example of this is the development of an international development degree (Master in Public Administration in International Development) at the Kennedy School of Government based on increasing demand in this area and created through a concerted effort by faculty members. Another is the recent formation of an "International" specialization at the Wagner School, which was described as a "natural evolution" due to the process of globalization.

The interviewees mentioned yet another common source of change in their curricula as being the turnover of faculty members within the professional school. If new people are hired who have different skills and specializations than those who preceded them, the U.S. professional schools generally adjust their curricula accordingly. Two examples of this are at SUNY Albany and the Ohio State University, where it was reported that new faculty members possessed knowledge in the fields of international security affairs and information technology, respectively. They were thus able to add these areas of study to their programs.

[71] These results statistically show how well the applicants from each institution did in the following areas of assessment: Problem Solving, Interpersonal and Team Skills, Resilience, Demonstrated Leadership, Adaptability, Oral Communication, Written Communication. The results are sent to the educational institutions of the participants. See http://www.pmf.opm.gov/ for more details.

In conclusion, U.S. schools of public policy and international affairs attempt to work together with the "buyers" or "consumers" of their programs to ensure the quality and value of their degrees on the labor market. They view such ongoing discourse and review as essential for all sides involved: students, employers, and academic institutions offering such programs. This is not to say that they design their degrees solely to meet external demand, but rather, they take the conditions and changes in the field into account in order to best prepare the students for their future field of work. This benefits the graduates, the employers who hire them and – in turn – the professional school itself. Perhaps our interview partner at the Kennedy School of Government sums it up best:

> *"There are certainly many different approaches that different schools take, but our graduates have met the market test: We send people out there and then we see how they do, and if somebody's hired one, it's often the case that they'll come back and hire more. So they're happy with our graduates."* (KSG)

Finally, it is important to remember that accreditation is a standard procedure in the U.S.: all major universities are accredited, and individual programs undergo accreditation from relevant agencies in their area of specialization. For example, ten of the programs in this study are accredited by the Commission on Peer Review and Accreditation (COPRA) of the National Association of Schools of Public Affairs and Administration.[72] This ensures that the programs are meeting self-defined objectives and serves as quality control, particularly in that it must be renewed after a certain period of time. This form of program evaluation is quite common in the U.S. and allows the directors and faculty members to obtain feedback from additional sources besides the three mentioned above.

4.2.2. Fields of study

Each of the degree programs included in the PROFIO study has a core set of courses all students must take. These varied widely depending on the general focus of the school, both in terms of the number of required courses (compared to the number of electives) and concerning the variety of fields that must be covered. Besides political science and international relations, at least one of which was an integral part of all the programs we examined, many other areas of study were required as well. A count of the total times other courses were required shows the full spectrum (cf. Table 4.1).

[72] http://www.naspaa.org/accreditation/document/Official_%20annual_roster_accredited_programs05-06.pdf, retrieved July 5, 2007.

Table 4.1. Fields of study in core requirements of U.S. schools

Required in 10-15 programs	... in 5-9 programs	... in 1-4 programs
– Political science – International relations – Economics	– Management (public, strategic, etc.) – Statistics – Foreign languages – Regional studies – Law	– Organizations/Institutions – Finance – Accounting – Culture – History – Security/Intelligence – Development

Source: Authors

The general structure of the degree requirements at most schools can be best described as a pyramid. At the bottom, a certain amount of theory (as determined in the curriculum design) should build the foundation for the students' knowledge of the field. On top of that, but to a lesser extent, the students must complete coursework that provides them with the tools for gathering information on their own, presenting it to others, and using it to solve real-world problems. These courses can include qualitative and/or quantitative research methods, policy analysis, program evaluation, budgeting, decision making, problem solving, ethics and values, information technology, and writing or speaking skills.

The next level of the pyramid would generally consist of the field or fields in which the students choose to specialize. Besides these competencies and in addition to the area of concentration, many programs (particularly international relations or diplomacy studies) require their students to acquire proficiency in a foreign language or complete a regional studies component.

Above this – and quite often toward the end of the program or at least after completion of a set of basic courses – we find those elements of the program that should impart practical skills and expertise on the students. This may include an internship, *pro bono* consulting work, an assigned group project, or even smaller-scale training sessions in certain areas such as intercultural negotiation or how to behave at a business lunch. In essence, these components should enable the students to put their knowledge to work and provide them the opportunity to learn and make mistakes within the program rather than on the job. Often, this is done through the use of case studies or simulations, which will be dealt with in more detail in Section 4.5.

Figure 4.1. Typical structure of curricula at U.S. professional schools

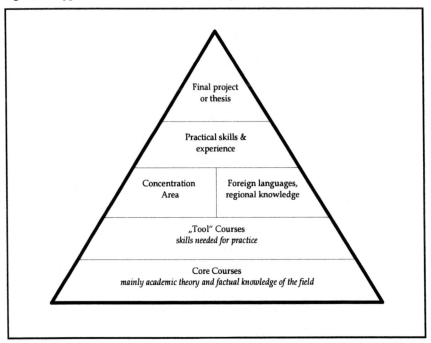

Source: Authors

Finally, the top of the pyramid consists of the final graduation requirements. Generally speaking, this may be one or a combination of the following: comprehensive oral examinations, comprehensive written examinations, a master's thesis, or a so-called capstone experience, which is a hands-on, problem-solving project related to the students' particular area of interest. Certainly not all curricula follow this pattern, but it is a common structure that allows for a great deal of flexibility, balance, and direction in the students' learning programs.

One final look at the core curricula at the schools of public policy and international relations in our study reveals that they require all their students to take anywhere between five and fourteen classes on topics considered to be of central importance. This total does not include any internship or paper requirements. Ohio State University has the most, and these are divided into 'streams'[73]:

---

[73] http://ppm.ohio-state.edu/handbook/handbook_mpa.htm, retrieved Juni 1, 2006.

– General
– PPM 893A Perspectives on Public Service (1 hr)
– Public Policy Stream
– PPM 801 Public Policy Formulation and Administration (5 hrs)
– PPM 802 Legal Environment of Public Administration (4 hrs)
– PPM 804 Program Evaluation (4 hrs)
– Public Management Stream
– PPM 810 Strategic Management (4 hrs)
– PPM 880G06 Strategic Leadership (4 hrs)
– PPM 811 Public Management & Human Relations (4 hrs)
– Public Sector Economics Stream
– PPM 830 Economics of Public Policy and Management (4 hrs)
– PPM 730 Public Finance (5 hrs)
– PPM 834 Public Budgeting and Spending Decisions (4 hrs)
– Decision Support Systems Stream
– PPM 820 Research Methods In Public Administration (3 hrs)
– PPM 821 Governmental Information Systems Administration (4 hrs)
– PPM 822 Data Analysis In Public Administration (3 hrs)
– PPM 852 Governmental & Nonprofit Accounting (4 hrs)

The core curriculum of the Kennedy School of Government consists of thirteen courses, and that of the Heinz School at Carnegie Mellon University has eleven. All others have between five and ten, though SAIS and the Fletcher School have unique designs that merit further elaboration. At SAIS, students must complete any two of the 20 different concentrations that are available. This means that no coursework is common to all students. The Fletcher School has a similar system called "breadth requirements". In the three divisions of the institution (Diplomacy, History, and Politics; International Law and Organization; and Economics and International Business), new students – beginning in 2006 – must take one or more courses from a narrower list of options. The objective is to expose them to each area, at least to a certain extent.[74] This is an interesting concept that allows the students a great deal of academic freedom and individuality. However, each program must determine for itself whether its graduates must all emerge with a certain base of knowledge or understanding.

To summarize, one of the most fundamental decisions when designing a curriculum is of which components or elements the core curriculum – those courses that all students in the program must complete – should

---

[74] Our interview partner at the Fletcher School of Law and Diplomacy said that they actually place the most emphasis on law because "law students are clear thinkers".

consist. Although great variations exist between the cores of the professional school programs examined in this study, they do, for the most part, share a general structure, and a certain range of fields of study tend to be comprised in them: (1) political science and/or international relations; (2) business, economics, and/or statistics; (3) law and/or institutional structures and processes; and (4) foreign languages and/or regional studies. This combination concurs with the results of the labor market study, showing that schools of public policy and international relations in the U.S. definitely offer an education relevant to the work of most international organizations, which is why they were included in the PROFIO study.

4.2.3. Areas of concentration

In addition to the academic or theoretical core, all professional schools in this study offer a variety of areas of concentration (also known as specializations, focus areas, majors, career tracks, areas of study, or PACs – Policy Areas of Concentration) to their students. Sometimes these are optional, which allows the students to receive a very broad education in several areas, and other programs require students to choose one or more of them to gain a certain amount of depth they would not otherwise have, as the following comment shows:

"We have lots of fields of concentration. That is a conscious choice on our part to allow students to have two things. One: cover the basic competencies, but two: have a field of expertise that they choose and that they will choose courses from, like international development management, budget and finance, urban and local government management, et cetera." (George Washington University)

The concentrations represent a wide range of policy areas. The three most popular (i.e., those offered by the most institutions) are development, economic, and environmental issues. Other well-represented topics include social policy, finance, policy analysis, public and non-profit management, and international relations or affairs. Among all concentrations offered (approximately 150 in total), 25 contain 'international' or 'global' in their titles. The Fletcher School at Tufts University even has a field of study specifically called "International Organizations". According to the program brochure, "Students who specialize in the field acquire a) basic knowledge of the nature and functions of international institutions – both formal organizations and less formal arrangements; b) an understanding of the role institutions play in the development of international law and policy; and c) an ability to think critically about the significance of inter-

national organizations to contemporary world affairs."[75] Three courses
from the following list must be completed:
- ILO L210 International Human Rights Law
- ILO L211 Seminar on Current Issues in Human Rights
- ILO L220 International Organizations
- ILO L221 Seminar on Actors in Global Governance
- ILO L223 Seminar on International Environmental Law
- ILO L224 Seminar in Peace Operations
- ILO L240 Legal and Institutional Aspects of International Trade
- ILO L242 Legal and Institutional Aspects of the IMF and the World
  Bank Group
- ILO L243 Seminar on International Legal Aspects of Globalization
- ILO L264m Non-Proliferation Law and Institutions
- DHP D224 International Multilateral Negotiation
- DHP P203 Analytic Frameworks for Public Policy Decisions

Another example of concentrations relevant for work in international
organizations are the two majors in the Master of Public and International
Affairs (MPIA) at the GSPIA (University of Pittsburgh). These are called
"Global Political Economy" and "Security and Intelligence Studies" and
could be quite useful for preparing for careers at financial or peacekeeping organizations, respectively. Other schools have established entire degree programs with a very particular focus in areas of high demand, such
as GSPIA's Master of International Development, KSG's Master of Public
Administration in International Development, and SAIS' Master of Arts
in International Development:

> "The other real change that happened in the last few years is a much broader interest
> -- or maybe we have actually opened up into -- international development. [...] And
> that is now our biggest program: the students coming just to focus on int'l develop-
> ment." (SAIS)

Although students could certainly specialize in a number of different
areas in order to become qualified for careers at international organizations (depending, for one thing, on the focus of their target organization),
these and other internationally-focused concentrations could serve as
positive examples in the search for best practices.

Regional studies (also called area studies) are often an additional component in master's programs of international relations or affairs. Sometimes they must be completed in addition to the more topical concentrations. They are considered to be important by some interview partners,
whereas others see a problem with specializing in an area that could later

---

[75] http://fletcher.tufts.edu/academic/fos/internationalorgs/, retrieved August 5, 2007.

become irrelevant for that person. The same applies to foreign language training. However, approximately half of the programs in this study require or at least encourage their students to select a region in which to specialize and a corresponding foreign language in which they must become proficient.

Some degree programs, in contrast, do not actually require that their students select a concentration. The Ford School (University of Michigan), the Heinz School (the University of Chicago), and George Washington University's School of Public Policy and Public Administration are of institutions that allow their students to complete 'generalist' degrees without selecting a field of concentration. In contrast, some programs allow or require more than one area of concentration (e.g., SPEA and SAIS). Finally, it is also possible at various schools to design one's own specialization based on the courses offered there or at other departments (e.g., SPEA and the Heinz School):

> *"We are different than many programs in that we allow students to take three to five courses just in their fields of concentration. [...] In our MPA, we even have always allowed people to actually design their own field. [...] Frankly, it is also a nice competitive edge in that students like to see that they are going to be able to choose a subset of courses to really help make them more competitive in the marketplace in health policy, for example." (SPEA)*

This opportunity might be useful to students planning to pursue a career in a very specific area of an international organization; however, they must first ensure that the courses they need are available at the school of their choice. In sum, areas of concentration should provide students with deeper knowledge in their particular areas of interest and thus help them be better qualified for a certain sector of the labor market. This is one specific way schools hoping to train their students for careers in international organizations can or could adjust their programs to better meet the needs of this professional path.

4.2.4. Interdisciplinarity

As described in the labor market study, a combination of different disciplines has proven to be an effective method for preparing future employees of international organizations for their tasks. Though related to the core curriculum and areas of concentration, interdisciplinarity is more than simply offering coursework in a variety of fields: The interconnections must be explained, and the content must be integrated.

The University of Michigan is an example of an institution that places a great deal of emphasis on interdisciplinarity in all programs – not just those at the Ford School. According to our interview partner there, the students have access to courses in other departments (e.g., law, public health, business, education, environmental studies, and international area studies)[76], which allows them to become experts on contents, regions, *and* methods. This is because "it makes sense to approach policy problems from different lenses." Those we spoke to at the Wagner School were of a similar opinion:

"The idea is to blur the boundaries between local, national, international... urban planning, health, and non-profit... and management, policy, and finance. [...] The more lenses you have with which to look at the world, the more facile and the more effective you can be in your various roles. So we are training folks ultimately to have influence in the field of public service, but we do not specifically define what that field is." (Staff member at Wagner School)

Other schools consider their interdisciplinary approach to be part of their comparative advantage:

"SPEA is the only institution in its league with an interdisciplinary character where students can combine science and public affairs." (SPEA brochure)

"The Heinz School integrates policy, management and information technology to create new ideas, policy solutions, inspired theory and innovative educational programs that serve the public interest. Our unique, interdisciplinary approach provides students with the depth and breadth necessary to formulate policy, manage and lead in today's world." (Heinz School brochure)

Law, economics and foreign languages or regional studies are, as stated above, commonly mentioned subjects built into the curricula of the MPP, MPA, or MA-IR programs. They are furthermore placed in the context of the program at hand, as in the case of "Statistics for International Analysis" at the Walsh School of Foreign Service or "Law and Public Affairs" at the School of Public Affairs and Environmental Sciences. The interview partners felt these were necessary to fully comprehend the policy area of the students' choice. This seems to be desirable from the students' point of view as well, as one can see from the recent increase in the number of students completing joint or dual degrees. A well-designed curriculum incorporates courses from various departments or disciplines that are tailored to the focus of the program while also providing the necessary explanation as to why these fields are relevant, useful, and related to one another.

[76] Source: Ford School Bulletin 2004-06, p. 3.

4.2.5. International focus

One of the major findings of this study has to do with the extent to which American schools of public policy and public administration focus on international policy and affairs. Clearly, those schools with 'international' or 'diplomacy' in their titles have always concentrated on teaching and research in foreign affairs. However, many of the others have recently decided to incorporate more global elements in their curricula. For example, the Wagner School just created an International Specialization last year. Our interviewee there described this development as follows:

"We have not shifted our core mission. We have just expanded to include the global interest on applicants' parts and the global expertise on faculty. It was a natural, an organic evolution. We did not shift our program to compete with SIPA at Columbia, for example; we are not an international affairs school. We are not training folks to be diplomats -- we are still training folks to be managers, policy analysts, and planners. It is just now with the international understanding that is behind that." (Staff member at Wagner School)

The educational experts we spoke to at Rockefeller College, Ohio State University, and GSPIA (the public administration program) made similar statements. Their programs are or were primarily domestically oriented, but as "everything in public policy is intertwined today" (Rockefeller College) and "globalization is a major force with state and local implications (Ohio State University), these schools are going through reform processes to make their curricula more international in focus.

"Rockefeller's profile is changing. In five years, it aspires to and will most likely place much greater emphasis on global issues due to the influx of new people, the press of 9/11, and the understanding that everything in public policy is intertwined today. Currently, there is a proposal to forge a specialty in global affairs that would possibly lead to the creation of a whole Master's degree in that area. [...] An international comparative focus was always there, but in five years, students would then gain more skills in global areas, and the balance of nationally to internationally-focused courses offered will change with the new global affairs module." (Staff member at Rockefeller College)

At Ohio State University, the discussion toward becoming more international is similar. However, they recognize that they need an area of comparative advantage and that they would not have one with international affairs due to the great deal of competition with many schools that have been active in this field for years. Their idea is therefore to have the program concentrate on the consequences of globalization at the local level:

"What do we need to know about other cultures in order to enhance ties locally? We could impart a world view that is very parochial." (Staff member at OSU, SPPM)

The GSPIA in Pittsburgh is already very strongly international, but according to our interview partners, the majors in the Public Administration program will soon be adjusted to include more global topics. Pending approval, a major in "Human Security" will begin this fall, in which students will look at issues dealing with the safety of humans rather than states. This sort of development came about as the threat of terrorism grew and the likelihood of war between nations decreased. At the Heinz School, on the other hand, the curriculum itself will not be changed in any way, but rather, there is more of a trend toward "putting the international bug in students' ears", especially in the career services office. Thus, even those programs that were primarily domestically oriented in the past are now or will soon be more global in scope, taking account of the increasing interest in – and necessity for – a combination of domestic and international offerings.

4.2.6. Program duration

The amount of time it generally takes to complete a master's program depends on many factors. One is, of course, how many credits or courses are required in total. Another is how intensively the students plan to study (i.e., full-time or part-time). Internships can play a role as well: For example, if students are allowed to complete them *during* the regular semesters in addition to their coursework, it can shorten the total length of the program as compared to having to do an internship by itself during a summer or additional semester. One major deciding factor is also whether or not the students enter the program with a considerable amount of work experience. Such "mid-career degree programs", sometimes called "executive education", typically take one year if done full-time or two years part-time. They are not the main focus of the PROFIO project but have still been included as long as the final degree is a master's. The majority of the programs in this study take four semesters to complete. As described in the section on Fields of Study, the first year is often reserved for academic or theoretical coursework that should provide the students with a broad knowledge base for the rest of the program. The summer between the two years is frequently meant to be used for doing an internship, though this is not the case in all programs. The third semester is generally a time for intensive study of an area of specialization or learning how to put theory into practice, and the last semester of most two-year programs is often dedicated to the capstone project or thesis research and writing. Table 4.2 shows the distribution of one-,

Table 4.2. Duration of MA programs offered at U.S. Professional Schools

Professional school (University)	1 yr	1,5 yrs	2 yrs
Elliott School of International Affairs and the School of Public Policy and Public Administration (George Washington University)	1	8*	0
Fletcher School of Law and Diplomacy (Tufts University)	2	0	1
Ford School of Public Policy (University of Michigan)	1	0	2
Graduate School of Public and International Affairs (University of Pittsburgh)	1	0	2
Harris Graduate School of Public Policy (University of Chicago)	1	0	2
Heinz School of Public Policy and Management (Carnegie Mellon University)	1	1	2
Kennedy School of Government (Harvard University)	1	0	4
Maxwell School (Syracuse University)	2	1	0
Nitze School of Advanced International Studies (Johns Hopkins University)	1	0	1
Rockefeller College of Public Affairs & Policy (SUNY-Albany)	1	0	1
School of International Service and School of Public Affairs (American University)	0	0	9
School of Public Affairs and Environmental Sciences (Indiana University - Bloomington)	0	0	1
School of Public Policy and Management (Ohio State University)	1	0	2
Wagner Graduate School of Public Service (New York University)	0	0	3
Walsh School of Foreign Service and BMW Center for German & European Studies (Georgetown University)	0	1	5
Total	13	11	35

Source: Authors
Notes: Not including dual and joint degrees, certificate programs, and degrees not relevant to the PROFIO project. *This degree can take anywhere between three and six semesters depending upon the students' enrollment (part-time, full-time, and number of courses completed per semester).

one-and-a-half-, and two-year programs among the schools of public policy and international relations examined in the PROFIO study.

Statements on the 'appropriate' length of master's programs can and should not be made here. This is a decision that must be made in the curricular development phase based on the established goals and methods of instruction chosen to meet these objectives. Those in charge of degree programs must also determine the most appropriate sequence of coursework and the pace at which it can realistically be completed. In this context, one must ultimately know what type of students will be participating in the program and how they learn most effectively (i.e., recent B.A. graduates, students who wish to change their career paths, or mid-career executives who wish to increase their knowledge in certain areas).

4.3. Additional components

All of the curricular elements mentioned above have to do with how the students can obtain relevant qualifications from degree programs at U.S. professional schools for a career in international organizations. This section will deal with other aspects of these programs that also play a role in their training or preparation but that do not come directly from the curriculum itself.

4.3.1. Foreign language requirements

Foreign language skills are, without a doubt, extremely important for those striving to work in the international arena. Yet some interview partners are of the opinion that it is better for students to acquire the necessary language skills as they move from one job to another. English is a common language for many people in international places of work, and it can later be supplemented by learning the local language in the country of the assignment. Still, however, as mentioned above, nearly half of the programs in this study require or at least encourage their students to become proficient in one or more foreign languages. It is interesting to note the typical conflicting opinions, even at two schools within one university, as the following quotes show:

> "We also have a foreign language requirement for all of our students. [...] It is above the course requirements, above the actual classroom requirements. [...] We think it is a really important requirement for anyone doing public policy anywhere in the world that they have at least one other foreign language at the intermediate level, minimal." (AU, School of International Service)

> "We do not have a language requirement. We debate that all the time. It is something I feel is a weak point [...]. Adding a language requirement is felt to be prohibitive in terms of getting students out in time to do something." (AU, School of Public Affairs)

> "Competence in a second language is especially important to success in a career in international affairs." (Maxwell School)

*"Language skills are obviously important, and we do not have a language require-
ment here, nor can students get credit for taking a foreign language at Wagner."
(Wagner School)*

*"Given the backgrounds of our students, almost all of them speak two, three, or four
languages when they get here." (KSG)*

Our interview partner at Rockefeller College mentioned lacking resources at the professional school as being an obstacle to a foreign language requirement; the students would then have to complete summer
courses elsewhere to earn the credits. On the other hand, he or she did
view foreign language skills as being helpful in finding employment after
graduation. The conclusion was thus that coursework in a foreign language should be "strongly suggested" in such degree programs. In sum,
therefore, it can be stated that comparatively few professional schools require their students to have or gain proficiency in a foreign language –
and those that do are typically schools of foreign service or international
relations.

The comparatively limited instruction of foreign languages at U.S. professional schools could reflect the common view that English is the main
means of communication in the international community nowadays and
that native English speakers thus have no need to learn foreign languages. However, this study and many others show that there is indeed a
great necessity to speak more than just English when working in the international arena, even if it is in one's home country. On the other hand,
one can concede that a master's program is not the appropriate time and
place for students to begin learning a foreign language; this must occur
earlier and simply be continued throughout one's education.

4.3.2. Practical, hands-on courses

Most programs included in our research offer skills workshops and additional practical training sessions for disciplines outside of the regular curriculum. Some of these exercises are related to the technical know-how
the students should gain in the program (political negotiations, consulting for clients, etc.), whereas others aim to hone the students' abilities to
communicate, manage, deal with people from other cultures, or master
other tasks or skills that will help them in their future careers but in an
auxiliary rather than a primary manner.

The format of such courses differs widely. Some professional schools
require that their students take these seminars, and others offer them on
an optional basis. Many of these courses are offered on campus, while
others take place in the context of excursions or studies abroad. The latter

options will be explored in following sections and therefore not mentioned here. The Maxwell School, for example, expects its students to spend an entire summer and their fall semester completing the program's "practical component" after having completed the "academic component" in their first two semesters of study. They are encouraged to spend this time off campus, be it in Washington, D.C., on one of the many exchange programs around the world, or at a location of their choice and arranged on their own. The context is also flexible: the students may do an internship, a study abroad program, or field research, as long as it is practical in orientation. Rockefeller College in Albany has "Professional Application Modules" meant to improve students' communication, presentation, teamwork, and group work skills. They include role-playing games on international development with a focus on economic growth and ethics and should provide immersion in and socialization to the public affairs field.

The SPPM at the Ohio State University also has the clear objective of giving its students practically-oriented coursework. Policy labs are mandatory and can be, for example, projects in which students work with government agencies or other organizations or guest speakers. This helps students to have greater contact with people and structures outside the university. The entire second-year curriculum is "organized around the policy papers, policy labs, and electives in a field of specialization," according to the brochure.

The Ford School has an "Integrated Policy Exercise" every year, which is a week-long simulation in which all students participate. Speakers and experts give talks and evaluate their performance. This allows students to put the skills learned in the academic courses into practice, such as how to research a topic, present their positions, and lobby for certain outcomes.

At the University of Chicago, the Harris School Office of Career Services recently began developing informal courses not offered in the actual public policy program based on the determined need for such skills-building courses. It is called the 'leadership curriculum' and includes such topics as presentation skills, media training, the U.S. legislative process, strategic thinking, and political memo writing. It is based on the realization that too many students were graduating from the program with the necessary analytical and problem-solving tools but lacking the people skills or knowledge of the system to implement their ideas. The same concept is being developed at Johns Hopkins and already exists at American University:

"We are hiring people to come to teach these courses like effective writing, briefing, presentation skills, some computer skills that they may not otherwise have, negotiation skills, and career preparation in the private sector." (SAIS)

"As a part of the research methods options, we offer something called skills institutes, [...] and those complement the students' studies by giving them hands-on skills, and they are taught by superb practitioners in the field. [These include] cost-benefit analysis, program evaluation, conflict mediation, and cross-cultural communication." (AU, School of International Service)

Finally, the Kennedy School of Government has a "Spring Exercise" which, according to the brochure, "is a unique course, providing practice in integrating the skills of the core by requiring students to develop and present a professional analysis of a real policy problem."[77] All of these course offerings have the same goal: to teach the students skills necessary for putting to work the knowledge they accumulate in the program. This is based on the assumption that universities can – and perhaps even have a responsibility to – provide their students a well-rounded education that enables them to be competent upon entering the work force and not still require a long period of training on the job in order to perform their tasks well. Some schools may not choose to offer a great deal of hands-on skills courses, however, because, as our interview partner at the Fletcher School put it, "Students learn these skills on the job." Yet most of the schools in our study offered them, at least as electives. One interview partner said, for example, that it is more important for a degree program to concentrate on "technical skills", as management skills and other soft skills can be learned on the job but cost-benefit analysis cannot.

4.3.3. Extracurricular activities

A wide range of extracurricular activities are available to the students taking part in the professional degree programs in the PROFIO study. (By extracurricular, we refer to all non-credit events and offerings from which the students can benefit, but do not have to attend if they do not desire.) The most frequently mentioned activity in this category is internships, which will be discussed in the next section. Other commonly offered activities outside the classroom include guest lectures, conferences and workshops, clubs, excursions, and community service. Examples of these from various programs follow.

The Kennedy School of Government calls the collection of activities and experiences outside the classroom in which the students take part the "Sixth Course": "the convergence at the school of an astounding mix of

[77] John F. Kennedy School of Government Catalogue 2005-2006, p. 15.

people, ideas, and agendas."[78] It (and most of the other institutions in our study) invites *guest speakers* on a regular basis to give formal or informal talks on their areas of expertise, often called "Brown Bag Luncheons". The Harris School in Chicago hosts numerous *workshops* throughout the year in areas such as Cultural Policy, Philanthropy, International Security Policy, and Human Potential. These are visited by students, staff, researchers, and practitioners from the field being discussed.

Our interview partners at SPEA spoke highly of their *student organizations*, as they are completely run by the students and help them meet others interested in a particular area. They are also of use for career orientation. These organizations include: Diversity Project; Environmental Management Association (EMA); Global & Comparative Affairs Group; Graduate Student Association (GSA); Indiana Health Student Association (IHSA); IU Graduate and Professional Student Organization (GPSO); IU Student Association (IUSA); Management Association; Nonprofit Management Association; Public Finance Association; Students Taking Active Roles Today (START); Urban Wildlife Habitat Project.[79]

Excursions generally take place during the winter or spring break and to places such as Washington, D.C., where the students can come in contact with practitioners in various areas of work. The Ford School has an interesting excursion program not found elsewhere. Every year, the International Policy Committee and a member of the faculty work together to organize a so-called "Developing Country Tour", on which students meet with representatives of several policy areas in a developing country. A class is held in the fall semester as an introduction, and the tour goes during winter break. It is not for credit, yet approximately 30 students take part each year, most likely due to the hands-on format.

Looking at examples of *community service*, GSPIA at the University of Pittsburgh has a so-called "Nonprofit Clinic" in which students advise a nonprofit organization on an issue of the organization's choice at no cost. The Ford School offers the same thing but calls them "Applied Policy Seminars", and the Kennedy School of Government requires the "Policy Analysis Exercise" of all students. This sort of service benefits both the students and the organizations involved. SPEA in Bloomington has a similar community service program called "Service Corps". It is a two-year assignment through which students receiving financial aid from the program are placed in businesses or organizations to do limited part-time

---

[78] John F. Kennedy School of Government Catalogue 2005-2006, p. 38.
[79] Source: http://www.iu.edu/~speaweb/academics/MA_studentorgs.php, retrieved July 5, 2007.

jobs throughout their studies. Clearly, this experience is much like an internship and gives the students the opportunity to gain professional experience and help others at the same time. Other extracurricular activities exist as well (debates, dinners, networking events, etc.), but these were the ones most often mentioned in our interviews.

4.3.4. Internships

As professional schools are mainly concerned with introducing their students to the ways and methods of their future field of work, internships are often incorporated into the programs to immerse students into the profession. Interestingly, about half of the participating institutions require them and the other half encourage them or only require them of students with less than a certain required amount of professional experience:

"We require all students who enter our program with less than two years of full-time relevant experience in their programmatic area of study to take a course called Foundations of Public Service Work, and it is one of the requirements of that course: They have to have an internship relevant to their field of study." (Wagner School)

Two factors seem to play a role in the decision of a professional school to require internships: duration and location. One-year degree programs are much less likely to have a mandatory internship than are two-year programs, as they can then be completed in the summer between the first and second year of the program. This could also have to do with the fact that many of the one-year programs are designed for mid-career professionals, who clearly do not need a short-term internship in order to understand the field. The other factor, location, might be less fundamental in whether or not internships should be compulsory but rather lead to the consideration of the program directors of how they can enable their students to do internships in places other than where the university is. For example, the schools of international affairs of the University of Pittsburgh, Syracuse University, and the University of Denver decided to cooperate on offering internships and courses in Washington, D.C. together. This reduces the cost to each school and enables students from areas with a limited number of interesting internship opportunities – particularly in the international arena – to go to a city with countless governmental agencies that deal with the whole spectrum of policy areas. Besides improving the infrastructure in a popular location, another means of assisting students is financial aid:

"What we do to try to help students perform those unpaid internships is that we have [...] a summer fellowship fund where we will give students money. I think the average grant is $2000." (SAIS)

Whether or not internships are mandatory, all interview partners agreed on their importance for students without work experience "to gain professional exposure," as the KSG brochure describes it.[80] Some interview partners even mentioned the ability of internships to lead to permanent employment later. For example, according to our interview partner at the Ford School, the World Food Program allows students to extend their internships for one semester (as opposed to the normal three-month duration in the summer) on so-called "detached study". This of course means that the students complete their studies one semester later than usual, but they reportedly do much better on the job market with longer internships than those students with two- to three-month internships. This not only has to do with the greater amount of experience, but also with their connections, references, and ability to 'work the network' over a longer period of time. Finally, the Maxwell School also claims that many of its alumni now have jobs in the UN System or other organizations because of their internships there. Those alumni in turn help future Maxwell School students to obtain internships within the organizations, so it is a productive spiral for the educational institution, its students, and the employers who hire its graduates. More information on the value of alumni involvement will be given in Section 4.7 on Career Services, but it suffices to state here that internships are a common means of easing students into professional life and showing them how their studies can be useful in the real world.

4.3.5. Studies abroad and joint or dual degrees

Exchange programs with universities around the world are available and marketed particularly by those professional schools that concentrate more on international relations, diplomacy, or international studies in general than those with a purely public policy or public administration focus. The people we interviewed at the latter institutions more often mentioned hosting students from foreign universities who hoped to learn more about the American system. Also, the IR and diplomacy schools were more likely to have studies, excursions, and/or internships abroad built right into their curricula than were the public policy schools. This, however, seems to be related to the somewhat more national focus of the pub-

---

[80] John F. Kennedy School of Government Catalogue 2005-2006, p. 21.

lic policy schools, and it does not necessarily mean that their students are not encouraged to spend time abroad in one context or another.

Here, as with foreign language requirements, around half of the examined programs offer study abroad experiences to their students. Those that promote them the most strongly (in their brochures as well as in our interviews) were SPEA and Maxwell. SPEA's "Overseas Study Experiences" take place on four continents, in countries such as Ghana, Senegal, South Korea, Romania, Croatia, Nicaragua, and El Salvador. There is also a tour of Western Europe called "The EU in the 21st century" that takes place each spring. Maxwell has exchange programs with Niigata, Tokyo, Seoul, and Capetown; Syracuse programs abroad exist in Santiago, Strasbourg, London, Geneva, Mysore, and Beijing. In addition, some offerings just for MA-IR students have been created in cooperation with international organizations to give students the chance to learn more about them from the inside:

"The Geneva Summer Program is an intensive seminar all about international organizations. [...] A Vienna Program is in development to establish more contact with the international organizations there. Then there is a UN Peacekeeping Program every January in New York City. The Washington Program, which takes place in the summer, deals with conflict resolution. The participants in that include the OAS [Organization of American States], the World Bank, and lots of NGOs. Then we have an EU program in the students' third semester or fall semester of their second year. The students go and live in a European city to take an inside look at European affairs, and through our alumni or practitioner faculty, we are sometimes able to get them internships and go around the Blue Book." (Maxwell School)

The Nitze School of Advanced International Studies at Johns Hopkins University has two locations abroad at which students can complete the same degrees as on the campus in Washington, D.C. These are the Bologna Center in Italy and the Nanjing Center in China. All the other exchange programs we encountered were bilateral agreements between the American and foreign institutions:

– The Harris School has an exchange with the University of Chile;
– GSPIA has programs in the Balkans, in Korea, and with Sciences Po;
– The KSG MPA/ID program takes students to India and various countries in Africa to teach them about development issues firsthand; and
– Fletcher School students can study at the HEI in Geneva or the HEC or Sciences Po in Paris.

Time constraints, language skills, and differences between curricula were two issues mentioned as causing difficulties in establishing exchanges. Many students interested in international relations furthermore already gain international experience during or after their undergraduate studies, which decreases the need for study abroad opportunities in their graduate education. Finally, students are generally welcome to arrange foreign studies on their own in order to create the ideal project or course of study, and as long as they discuss their plans with their advisors beforehand, the credits can be applied toward their home degrees.

Almost all of the professional schools in our study have created -- or at least allow -- joint and/or dual degrees with programs in various disciplines. One of the most common is law (MPP/JD or MPA/JD), and another is business (MPP/MBA or MPA/MBA). Other fields in which dual degrees are available are social work, medicine or public health, regional or urban planning, information science, and natural sciences. These results correspond closely to those on interdisciplinarity in programs, except that here, much more different disciplines can be combined, as they are offered by entirely different institutions or schools.

One particularly interesting degree combination for those wishing to work for international organizations is the Master of Arts in International Relations and Master of Arts in Public Relations, which is currently only available at George Washington University and the University of Southern California. The Maxwell School hopes to open up a similar program this fall, pending state approval, which would be in cooperation with the Newhouse School of Communications and called "Public Diplomacy". Our interview partner there said that this is "something international organizations really need and that is currently not available in many places." Its creation was largely based on the results of an internal survey asking current students whether or not they would be interested in such a degree.

The Maxwell School's two most popular existing joint degrees are Public Adminstration/International Relations (PA/IR) and Public Administration and Law (PA/JD). These are said to be very useful combinations for jobs that combine law and administrative components, and the PA/IR in particular can be very useful in the public sector, international organizations, and NGOs. The Econ/IR gives students the opportunity to earn two degrees in two years and could be a good idea for students interested in international trade, economic development, financial institutions, banking, and finance.

At the Harris School, joint degrees programs have been created with all other professional schools at the University of Chicago. Students reportedly often see them as wise in terms of time but not really compatible in terms of subject matter. The MBA/MPP is most popular there. SAIS also encourages its students to pursue joint degrees because of the broader range of skills they acquire, and according to the brochure, approximately ten percent do combine their M.A. International Relations with business, law, public administration, or public health. Finally, the SPEA offers its students similar opportunities, some even within the school:

> "We have joint MPA/MA degrees with a number of area studies programs. One of our strongest and oldest is with the Russian and East European Studies Institute. [...] We have some of our area studies joint programs with Caribbean and Latin American Studies, West European Studies, Central Asian Studies, African American Diaspora Studies... The ones [dual degrees] that are with other units on campus we administer cooperatively. We also have joint degree programs between our own degrees [in Public Affairs and in Environmental Science]." (Staff member at SPEA)

Our interview partners at many schools mentioned that this is becoming a popular option with their students, and one said that there must be a major value added that could explain this new trend, although he or she had not yet seen any job placement statistics that prove that dual degrees help students on the labor market. In the American system, of course, students who earn joint degrees also save time and therefore money as opposed to completing them consecutively.

4.4. Balance between academic and practical training

Whether professional programs should place the main emphasis more on the theoretical or more on the practical components is a controversial question. Students and non-academic faculty and staff members tend to favor the practical aspects, whereas academic faculty feel strongly about the continuation of theory instruction. However, there is overall consensus that both types of teaching and learning must remain a part of the professional programs. In this section, we will discuss the level of importance attached to academic and practical elements within the programs in our study. The appropriate combination of these elements is, according to the results of the labor market study, a very important factor in the preparation of future employees of international organizations (cf. Sections 3.6.3 and 3.6.4).

Our interview partners agreed, in general, that theory and application are both essential parts of any professional education, and that all theory should be placed in the professional context and not taught simply for the sake of teaching theory:

> "The main draw to our program is the combination of practical and academic training. We offer theory in a way that relates to practice. And after they get the basic knowledge, we send them out into the world [concerning the practical component in the summer and third semester of the program]. We try to help build the students' network of contacts and field experience." (Staff member at Maxwell School)

"We are an academic institution, so knowledge- and theory-based learning will always be part of what we do. [...] What you learn in the classroom will help inform what happens in the field. And what you experience in the field will help inform your ability to participate appropriately in the classroom. [...] Providing them with the opportunity for practical and relevant experience while they are in school to help inform the other parts of their academic education is key. Finding ways to marry those two is not always easy – especially with international development, because a lot of that work means you have to do it in the summer." (Staff member at Wagner School)

"Our program is very much a combination of theory and practice, academics and practical application of those academics. [...] You learn something, but you learn it for something." (Staff member at SAIS)

"There is a continuing theory, I think, that if we in fact let internships be included in professional schools, the academics somehow get watered down." (Staff member at SAIS)

"It's always a discussion: 'Where's the balance between the academic part and the professional program part?' [...] Right now, it seems like the students are the ones pulling in the pre-professional direction, and the faculty are kind of holding on to some of the academic side. [...] Many of them feel that the students really cannot go into the professional world without having tools for thinking, and I know they believe in some of the academic courses with theoretical approaches – that that is where they are going to get those skills, and not necessarily in the other types of courses." (Staff member at Georgetown University, SFS)

"Fletcher's philosophy connects theory and practice. We train broadly knowledgeable and curious leaders to develop a thorough and nuanced grounding in the latest political, economic, business, and legal thinking and translate it into practical, successful actions that shape international issues and events." (Staff member at Tufts brochure, p. 1)

"I try to mix theory with practical considerations. To be only theoretical is a mistake, because theory is a way of ordering." (Staff member at SPEA)

"I would like to think that in the upper-level seminars and upper-level courses in a particular concentration, there is more and more case work because of the expectation that the students have picked up the theoretical material earlier in the coursework. [...] Probably, there are more practical examples as you move through your career in this program." (Staff member at SPEA)

"We do not do a whole lot of pure theory. Everything is for a particular applied reason. I believe that goes through all of our courses. It does not mean that we do not do some theory, but we follow it up with, 'This is how it applies'." (Staff member at SPEA)

These opinions clearly show that although no one answer exists to the question of how to best combine theoretical and practical elements in a public policy or international relations curriculum, the programs in our study have found solutions that work for them. The key seems to be teaching theory in a manner that allows the students to comprehend its real-world implications right away, rather than having to discover this for themselves later. Other factors include the order in which courses are taught, the combination of theory with the skills needed to use it (e.g., the core course 'Statistics for International Analysis' in the MSFS at Georgetown University), and the teaching methods used to impart the theory. We will deal with this last point in the following section.

4.5. Teaching and examination methods

A central purpose of a professional school is to help a student to acquire specific knowledge, skills and attitudes. Thus, we feel it is necessary to discuss *how* the educational institutions in our study choose to impart the chosen contents and substance to their students.

Lectures were mentioned by many as one of their methods of instruction, but always with the caveat that they are moving toward "active learning" or "experiential learning techniques" and only use lectures where they are the most appropriate method. Among the other methods used at these professional schools are classroom discussions, Socratic dialogue, simulations, role-playing games, group projects, team teaching (when a scholar and a practitioner take turns instructing a course), presentations, debates and ethics debates, problem sets, collaboration between students and professors, peer review of papers before they are submitted, and work in the field by internships or assisting a client. Below are various quotes describing the teaching methods used in the programs we examined as well as, wherever possible, a brief statement about why these particular methods are preferred.

"Lots of emphasis is placed on case studies, at least in courses outside of the core curriculum. [...] We also have group projects as another form of teaching within a lot of the courses. [...] The assignments are practical and relevant [even in courses in which theory is taught]. [...] Write a policy memo in the area that you want to work, and then you will be able to use that knowledge when you are in the interviews and say that you have already written something about that topic that impacts your organization." (Staff member at Wagner School)

"We focus on so-called 'active learning' to teach the basic theory, knowledge, and 'science' necessary to understand public policy. Courses tend to be a combination of, 'What do we already know, what's the proper technique, and how can it be applied to the problem to come up with a solution?' Our teaching methods include case studies, simulations, and briefing papers." (Staff member at Rockefeller College)

"Teaching methods for quantitative skills are lectures and labs. For qualitative skills, it's hands-on. We have lectures for history and economics. For UN topics, we do lots

of role-playing games. We also do team teaching to take advantage of areas of common interest and to expand students' knowledge beyond the sphere of political science, public policy, etc." (Staff member at Maxwell School)

"[We have] applied assignments in the classroom where you have responsibility beyond just to your grade: to teammates, to a client, and where you are working in a real-world situation or environment. [...] We also have group work because we all believe that in the real world, to get anything accomplished, you're going to be working in teams. [...] There are some cases -- in some cases more than others. [...] Literally every week, we have ethics debates which again would be something perhaps more likely in a professional school." (Staff member at George Washington University)

"Our teaching methods are very interactive [...]. We use case studies, teamwork, simulations. But each faculty member is unique and brings their own pedagogy. [...] It really has to go on beyond the lecture to include Socratic dialogue with questioning and not just expected answers but real, interactive learning and the synergy of minds working together. Simulations, collaboration, action learning projects where we send students where they are in the workplace..." (AU, School of International Service)

"During their paper-writing support seminar, they have to present their work in progress and get feedback from their peers and, on the other days, provide the feedback to their peers in turn so that again, they have had practice doing exactly what you said, of not only coming up with the results, and not only writing about the results, but communicating and representing them to an audience. [...] Our students never write a research paper in the sense that you would in an undergraduate school the whole time they are here. [...] We start out in the first semester teaching them to write policy memos for those who have not had that experience. [...] It has to be one or two pages; it has to be in non-technical language... the usual sorts of things." (Staff member at KSG)

"We have lectures, discussion seminars, case exercises, problem sets, field work. It's all over the place. [...] Obviously, the pedagogies may differ across the board, but again, we like to see if the students are being moved to the same place in the end." (Staff member at SPEA)

"The case studies are based on real-world experiences of a company or a government. They are written in prose form -- that is, a narrative -- and then tables and data and so on. Some of them are fairly complex. Oftentimes, data is missing, and they have to just use their best judgment, but they are real-world problems. [...] I think that case studies help, and I think that this school tends to underutilize case studies. [...] My problem is that there are very few good case studies that are really about environmental economics." (Staff member at SPEA)

Of the programs examined in this study, the vast majority require their students to do an applied project in their final semester(s) before graduation. These *final graduation requirements* vary greatly: Some programs allow students to choose the project, and others assign one to them. Some students must work in groups, whereas others work alone. The strength of this requirement – often called a capstone course – lies, in the opinion of the faculty members we interviewed, in the preparation for students' future careers and endeavors in the non-academic working world. They must deal with missing information, changing goals and circumstances, and very real pressure to succeed and solve a problem. This requirement is sometimes supplemented by comprehensive oral or written exams in the students' focus area(s). Some programs have different graduation requirements for their different degrees or allow the students to choose what type of paper to submit based on their future career plans (those with an academic orientation may opt to complete a traditional master's thesis). However, the overall trend is to have students gain real-world experience before they finish the program in the form of a final "capstone" project.

"Students do a capstone project in which a region and an issue are identified and the students then 'solve the problem' in order to bring together quantitative and qualitative skills and knowledge learned in the program. It should be in the form of a policy briefing memo rather than the long research papers required in most programs. Students are expected to make a transition in their writing throughout the program from scholarly or academic papers to the style used in a work setting. This is reflected in the curriculum." (Staff member at Maxwell School)

"We think the Capstone is learning in action. It is a core requirement of all of our students. It is an academic year-long, team-based project for an outside client. It has faculty oversight and theoretical learning. But most of it revolves around a project that they are doing for a client who has requested that project. [...] We find when our students get through the Capstone, employers love it. They use their Capstone experience in their interview. They talk about the challenges of real-world experience. [...] The students may not necessarily adore it while they are in it, but they certainly get it afterwards." (Staff member at Wagner School)

"In our Capstone for our Master of Public Policy, they have clients and they do public policy analyses. [...] It is another three-credit-hour course that you would be working on to fulfill the requirements of the course." (Staff member at George Washington University)

"The faculty very much believes that the experience [the Master of Arts in German and European Studies project] should be part of any graduate work, basically pulling together all sorts of different resources, information, and making something publishable at the end. Our students work on it for about a year. [...] They can work either individually or as a team. The idea is that all the students are part of the seminar, and they read each other's papers before they hand them in." (Staff member at Georgetown University, BMW Center)

"They write a second-year paper, which we do not call a thesis because it is more applied than that. They need to select a real problem that is being faced by a real or-

*ganization. [...] That can be a real segue into the professional nice that they are try-
ing to get into. [...] The second-year paper is an extended policy analysis and recommendations. But even that is limited to 40 or 45 pages." (Staff member at KSG)*

*"Then there is the capstone course at the end of their two years, which is a little bit
different, I think, from some of the other schools, where you are trying to really be
very explicitly interdisciplinary. [...] The capstone course that I mentioned, which is
this integrating exercise, often has students working for a client. [...] The assignment is a very professional assignment: They are really acting like young professionals and not simply students. It is a bridge assignment between being a student in the
school and being a professional in the working world. [...] Students with different
interests, different skills, and different concentrations work together on a common
project -- ideally, a common project involving a topic that is foreign to all of them so
that they can learn organizational skills, teamwork, to be quick studies in their basic
foundation. [...] After they have been out on the job, they understand the evaluations of the capstone experience improves with age." (Staff member at SPEA)*

Two programs in our study had particularly interesting capstone experiences that we would like to describe here in more detail. The Wagner
Graduate School of Public Service sends out "Requests for Proposals"
each year to various businesses and organizations, which can then submit
ideas of projects they would like the Wagner School students to do for
them. Faculty members then select a number of different projects and assign three to five students and one faculty advisor to each. Although the
projects are not urgent, they are important to the client, and the students
are expected to do them well. Examples of past projects include urban
planning assessments of infrastructure systems in Cambodia, financial
management of governmental systems in Guatemala, assessing programmatic effectiveness or outreach methods of United Nations departments,
and helping NGOs to increase their funding streams.

The students at SPEA in Bloomington, Indiana, tend to have more local
or national projects, but they are nonetheless an interesting means of im-
mersing students into professional life. All students in one class work together on a major project, such as determining how the city of Bloomington could better promote sustainable development within the community. As the students all have different strengths and interests, they are
expected to work together to find solutions to all the problems involved,
including matters of time, money, and communication. They act as young
professionals rather than students and provide a real service to an actual
client. As with the Wagner School (and most likely other capstone
courses), the SPEA students might not appreciate the value of this chal-
lenging experience right away, but they usually do later when they begin
working after graduation.

Finally, it is interesting to see which of the programs in our study require theses, capstone projects, and/or oral or written comprehensive exams of their students before graduation. Table 4.3 clearly shows the predominance of capstone projects as the final graduation requirement over theses and comprehensive exams. Our interview partners firmly believe in the advantage of such application- and career-oriented assignments, as we saw in the section on teaching methods. It is true that many students have trouble with the capstone or rate it as a negative experience while still in the program, but program directors indicated as soon as the graduates enter the labor market, they begin to appreciate the value of what they learned – in terms of both hard skills *and* soft skills. Immersion in the reality of the professional world is an effective, though not always easy, method of preparing students for their future careers, and it is in no way less demanding than a thesis or knowledge-based exam would be.

4.6. Faculty and student body composition

At any educational institution, the faculty members have a great impact on the quality and general direction or focus of the programs they offer. Their degree of commitment, teaching styles, and individual professional and academic backgrounds very much influence the experience students who go through the program will have. Also, the students bring in a variety of viewpoints and personality traits that play a role in all classroom interactions and, in essence, affect each others' learning as well. This is why these two factors were examined in the PROFIO study as well, even though we recognize the fact that universities do not have complete control over their applicant pools – and of course, they can only choose from those who apply, both as students and as faculty members.

4.6.1. Faculty

The opinions of the interview partners varied widely on the ideal composition of faculty members. Permanent faculty always teach at least 50% of the classes in an entire program, but the number of adjuncts and the extent to which students have contact to them is quite different. Maxwell has a summer program at which all instructors are practitioners, whereas the Harris School's students take classes with only one or two practitioners throughout their degree program. Our interview partner at the Rockefeller College admitted that the national accreditation agency puts limits on the number of courses non-permanent faculty members – at least those without Ph.D.s – may teach. Other interview partners men-

Table 4.3. Graduation requirements of the U.S. Professional Schools

Professional school (University)	Thesis	Capstone project	Comprehensive exam
Elliott School of International Affairs and School of Public Policy and Public Administration (George Washington University)		✓	
Fletcher School of Law and Diplomacy (Tufts University)	✓		✓
Ford School of Public Policy (University of Michigan)			
Graduate School of Public and International Affairs (University of Pittsburgh)		✓	
Harris Graduate School of Public Policy (University of Chicago)			
Heinz School of Public Policy and Management (Carnegie Mellon University)		✓	
Kennedy School of Government (Harvard University)		✓	
Maxwell School (Syracuse University)		✓	
Nitze School of Advanced International Studies (Johns Hopkins University)			✓
Rockefeller College of Public Affairs and Policy (SUNY-Albany)		✓	
School of International Service and School of Public Affairs (American University)			✓
School of Public Affairs and Environmental Sciences (Indiana University – Bloomington)		✓	
School of Public Policy and Management (Ohio State University)		✓	✓
Wagner Graduate School of Public Service (New York University)		✓	
Walsh School of Foreign Service and the BMW Center for German & European Studies (Georgetown University)		✓	
Total	1	10	4

Source: Authors

tioned that even their permanent faculty members have "mixed careers" and have worked in the field or even do so in addition to their work as professors. The Kennedy School of Government and American University call their adjunct faculty "practitioner-scholars" or "scholarly practitioners", which describes their involvement in academics and research as well as in the field.

"Our faculty members are at many different international organizations and EU institutions, such as the European Court of Human Rights, the European Parliament, and the Council of Europe. One professor worked for the UN for 30 years and now teaches a course on the relations between international organizations and NGOs. [...] The instructors here in Syracuse are mostly academics, but with mixed careers. The ones who teach for us in [Washington] D.C. and Strasbourg are all practitioners. Some of our faculty members are four-star generals, former ambassadors, and UN or EU employees. [...] All our statistics and internationally-focused classes are taught by practitioners." (Maxwell School)

"We have faculty who are actually full-time on staff at a UN agency who are adjuncts here, or full-time faculty who are full-time here and who are doing consulting work for a UN agency, NGOs, or the World Bank. So they have that practical experience to know what international agencies are looking for. [...] But everyone who teaches at Wagner – certainly our international faculty – have practical, relevant experiences in the field." (Wagner School)

"We have 50 full-time faculty members and about 150 adjuncts. Many of these adjuncts come from jobs during the day, where they are in international organizations here in Washington. [...] Almost all of our adjuncts are Ph.D.s or lawyers working in the field. But across the board – even for our tenured faculty members – almost all of them have been involved in policymaking at some point or are involved in policymaking currently while they are tenured full-time professors as well." (SAIS)

"We have approximately 63 full-time faculty and over 40 adjuncts, who are practitioners... We have some extraordinary practitioner-scholars – that is what we like to call them. [...] Our adjuncts just make the difference in providing networking for our students – not just for internships, but for jobs." (AU, School of International Service)

Some of our interview partners expressed the opinion that practitioners should not teach courses in higher-level education ("Graduates need to be trained by Ph.D.s, not by MBAs") and that universities should focus on academic education and not vocational training. Overall, however, we come to the conclusion that the advantages outweigh the disadvantages of having practitioners teach at least some courses in a given program. The comment made on networking, for example, shows that the students not only benefit from the practitioners' experience in the field but also from their contacts and assistance in finding internships or jobs. In the end, it is up to the directors of a program to determine for which courses and to what extent they wish to allow non-tenured faculty members to instruct the students. They can also provide services to help their external instructors improve their teaching methods, as American University does at its Center for Teaching Excellence and its review of syllabi in advance:

"We also have across the university an orientation for our adjunct faculties, and in addition, we work with them as they're developing syllabi by giving them guides and having templates for syllabi so that they know the sorts of rigor that we require. We strongly encourage them to go through this orientation process with the Center for Teaching Excellence and with us, learning about what's required, what's expected, the sorts of substantive materials that are expected to be covered on a weekly basis and by the end of a course, and the different teaching methodologies with which they may not be familiar. [...] Another thing I have learned is that you want to actually review practitioners' syllabi in advance and before they hit the classroom, because you don't want them going in and telling war stories. Stories are great – you can learn from stories – but you really want to be sure that that's not what's happening. And they're fantastic people who are really great teachers: We have some former ambassadors, and they're marvelous in the classroom. But truly, that mechanism will prevent challenges a little bit later on in the process." (AU, School of Public Affairs)

Therefore, in sum, the faculty certainly plays a role in how a program meets its learning objectives, but this does not mean that only academic professors or experienced practitioners are the most suitable instructors; rather, the composition should include a fair number of each.

4.6.2. Students

The typical size of the entering classes at the professional schools in our study ranges from 80 to 400 new students per year, with the average around 150.[81] The internationality of the student body also widely differs: The greatest number of international students take part in the MPAID (KSG) and MAGES (Georgetown University) programs (60% and 48% respectively), and the least (11%) are at the Wagner School. Some institutions had higher ratios of international to domestic students before restrictions were made on student visas after 9/11.

Our interview partners further gave a wide range of answers to the question what types of students are attracted to their program, especially with regard to their career aspirations when they begin their studies there. One could almost consider this to be irrelevant, however, as it was reported that many students end up in entirely different work areas than they originally envisioned. Another interesting factor is the amount of work experience most students have when they apply. Some programs

---

[81] This includes all students registered for all master's programs at a given professional school, as we were not always provided the numbers for the individual programs.

require two, three, or even more years of relevant work experience for admission, whereas others (such as SPEA in Indiana) also accept applicants directly after completing their bachelor degrees. The quotes below exemplify the types of students in highly-ranked public policy and diplomacy programs in the U.S.

"Most of our students aspire to work for local, state, or national governments. Only a small percentage of students are here in an international context. Students who go to IOs do so candidly. I would say that six to ten students per year interested in international work or in capability building." (Rockefeller College)

"The goal of the students who come here is to be trained to be professionals. [...] Our students often do have the goal of working for international organizations but find that it's hard to break in and go to NGOs instead." (Maxwell School)

"Many American students want to work internationally – World Bank, IMF, State Department, consular or foreign service. [...] More students are coming in with the specific goal of working for international organizations since 9/11." (Harris School)

"90% of our students are career changers: They come to the school in order to change the career that they are in." (SAIS)

*"Some of our students end up in international organizations not thinking they are going to because of internships they do in Washington or professors they have from the World Bank or an IO. Some of our **students** come in thinking they are going to be international and end up doing domestic work. [...] It is a self-selecting group. The people who apply here are really committed to making a difference."* (AU, School of Public Affairs)

"I think the average age of incoming students for that program [MSFS] was 27 or 28, and they are very professionally oriented: They want to go on to careers in government and international organizations and business sometimes as well. [...] Our classes partially consist of U.S. citizens, but partially of European students, so we are also recruiting in Europe." (Georgetown University, SFS)

"The average age when they come in is about 28, although it ranges from 22 to 42. They tend to be 28 or so with several years' work experience and possibly a previous master's. [...] Because our students have come from so many different places, they often add value to the discussions on these particular subjects." (KSG)

"Something that distinguishes our program from our competitors is [that we are] often willing to take a student right out of an undergraduate institution, because we believe that not only our curriculum and our concentrations work, but also that applied piece can prepare them to step into these positions that you describe." (SPEA)

The programs are somewhat heterogeneous with regard to the students who apply and decide to attend them, yet this of course relates to the goals and profile of the institutions. In general, we can say that the majority of master's students in public policy and international relations have earned a bachelor and often a master's degree already and have gained work experience (possibly through internships or in the Peace Corps). They also have career goals that go beyond work at international organizations to include domestic government agencies, NGOs, and private companies. Apparently, 9/11 seems to have been a catalyst for American students' new wave of interest in careers in international organizations. Finally, the students contribute to the program while they take part as well as after graduation as alumni, as we will discuss in the next section.

4.7. Career services

Career services offices are very common at American institutions of higher education and serve various roles and functions. Many professional schools even have their own career services offices. The services they provide commonly include counseling; job/internship postings; courses on how to write résumés and do well in job interviews or business lunches; and career fairs, workshops, or information sessions. Alumni of the school or program can provide assistance in various ways as well. These include networking, giving feedback on the curriculum, holding skills-building sessions, providing information on job and internship openings at their places of work, marketing for their alma mater, and mentoring. This way, it is not solely up to the students to find employment after finishing their professional school degree – which benefits the school as well, as the students are then later likely to help fellow alumni from the same institution in turn. Also, in order to become a full member of the Association of Professional Schools of International Affairs (APSIA; cf. Section 4.8.1), the institution must have its own career services office and not simply rely on the career services office of the whole university. For the schools, these offices are crucial, as the following exemplary statements show:

> "Our job is to drum into students' heads that few employers visit the school [15 to 20 go to the Heinz School per year, whereas approximately 75 go to the business school] because it is not as attractive to big firms. We try to explain the need for networking and general proactiveness in their job search. Also, it's our job to create events or occasions that bring students in contact with potential employers. Finally, we try to teach students to read job ads loosely: fifty percent of hiring is about chemistry and one's ability to learn the ropes." (Heinz School)

> "The main objective of the courses and workshops offered by Career Services is to energize students, give them a glimpse into what they can do, help them with networking, and reinforce the Harris School's connections to these institutions [those that send representatives to lead a career session]. We also try to help students 'stake out what they want to do' and let them know they should be aware of all aspects of their future jobs." (Harris School)

"The Career Services Office here was originally created to generate international connections. [...] We track all students after graduation. We show them how to get their materials ready and teach them how to develop their own internships [how to research and approach an organization]. We also identify ongoing internship programs and develop partnerships with organizations of broad interest to students but where access is harder. Finally, we contact employers to ask about their hiring needs and tell them what skills our graduates have." (Ford School)

"We have a number of services and resources that are available to our students to find full-time, part-time, paid, unpaid jobs, internships, fellowships, and volunteer assignments. What we do not do is match them up. [...] We help build their capacity, so that they understand how to frame themselves from the employer's perspective, because we want to teach them life-long skills." (Wagner School)

"We place a very large emphasis on career development. [...] Each of the six programs has one person in the program, an administrator, who is responsible for career services for the students." (Georgetown University, SFS)

"We tell our students from the point of stepping on campus for orientation that their career search begins then. They are introduced to our career service area and the staff the very first day of orientation, and they have individual meetings immediately with our director and her staff. [...] Her strategy is to attack, if you will, the students along their professional student organizations. [...] The students have grouped themselves already along professional lines. Therefore, she approaches them there and meets them where their needs are: asks them, 'What would you like to hear? How can I help you?' [...] She also plans a couple trips a year for students to engage in. We take a DC trip every spring break for them to go and experience DC and have information sessions for the students. Then in the fall, they take a trip to Chicago." (SPEA)

As such services are becoming a major expectation of the students, some institutions without their own career services offices reported that they were beginning to hire full-time staff members for this purpose. One faculty member commented on the ability some schools have to offer events, databases, and publications to their students to help them find jobs because they charge a fee to each incoming student (in this case, $5000) and therefore have extensive financial means that allow them to do so. It is clear that staff working full-time solely for the purpose of career services will be able to provide a different level of assistance than those who teach, research, and advise students on career issues on the side.

As mentioned, the organization of *alumni involvement* is often a major responsibility of those working in the career services office. It is useful to maintain contact with as many graduates of a program as possible, as they can later return a great deal to the school or institution. Their roles and functions can include – but are not limited to – networking, providing feedback on the curriculum, offering skills-building sessions, giving information on job and internship openings at their places of work, and marketing for their alma mater. Our interview partners at some of the schools mentioned that students were welcome to contact alumni in their database concerning job-related questions, and that many alumni were quite willing to meet with students over a cup of coffee to discuss their career goals and paths. The Harris School even arranges for a limited number of students to have mentors in the area (among the members of the Visiting Committee), which has proven to be very effective in helping students find employment.

"Alumni do lots of things to help our current students. They send job postings; they advise students; sometimes they hire interns. They also provide access points, because they can tell the students, 'Try talking to so-and-so.' We have them give presentations on campus, and some attend the Washington event. We also send résumé books for full-time jobs and internships to our alumni in key positions – one to two graduates per year find jobs just because of that. Another advantage of the résumé books is that it gets the students' resumes done very early." (Ford School)

"We do have a practice of bringing alumni back from various jobs in various sectors, and they run sessions for current students to talk about where they are, how they got there, what they found on the job, what things are working, what things are not working, what things you need to succeed..." (KSG)

The collection and analysis of alumni placement statistics is another common task of career services offices. However, such statistics were not available from all institutions in this study, and those we did receive are not all directly comparable with each other. For example, some schools simply categorize their alumni placement statistics in general sectors: public sector, private sector, non-profit organizations, and further study. For these reasons, we cannot make any specific conclusions on which professional schools are most effective in preparing their students for careers at international organizations (and actually sending them there). The job placement at international organizations ranged from five to twenty percent, though in some cases it was unclear whether these numbers also include positions in foreign governments or multinational corporations. The Kennedy School of Government reports that 63% of its alumni work in the international public and non-profit sectors combined but gives no precise percentage for those working at international organizations. It is therefore safe to say that while none of these programs primarily educates its students for international organizations, many of them certainly do have this career goal in mind and thus give their students the opportunity to complete coursework in this area.

4.8.   Cooperation agreements

Another point of interest is the educational institutions, employers, or associations with which a particular program of study chooses to cooperate. This can be useful in providing the students with opportunities they would not otherwise have, and it can also help several higher education institutions to use their resources more wisely. Finally, direct cooperation with future employers benefits all three sides: the students gain easier access to internships and jobs, the study programs receive feedback from employers on their curricula, and the employers have the opportunity to scout out future talents for job openings.

4.8.1.   Academic cooperation agreements

Most of the professional schools have close ties to research or policy centers on campus that specialize in certain areas too specific for the schools. One advantage of these is that they can be a source of additional instructors who are specialists in other areas, and another is that students can often take part in the research there as well. Another common form of intra-institutional cooperation is when a program at one professional school allows students to take relevant courses offered by other schools or departments at that university or others in the area.

Some professional schools have chosen to cooperate with each other on projects of common interest, such as offering joint recruiting events or coursework alongside internships in a location like Washington, D.C. One school also mentioned having offered joint coursework via video conferencing, but this seemed to be the exception rather than the rule. Also, location seems to play a major role in the extent to which universities see the need to cooperate: the professional schools in Washington, D.C., and New York City did not mention cooperating with any other institutions in the U.S., whereas those in Pittsburgh, Syracuse, and Albany did.

Three organizations[82] were mentioned by our interview partners as being useful for linking schools with common goals and objectives: the National Association of Schools of Public Affairs and Administration (NASPAA), the Association for Public Policy Analysis and Management (APPAM), and the Association of Professional Schools of International Affairs (APSIA). The member institutions work together in different ways. For example, NASPAA has an accreditation institute by which the

[82] The Transatlantic Policy Consortium (TPC) is another cooperation network in which several of the institutions in our study are members; however, this will be dealt with in greater detail in the section with results from Western Europe. For more information on the TPC, please see http://www.spea.indiana.edu/tac/.

member schools can have the quality of their degree programs tested (see Section 4.2.1). Also, our interview partner at the University of Michigan told us that APSIA career staff share best practices with each other in yearly meetings and visit businesses and organizations in collective trips (employer outreaches) to "promote the general mission of education in international affairs." These activities are said to benefit all members despite the competition that exists between them, as they simply want to let hiring managers know of what public policy and international affairs graduates are capable.

The missions of these three associations are as follows:

"The National Association of Schools of Public Affairs and Administration (NASPAA) [...] serves as a national and international resource for the promotion of excellence in education and training for public service. Its institutional membership includes 253 U.S. university programs in public affairs, public policy, public administration, and public management."[83]

"The APPAM Policy Council has approved the following language pertaining to the Association's mission: APPAM is dedicated to improving public policy and management by fostering excellence in research, analysis, and education."[84]

"The Association of Professional Schools of International Affairs (APSIA) comprises 29 member schools in the United States, Asia and Europe dedicated to the improvement of professional education in international affairs and the advancement thereby of international understanding, prosperity, peace, and security. APSIA members work to promote excellence in professional, international affairs education worldwide by sharing information and ideas among member schools and with other higher education institutions, the international affairs community, and the general public."[85]

Interestingly, the professional schools in our study were often members of more than one of these associations. This would indicate that the benefits of membership thus vary greatly enough between them to make paying dues to more than one worthwhile. Table 4.4 lists which schools or institutions are members of which of the three associations.

[83] http://www.naspaa.org/about_naspaa/about/overview.asp, retrieved July 5, 2007.
[84] http://www.appam.org/information/index.asp, retrieved June 1, 2006.
[85] http://apsia.org/apsia/aboutus/aboutUs.php, retrieved July 5, 2007.

Table 4.4. Professional School membership in cooperation organizations

Professional school (University)	Member of NASPAA	Member of APPAM	Member of APSIA
Elliott School of International Affairs[a] and School of Public Policy and Public Administration[b] (George Washington University)	✓ b only	✓	✓
Fletcher School of Law and Diplomacy (Tufts University)			✓
Ford School of Public Policy (University of Michigan)	✓	✓	✓
Graduate School of Public and International Affairs (University of Pittsburgh)	✓	✓	✓
Harris Graduate School of Public Policy (University of Chicago)	✓	✓	
Heinz School of Public Policy and Management (Carnegie Mellon University)	✓	✓	
Kennedy School of Government (Harvard University)	✓	✓	✓
Maxwell School (Syracuse University)		✓	✓
Nitze School of Advanced International Studies (Johns Hopkins University)		✓	✓
Rockefeller College of Public Affairs & Policy (SUNY-Albany)	✓	✓	
School of International Service and the School of Public Affairs (American University)	✓	✓	✓
School of Public Affairs and Environmental Sciences (Indiana University – Bloomington)	✓	✓	
School of Public Policy and Management (Ohio State University)	✓	✓	
Wagner Graduate School of Public Service (New York University)	✓	✓	
Walsh School of Foreign Service and BMW Center for German & European Studies (Georgetown University)		✓	✓
Total	11	14	9

Source: Authors

4.8.2. Cooperation agreements with international organizations

Only two U.S. professional schools mentioned having formal cooperation agreements with international organizations, and even informal arrangements were less common than those with other educational institutions or state governments. One interview partner (Ford School) mentioned the Diplomat-in-Residence program through which senior officers are placed on university campuses to advise students on careers in international policy and diplomacy. The numbers of students having internships and jobs with the U.S. Department of State reportedly 'skyrocketed' when this program began.

Besides this, which is more of a form of cooperation with the federal government, two of our interview partners mentioned cooperating with actual international organizations. The Maxwell European Union Center of Excellence (Syracuse) is funded by the EU Commission in Washington, DC, and offers advanced coursework (e.g., simulations), guest lectures, special events, and research opportunities to those interested in learning more about the EU. Also, the Heinz School at Carnegie Mellon University has created a partnership with the United Nations Development Programme via personal connections that allows students to secure internships there and receive funding for them through the School. This is a prestigious opportunity that attracts the Heinz School's best students, who then provide services to the organization based on the strong quantitative skills they learn in the program. Recently, several of the interns did their capstone projects in cooperation with the UNDP after returning to Pittsburgh and created measuring tools for program evaluation. Finally, according to our interview partner,

> "The majority [of the Heinz School interns at the UNDP] have been made to understand that if they wished to pursue a longer engagement with the UNDP at a later point, their applications would receive the endorsement of the managers for whom they worked. There are of course no guarantees; the managers were sufficiently happy with their work results to offer to serve as references." (Heinz School)

In other words, such positive internship experiences can help students to obtain full-time employment after graduation. Such partnerships are not easy to establish, but if they go well as in the case of the Heinz School, they benefit all parties involved.

4.9. Conclusion on the U.S. programs

As was shown in this chapter, each master's program has a somewhat different focus and concept of the skills and competencies their students must learn. However, their programs are quite similar in terms of their general structure and content. Overall, it can be stated that the degree programs in the U.S. attempt to combine the following elements in a manner that fits with the focus area of the particular school: *topical* (dealing with issues, policies, and affairs), *geographical* (regions, languages, or institutions), and *methodical* elements (tools-based, hands-on, analytical). Besides political science and international relations, the primary fields of study in the core curriculum, the concentrations, or both were law, economics, statistics, foreign languages, and area studies. The programs also all attempt to impart – either inside or outside of the core curriculum – management skills, communication skills, and career-finding skills to their students.

The findings further reflect the fact that American professional schools are in constant contact with their alumni and various employers and incorporate the feedback they receive from them into their curricula. They see the increasing importance of international and interdisciplinary orientations and implement these as fits with the objectives of the institution. Often, they leave the amount of depth and internationality to the students by giving them the opportunity to earn a joint or dual degree or to study in a foreign country. The length of the master's programs is also determined on an individual basis, though none takes less than one or more than two years to complete. Students can or must do internships, and they may extend their internship or gain additional experience through pro bono consulting or a capstone experience. This and other teaching methods used at U.S. professional schools tend to be mainly interactive (with the professor and with other students), and guest lectures or workshops with practitioners further aid in their immersion into real-world practice. It is also common to introduce the students to their future fields of work by taking excursions to major political centers and inviting employers to campus.

In conclusion, the findings in the U.S. part of the curricular study greatly correlate with those in the labor market study. By selecting an internationally-oriented program and planning one's curriculum and extracurricular activities wisely, students can obtain a solid preparation for careers in international organizations according to the opinions and expectations of those who already work there.

5. Results of the curricular study – Western Europe

In this section, the findings of the study in Western Europe will be discussed in detail. Here, it is important to mention that the results presented below give a rather incomplete picture of European educational offerings that aim to prepare students for the international public service. However, although we examined a heterogeneous selection of educational programs in Western Europe, most of the crucial categories (e.g., practicality, international orientation, and cooperation agreements with international organizations) are relevant to all programs so that a systematic analysis of best practices was possible even if not all programs aim similarly to qualify their students for the international public service.

5.1. Core components of the curriculum

In this section, the core components of the educational programs examined in this study are described and analyzed in detail. Here, we were mainly interested in the core courses students are required to attend and which areas of concentration are available. However, before describing the core elements of the programs examined, the process of curriculum development and evaluation should be considered.

5.1.1. Curricular development and evaluation

In the PROFIO study, we were interested in how the curricula of the educational programs examined were designed. Only very few program coordinators interviewed made specific statements on this topic. However, those who discussed how their program was designed stressed that the curriculum was mainly developed by experienced academic faculty members who have a great deal of expertise in different fields of study and also to a certain extent work experience in the professional field for which the program prepares students:

> "An economist and a political scientist developed this program, and we both have a great deal of knowledge of public and international law. We were the core group but called on others from the beginning, such as someone in the area of Public Management, people from the business side of things, and more economists." (University of St. Gallen)

In addition to the input from the faculty members, some interview partners admitted that they studied the curricula of European and other educational programs that have a strong reputation in preparing students for the national or international public service, mainly those at professional schools in the U.S. Only in very few cases were practitioners systematically involved in the curriculum development with the purpose of ensuring that the demands of the professional world are sufficiently considered. At the University of Konstanz, for instance, the curriculum was developed by taking into consideration recommendations from outside of academia:

"It was really our own creation, also in that at that time – at least in Germany – there were no offerings in this field. It was our idea to do something like this, and then we gathered more information from discussions with experts and various analyses. That is also where we got our structure from." (University of Konstanz)

Furthermore, program coordinators at the Hertie School of Governance and the European School of Governance in Berlin conducted interviews and surveys among educational experts in Germany and abroad as well as among practitioners working in the private and public sectors. Other educational institutions were advised by national administrations. For example, the Diplomatic Academy of Vienna consulted with the Austrian Federal Foreign Office concerning its curriculum development.

"We received advice from the Ministry of Foreign Affairs, and the Ministry of Foreign Affairs is of course represented in international organizations in Vienna, so they come here and advise our curricular committee." (Diplomatic Academy of Vienna)

It is further apparent that the process of curriculum development is an ongoing process, as there were continuous evaluations by practitioners and within the faculties which often led to substantial changes in the design. Our interview partner at the Hertie School of Governance described it as follows:

"[Curricular development] is basically [...] never finished, because it's always dynamically being developed further. This is the process in a nutshell: first draft, consultation with representatives from corresponding fields, second draft, consultation with stakeholders, third draft, consultations with peer institutions. Then the faculty came. And then the finishing touches, so to speak." (Hertie School of Governance, Berlin)

However, there is no information available as to what extent evaluations of curricula are institutionalized, meaning whether the program directors have set up special committees or invited external experts specifically for the purpose of reviewing the curriculum on an ongoing or intermittent basis. According to the information we received, only the Erfurt School of Public Policy organizes meetings of its entire teaching staff once per semester in order to discuss the quality of the curriculum. Some programs receive feedback from potential employers, program alumni and students. The curriculum of the German Development Institute in Bonn, for instance, is assessed and improved every year by potential employers such the German Federal Ministry for Economic Cooperation and GTZ. Other programs receive feedback from their students or program alumni, as the following comments show, but it is apparent that only very few programs are systematically evaluated either by academic staff or practitioners, although many interview partners highlighted the importance of evaluations on an ongoing basis:

"The alumni, and especially the fellows, give us feedback on what they would like to have in addition. And we are happy to hear it. Not changing anything would be like taking a step backwards in today's market. You definitely have to take that into account. You also have to watch what's a trend at a given point in time." (Center for European Integration Studies, Bonn)

"You can really always change something. You can improve and optimize everything. We have done just that, of course through continuous feedback we receive. There are always a few aspects of the program that the various stakeholders don't particularly like. One example of this is the proportion of theoretical and practical elements in the program." (University of Potsdam)

Only a few of the educational institutions examined cooperate with other institutions in the country or abroad concerning their curriculum development and assessment. The University of St. Gallen, however, receives informal feedback on aspects of their program from Sciences Po in Paris:

"We get this feedback through our cooperation with Paris. It's quite interesting to us, as Paris has a different educational culture. It [the feedback] especially comes from problems we discuss with each other, such as 'How do you deal with that?' 'What kinds of problems do you have?' We learn lots of things from this cooperation. But it's not that we are involved in a dialogue that would allow us to change anything specific about the program, but we do take various suggestions and think about incorporating them into the program." (University of St. Gallen)

Another assessment tool mentioned by most interview participants are the criteria set by the accreditation bodies. Many interviewees stressed that they had to revise the program's curriculum to meet the criteria for accreditation. The programs examined in this study are mostly accredited by different European agencies (e.g., FIBAA, ACQUIN).

5.1.2. Fields of study

The educational programs examined in the PROFIO study have a core set of courses all students must take. However, these vary considerably depending on the educational objectives of the institution, both in terms of the number of required courses (compared to the number of electives) and concerning the variety of fields that must be covered. With regard to the core courses, most programs require their students to attend courses

in the fields of political science, economics, and law. These courses are mainly taught with a European or international perspective and are characterized by an interdisciplinary orientation. The program "Master of European Studies" at the Center for European Integration Studies in Bonn, for instance, requires the students to complete the following basic courses:
– Political Science
  – Introduction to the History and the Political System of the EU
  – The European Union as a Global Actor
– Economics
  – Economic Principles of European Integration
  – The Economic and Monetary Union
– Law
  – Introduction to the Institutions, Procedures and Law of the EU
  – EC-freedoms, Fundamental Rights and Protection of the Individual[86]
In comparison to the programs with a strong European perspective, the International Organizations M.B.A. at the University of Geneva offers core courses with a strong international and practical orientation, including:
– Business and Public Policy
– Social Entrepreneurship (part 1 & 2)
– How Organizations are Governed
– The Business Underpinning of International and Non-governmental Organizations
– Strategy in the Global Environment
– Microeconomics for Managers
– Finance for Managers
– Management Accounting
– Resource Management
– Fundraising
– Business Simulation Game
– Financial Accounting
– Project Management
– Organizational Behavior and Change Management
– Communication Skills[87]
In addition to courses in certain fields of study, most programs also require their students to attend courses on qualitative and/or quantitative research methods, policy analysis, project management, budgeting, and

---

[86] http://www.zei.de, retrieved July 5, 2007.
[87] http://hec-executive.ch/iomba//www/index.php, retrieved July 5, 2007.

strategic or human resource management. Here, students should acquire essential tools which enable them to perform empirical research, program evaluation, and financial and administrative management required for successful performance in national administrations and international organizations. Some programs offer comprehensive moduls that combine courses which introduce students to a certain field of study (political science, public policy, law, etc.) and courses that focus on professional skills and competency development (qualitative/quantitative research methods, project management, policy analysis). It comprises four courses: Introduction to Public Policy, Quantitative Analysis and Empirical Methods, Economic Analysis and Modeling, and Comparative Public Policy[88]. Other programs require their students to carry out an applied project so that they can develop their analytical, problem-solving, and methodological skills. However, many one-year programs assume that students have already acquired the basic research methods and analytical skills in prior academic programs, as the lack of time that does not allow them to include this training component into the curriculum.

In general, it can be concluded that courses that aim to develop a broad or specific knowledge base *and* courses which focus on the training of methodological, analytical, and problem-solving skills are very often an essential part of the core curriculum in the programs examined.

Furthermore, in addition to these courses, some programs offer a variety of areas of concentration or specialization courses through which students can deepen their knowledge in a chosen field of study. The specialization courses students can attend at the programs examined are described in detail in the next section. Another core component of the curricular examined are courses which primarily focus on the reflection and application of background knowledge and skills gained in prior academic training and courses which aim to develop certain professional skills, such as communication, teamwork, and project management skills. Here, students are often required to carry out hands-on projects, case studies, and internships. Finally, another important core component of almost all curricula examined is the final master's thesis.

When summarizing the information obtained on the structure and core components of program curricula, it can be concluded that many programs are primarily designed on the basis of three overarching educational objectives: (1) The first objective comprises the development of a systematic knowledge base, largely, though not exclusively, based on contributing academic disciplines, such social and political science, law,

---

[88] http://www.espp.de, retrieved July 5, 2007.

economics, and business administration. (2) The second objective focuses primarily on the application of knowledge aquired under the first educational objective and the development and application of analytical, methodological, problem-solving and management skills. It further covers the range of professional activities in the field the program aims to prepare for. (3) The third objective involves the opportunity for work-related learning (e.g., internships). Many curricula examined are marked by the interrelationship of these three educational components, although they differ concerning the measures applied to achieve these educational objectives and how much emphasis they place on each. In general, it is apparent that the curricula of the more practically-oriented programs which primarily aim to prepare students for work in the national or international public service are similarly structured to those of the U.S professional schools (cf. Section 4.2.2).

The training program at the German Development Institute in Bonn, for instance, clearly reflects these educational components in its program structure: The first training period in Bonn includes courses on development-related subjects as well as methodology workshops, courses on report writing, and courses designed to improve communication and social skills. In the second training, period students are required to carry out an empirical and consulting-oriented study project (so-called country working groups) which clearly focuses on knowledge application and workplace learning.

The curriculum of the program "Master of European Studies" at the Center for European Integration Studies in Bonn is built on three basic pillars:

"The curriculum has three pillars. The first is instruction on the subject. The second is the Europe Dialogue, which also includes excursions to the institutions. And the third is 'career development' [...]." (Center for European Integration Studies, Bonn)

The two pillars "European Dialogue" and "Career Development" are designed to guarantee the practical application of theoretical knowledge acquired in the first pillar.

When analyzing the structure of the program "Master of Public Policy" at the Hertie School of Governance in Berlin, it is also apparent that the educational objectives identified were the underlying guiding principles for the curriculum development. Here, the curriculum is divided into the following parts:

- Core Curriculum: The Core Curriculum is structured by the two central fields of competence: "understanding" and "changing". In four so-called U-courses and four C-courses students are introduced to topics such as the historic development of public affairs, applied economics, political economy, the logic of political action, scientific methods of information processing, public management and the skills necessary for successful negotiation, mediation, and political communication.

- Advanced Curriculum: The aim of the Advanced Curriculum is to coach students in the practical application of the skills and methods acquired in the Core Curriculum. Students have to complete a total of eight electives half of which have to come from one of the areas of concentration the Hertie School of Governance is offering: "European and International Governance", "Economics, Welfare, and Sustainability" and "Public Management".
- Integrated Workshops: The objective of two mandatory Integrated Workshops is to familiarize students with various kinds of problems they may encounter in their professional work. The integrated workshops are organized as seminars, in the course of which numerous guests from public, private or civil society institutions present problems of their day-to-day business.
- Internship: The six-week internship at an institution in the public, private or civil society sector has to be completed during the summer break between the first and the second year of study. The Hertie School of Governance pre-negotiates for its students a range of offers in relevant institutions and ensures the assignment of meaningful tasks during the internship.
- Student Project: The internship can be linked to the Student Project which concludes with a thesis-type policy paper in the service of an institution from the public, private or civil society sector. The aim of the project is to prove the candidate's ability of analysing practical problems within a specified time limit and limited amount of resources using the skills and knowledge gained in the programme. Work on the student project is carried out during the second year of study; the finished paper is handed over to the respective institution free of charge.[89]

The curriculum of the Erfurt School of Public Policy also reflects that the development of a systematic knowledge base and professional skills and the practical application of it are the basic educational objectives of the program, as Figure 5.1 shows.

When examining the curricular design of the M.A. in International Affairs and Governance at the University of St. Gallen[90], it is apparent that the program aims to achieve the following objectives: develop a specific

[89] http://www.hertie-school.org/en/3_mpp/curriculum/index.html, retrieved July 5, 2007.

182

Figure 5.1. Curriculum of Master of Public Policy, University of Erfurt

Term	Master of Public Policy (M.P.P.)			
4	Master Thesis (30 credits)			
3	Leadership Module (12 credits) − Pol. Advocacy − Ethics	2 Specialization Modules (2 x 9 credits) including − Int. Affairs − EU − IPE	Practical Training Module (15 credits) − Internship − Project Group	2 Specialization Modules (2 x 6 credits)
2	Management Module (12 credits) − Financial M. − Strategic M.			
1	Policy Analysis Module (24 credits) − Introduction to Public Policy − Quantitative Analysis and Empirical Methods − Economic Analysis and Modeling − Comparative Public Policy or an elective course			

Source: *Erfurt School of Public Policy, http://www.espp.de. Adapted by authors.*

knowledge base in the fields of political theory, economics, law, and business administration; strengthen the interdisciplinary manner of thinking, and the study and practice of interdisciplinarity; develop methodological and intercultural skills; and reflect and apply skills and knowledge (cf. Figure 5.2).

5.1.3. Areas of concentration

As mentioned before, in addition to specific core courses, many programs examined in this study offer areas of concentration (also known as specializations, focus areas, and clusters). However, most one-year programs rather provide their students with a fixed curriculum which only includes few electives. The vast majority of programs require their students to choose a thematic specialization at the beginning of the second semester, whereas during the first semester, the development of a broad knowledge base is usually the main focus. The thematic concentrations most often of-

---

[90] The program has been modified since our study has been conducted. These changes are not reflected here.

Figure 5.2. Curriculum of MA International Affairs & Governance, St. Gallen

Term	Core Area International Affairs & Governance			Independent Options	Context
3	Political Science, Economics, Law Interdisciplinary courses (6 credits) Disciplinary courses (6 credits) Electives & Independent Study (11 credits)			Independent Optional Courses (10 credits)	Action Competence (6 credits)
2					Cultural competencies (12 credits)
1	Interdisciplinary core course (9 credits)	Political Theory (6 credits)	Research Methods (6 Credits)		

Source: University St. Gallen, http://www.master-stufe.unisg.ch/org/lehre/ms.nsf/wwwPublnhalte-Ger/MIA:+Curriculum?opendocument, retrieved February 25, 2006. Adapted by authors.
Notes: In the meantime, the program has been modified. The link above leads to the new program.

fered in the programs examined were as follows: International Relations/International Affairs; International and European Economics; International and European Law; Public Policy/European Public Policy/Public Policy and Governance/European and International Governance; and Public Management. In general, we can see that many elective courses are characterized by a strong "European" and "International" perspective.

Furthermore, our study has shown that some programs even offer specific concentrations on the development, structure, and functions of international organizations. At the University of Konstanz, for instance, students can choose within the program "Master in Public Policy and Management" an area of concentration called "International Organization and European Integration" that has the following objective:

"The policies and politics of international organizations like the United Nations and, most notably, the European Union affect an ever-increasing number of individuals. To understand these effects, we need to study the decision making processes and patterns of policy making of these organizations in a systematic and detailed fashion. Students who are enrolled in the program European Integration and International Organization will receive a rigorous training in the social scientific study of the European Union, the United Nations and other international organizations. They will explore the main theoretical debates in international governance and develop their methodological skills substantively. This theoretical and practical knowledge will enable them to evaluate contending arguments on the achievements and failures of international organizations in a scientific way."[91]

In the program "International Studies" at the Diplomatic Academy of Vienna, students can also attend courses that deal primarily with the function and instruments of international organizations:
– National and International Parliamentary Bodies with special emphasis on the European Parliament
– Law of International Organizations and Multilateral Diplomacy
– European Law: External Economic Relations and Foreign Policy in the EU
– Case Study: The United Nations and Compensation for Gulf War Losses and Damage
– EU Institutions and the EU Decision Making Process[92]

The program "Master of Arts in International Relations" in Berlin und Potsdam offers a thematic concentration called "International Institutions and Transnational Politics":

"International institutions in the broader sense are a major focus of our curriculum, meaning in the core thematic area of the program. Specifically, there is a basic module, one of four, that is called 'International Institutions and Transnational Policy'. Therefore, it is one of the main foci in our curriculum." (Master of International Relations in cooperation between the Humboldt University of Berlin, the Free University of Berlin, and the University of Potsdam)

Another interesting area of concentration is offered by the program "EU International Relations and Diplomacy Studies" at the Collège d'Europe in Bruges. In cluster 4, "Professional Skills", students can choose courses on International Negotiation Analysis, Project Management and Fund Raising, Political Risk Analysis, and Public Relations. According to the information we received, none of the programs offer regional concentrations.

5.1.4. Interdisciplinarity

All the programs we analyzed in Western Europe are strongly committed to the practice of interdisciplinarity. A broad interdisciplinary education

[91] http://www.uni-konstanz.de/sektionen/polver/en/ma/?cont=program&subcont= program_ireint, retrieved July 5, 2007.
[92] http://www.da-vienna.ac.at/userfiles/SPIS0506.pdf, retrieved July 5, 2007.

is not only considered by professionals at international organizations as very beneficial for one's career development, but also the educational experts interviewed suggested that students should be familiar with approaches and, in particular, with the language of different disciplines if they want to be successful in a professional field that requires not only experts but also generalists who are able to interact and communicate in a multidisciplinary working environment. Therefore, it is a fundamental educational objective of many programs to familiarize the students with the knowledge and methodology of different fields of study so that they are applicable in various fields of work. The national and international public service needs people who are able to deal with multidimensional problems not specific to certain disciplines. Therefore, a strong consensus emerged among our interview participants that a practically-oriented education should not primarily consider disciplinary or subject-oriented questions, but rather also take into account the kind of problems students may encounter in their future professional life, as the following statements indicate:

"We view it as our responsibility to prepare students for such careers with a good general education in the areas of economics, social studies, law, and politics, of course. A certain structure automatically follows from being a generalist program. We are of the opinion that we should offer a multidisciplinary program or interdisciplinary program to reach these goals. That means that we have various subjects that are weighted and distributed about equally. The students should get a good basic education in these disciplines and, in addition, gain the ability to think interdisciplinarily. That means they should be able to understand the various perspectives of the specialists they will deal with in the future and to be able to integrate these perspectives in certain cases. That is the basic idea of the program." (University of St. Gallen)

"For international organizations, I think an interdisciplinary approach is a good idea, in that it provides a good foundation for a career in international organizations – even if one actually works there as a specialist." (Master of European Studies in cooperation between three universities in Berlin)

Through interdisciplinary studies, students would be enabled to think beyond disciplinary borders and consider different solutions and approaches drawn from various disciplines and diverse perspectives. Interdisciplinary programs are regarded as one central 'tool' for the development of creative and holistic problem-solving skills. Our interview partners described the relevance of problem-based in contrast to subject-based teaching:

"Political reform cannot be viewed from the disciplines but rather from the point of view of the problem. We must educate people to solve problems and not to understand one subject. What good is a good business administrator if he does not under-

stand most problems? What good is a good law school graduate if he does not under-stand most problems? The students are trained under major duress to work transdis-ciplinarily. That is not easy, because nobody is used to it – including the instruc-tors." (Zeppelin University, Friedrichshafen)

"Problem-oriented meaning that we want to teach our students to understand differ-ent problems from different perspectives and to be able to solve them. [...] [We want to] help them understand different perspectives, even though these may by all means contradict each other. [...] There is a lovely image to describe this: that you can throw the participants out of a plane with a parachute, and that no matter where you fly them, they will know how to navigate the terrain. They do not have their tools with them, so to speak, but they know how to identify the terrain and how to get around there and which models they can use to solve problems in it." (Master of Arts in In-ternational Relations in cooperation between the Humboldt University of Berlin, the Free University of Berlin, and the University of Potsdam)

Many programs are intrinsically interdisciplinary, as they combine the study of different disciplines in their academic core curriculum. Other programs offer a core set of interdisciplinary courses. At the program "Master in International Affairs and Government" at the University of St. Gallen, for instance, students are required to attend an integrative core course with faculty members from political science, economics, and law. In addition, experts from the business world are brought in for guest lec-tures or to mentor projects.

As mentioned before, the disciplines most often included in the curric-ula of the programs examined are political science, law, and economics. However, the combination of these disciplines and how much importance is placed on the teaching of each discipline varies considerably by the in-stitutions and depends on many factors, as the following statements made by two of our interview partners indicate:

"The subjects we offer are economics, international and European law, international relations, comparative political science, and history. The distribution depends on the department chairs. I have the first chair, and that caused the program to be a bit heavy on economics at the beginning. Now, though, we also have a chair for interna-tional law and one for history. These three are about equally represented in the pro-gram, and political science and international relations are also about equal... I believe these four are basically equal." (Diplomatic Academy of Vienna)

"The skills we would like to develop are in the areas of politics, management skills, economics, and, to a lesser extent, law. The economic component is especially well-developed, as we must recognize that discourse is often very economic in this day and age. If you can handle terms like marginal utility or marginal cost and can un-derstand the language of budget policy, then you can prove yourself in the political arena." (Erfurt School of Public Policy)

It is often the basic orientation of the university, the institute, or even the faculty members' preferences that determines whether a master's program focuses more on law, economics, political science, or other disciplines. Besides the three abovementioned disciplines, business management courses, history courses, management courses, and courses on cultural or language studies are also represented in the curricula of some programs.

5.1.5. International focus

Our analysis revealed that the programs examined in this study differ considerably regarding their international orientation. This is due to the fact that we included entirely different programs in our study, from "Master of Arts in International Relations" or "Master of European Studies" to "Master of Public Policy". It seems that programs that specifically aim to prepare students for international work are for the most part entirely internationalized, which means that they tend to deal with a thematically broader range of issues than programs aiming to prepare students for work in national and European administrations. However, there are ongoing discussions among all educational experts interviewed that programs – regardless of their educational objectives – should include more international elements to better prepare students for the professional world. Our study has shown that the institutions examined made efforts to systematically integrate an international dimension into their programs. The processes of European integration and globalization foster the interdependence of countries worldwide through an increasing volume and variety of cross-border transactions. Therefore, national, European, and international administrations require professionals who are prepared to deal with developments on the European and international level. They must be able to live and work at home and abroad in contexts were cross-cultural awareness and understanding and international perspectives are essential. The line between national and European or even the international public service cannot be clearly drawn anymore, especially when one considers the frequency with which civil servants are now seconded as national experts to international organizations. Therefore, educational programs which aim to prepare students for today's professional world must take into account the dynamics of national, European, and international policy-making. Many of the educational experts interviewed regarded an education which focuses solely on national issues or even regional issues as no longer sufficient.

However, as mentioned before, only some of the programs examined have a strong international orientation, whereas other programs tend to deal primarily with national and European issues. Programs with a strong international orientation, such as the "International Organizations M.B.A." at the University of Geneva, the "Master of Arts in International Relations" in Berlin/Postdam, the "Master of Advanced International Studies" at the Diplomatic Academy of Vienna, and the "EU International Relations and Diplomacy Studies" at the Collège d'Europe in Bruges, are marked by diversification through a thematically broader range and a strong interdisciplinary orientation. In these programs, students learn widely from the other regions and countries; the practice of cross-national comparison is an essential indicator for the level of the international orientation. Furthermore, internationalized curricula often show a strong link to new professional fields (e.g., conflict management, area studies).

In most cases, where curricula are partly internationalized, students can make their own decision about their international orientation by choosing internationally-oriented modules as electives. This is the case in Erfurt, Konstanz, Speyer, St. Gallen, and at the Hertie School in Berlin.

Another measure taken to achieve an international orientation is that programs are taught entirely in a foreign language. At many of the programs we examined, the language of instruction of most or all of the courses is English. In this way, universities seek to make themselves attractive to foreign students and provide their students with an intercultural learning environment. Many programs are open to a diverse and international student body[93], which sets the context for helping students to develop their intercultural and foreign language skills. Another indicator for international orientation is that educational institutions offer exchange programs, which can serve as a means of enhancing students' mobility and international perspective.

Summarizing the results obtained, it is apparent that some programs examined in this study are significantly more internationalized in substance and structure than others to better prepare students for work in the European and international public service. The expansion of course offerings (geographically, by discipline, and by the introduction of comparative and multicultural materials into existing courses) is one measure taken to enable students to deal with complex issues and global developments. The addition of foreign students and faculty is enhanced by teach-

---

[93] On average, 30 to 50 percent of the students who study at the programs examined in this study come from aboard.

ing the entire program in English as well as by offering exchange programs. One interview participant described the strong international focus of its program as follows:

"Then in the third step, there is the formal international orientation, not just in terms of content, but also formally in the sense of a required study abroad experience within the curriculum. And if you look at the admission requirements, they must have a very high level of proficiency in English to get in. Half of the courses in the basic modules must be taken in English, so they are also offered in English." (Master of Arts in International Relations in cooperation between the Humboldt University of Berlin, the Free University of Berlin, and the University of Potsdam)

5.2. Additional components

This section will deal with other aspects of the curricula of the programs we examined that also play an important role in training students for careers in the national and international public service. Some of these components are included in the core curriculum, whereas others are considered additional elements.

5.2.1. Foreign language requirements

All educational experts interviewed shared the opinion that foreign language skills are a basic requirement for a career in the national and international public service. In our study, we identified three means of integrating foreign language requirements in the program: (1) Proficiency in English and/or other foreign languages is a formal admission requirement for potential students. (2) The program is taught entirely or partly in a foreign language. (3) Foreign languages courses are a compulsory component of the curriculum.

Many programs examined in this study require excellent English skills for participating in the program (between 213 and 260 on the computer-based TOEFL test):

"The average student in this Master's program speaks three languages fluently. We are not talking about English. That is the basic language, the language of instruction. It's really two different things." (Center for European Integration Studies, Bonn)

Our study has shown that English is about to displace the national language, German or French, as the primary language of instruction. In the process of the internationalization of higher education, many programs have decided to teach their entire programs in English, whereas some programs only teach one part of the curriculum in English. The importance attached to professional English skills is not all that surprising when one considers the greater role it plays in the international field compared to other languages.

However, some programs also require proficiency in another foreign language (mainly French or German), but only a few programs expect their students to develop a high level of competency in other foreign languages and provide them with professional language training accordingly. Foreign language courses are only a compulsory component in the curriculum at strongly internationally-oriented programs which specifically aim to train students for careers in the European and international public service. According to the information we obtained, language courses are compulsory, for instance, in the programs of the Diplomatic Academy of Vienna, the program "EU External Relations and Diplomacy" at the Collège d'Europe in Bruges and the program "Master of European Studies" at the University of Vienna. At the University of Vienna, students must take at least two of five possible languages. Here, students can choose between English, French, Polish, Czech, and Hungarian. During the first semester at the Collège d'Europe, students are required to take an obligatory language course as well: French, or, if a sufficient level of French has already been acquired, German, Spanish, or Russian.

Few programs offer language courses as electives. In general, the majority of the programs examined do not offer further language training. One reason for that is that most of the one-year programs do not have enough time. The lack of financial and human resources to offer foreign language courses is another reason for not providing students with further training, although all interview participants regard it as an important factor for preparing their students for international work.

5.2.2. Practical and hands-on courses

As mentioned in Section 3, professionals at international organizations were of the opinion that higher education institutions could do much better in providing students with certain key competencies such as leadership, intercultural, teamwork, and project management skills, needed for a successful application and work performance. In addition to academic training, courses which focus on skills building and knowledge application should be an essential component of each educational program that aims to prepare students for work both in the national and international public service. Most of our interview partners shared this opinion and integrated key skills into their curricula:

"We have quite a few courses for soft skills [...], because we think it's very important not just to teach them about European law but also to prepare them for the real world." (University of Saarbrücken)

Our study revealed that a vast majority of the programs examined in Western Europe incorporated courses for the development of professional competencies into their curricula, although the means are extremely heterogeneous. For instance, the programs "Master of Public Policy" in Erfurt, "Master of Public Policy" in Berlin, "International Organizations M.B.A." in Geneva, and 2EU International Relations and Diplomacy Studies" in Bruges place a great deal of emphasis on skills development and offer comprehensive modules ("practical training module"), a whole section ("Transforming Theory into Practice") or a concentration area ("Professional skills") that specifically include courses on "Intercultural Communication", "Presentation Techniques", "Report Writing", "Management across Cultures", "Leadership Skills", "Fund Raising" and "Project Management Skills". Other programs offer practical training courses on negotiation skills, project management skills, public diplomacy, and presentation techniques:

"There is a course that I have taught for seven years. It is called 'Management Skills in Behavior'. I have placed emphasis on different areas in the past. But the main goal is always to introduce students to management skills and train these skills. In addition to our excursions, which also have a major practical component, we have had optional courses on project management, change management, and human resource management. These are the main courses that are offered on a regular basis that teach students practical behavior. It's not just about practicing skills but also about sensitizing them and allowing them to reflect on their own behavior. We attach great importance to this." (Master of International Relations in cooperation between the Humboldt University of Berlin, the Free University of Berlin, and the University of Potsdam)

"In the first year, we teach practical skills such as negotiation, project management, public diplomacy, protocol... things that field experts come and teach. Former protocol leaders or external trainers, presentation techniques, all these things." (Diplomatic Academy of Vienna)

In addition to specific training courses, other important tools used at many programs examined to develop students' skills are simulations of international conferences, case studies, and hands-on projects. These require students to work in teams, solve problems, make decisions, give presentations, deal with uncertainty, and write reports as would be the case in the workplace. For instance, in the program of "Master of International Affairs and Governance" at the University of St. Gallen, students can attend an applied project in the field of development politics. The program cooperates with the Swiss Agency for Development and Cooperation to enable students to apply their theoretical knowledge and improve their project management skills. Budgeting and fundraising are essential components of this learning experience:

"A practical project in development cooperation at the Swiss DEZA [Department for Development Cooperation], like the BMZ in Germany, where a former official of the DEZA offers a course in which students work on current dossiers that are then presented to and discussed with the officials in Bern. Just like the WTO seminar and a practical project called 'World Bank Projects', where students go all the way to Washington and present their projects to the World Bank." (University of St. Gallen)

The Hertie School of Governance in Berlin offers a similar project – the student project – which is mainly carried out in cooperation with public service officials and is part of the final graduation requirement. Through this project, students should improve their ability analyze real-world problems within a specified time limit and a limited amount of resources using the skills and knowledge gained in their prior academic training:

"The final element of this curriculum is the so-called Student Project. [...] This Student Project is completed with a final paper that is at the same time the final thesis. But this paper is not a traditional thesis in the academic sense, but rather a piece of commissioned work for an institution in the field." (Hertie School of Governance, Berlin)

The German Development Institute requires its students to carry out practice- and consulting-oriented study projects (so-called Country Working Groups) in cooperation with institutions in developing or transition countries. The goal of the study is to deepen the knowledge gained in prior academic training and provide experience of interdisciplinary teamwork, working in a different cultural environment, and cooperating with governmental agencies, social groups, other donors, German embassies, and other experts. As the main educational objective of the Institute is to train professionals for work in the field of development cooperation, it is no surprise that these Country Working Groups are considered the most important part of the training program. In other programs, students are required to carry out a practice-oriented research project to develop analytical, problem-solving, and methodological skills:

"Then there's another module called the Project Course Module. Project Courses are two-semester courses in which the students basically carry out a small, individual research project under the supervision and in the context of the course in preparation for their master's thesis. They thus engage in hands-on learning and reinforce the methods they need for their master's theses. That should enable students to analyze and solve matters and problems of international politics using their acquired methodical competence and theoretical foundations independently of the concrete empirical questions that they have researched during their studies." (Master in Interna-

tional Relations in cooperation between the Humboldt University of Berlin, the Free University of Berlin, and the University of Potsdam)

In conclusion, many programs examined in this study are placing more and more emphasis on knowledge application and skills development to equip students with the expertise they need for their future work than traditional or research-oriented programs. With regard to the structure of the curriculum, practical hands-on courses mainly take place during the second period of study. According to most educational experts, during the first period of study, the emphasis is on the development of analytical and methodical skills as well as on the development of a knowledge foundation.

5.2.3. Extracurricular activities

Another measure taken by many programs examined in this study to enhance the practical orientation of education is to offer a range of extracurricular activities. Many programs organize study trips or excursions to national administrations and international organizations, speakers' series, and meetings and conferences with practitioners to provide students with information on the function of national administration and international organizations, working conditions, recruitment strategies, and selection procedures:

"We invite people from the field – from Brussels and ministries – who give talks on various topics and discuss them with the students in large groups." (Master of European Studies, cooperation between three universities in Berlin)

"We take excursions: one week in Luxembourg, Brussels. One day at the European Central Bank in Frankfurt. One or two days in Strasbourg with the Parliament, at a plenary session, with the European Council, at the Court of Human Rights." (Master of European Studies, University of Tübingen)

"In addition, there are excursions that teach the people about the different institutions. We have an excursion each year that goes to Strasbourg, Luxembourg, Brussels, and Frankfurt and where the students really go to the institutions. There are actual lectures everywhere because some of our instructors work as officials in the Commission in Brussels. [We take] excursions here as well, such as to the United Nations, the UNODC, and others. [And we also have] close cooperation with the Representation of the Commission in Vienna, where evening talks take place at least twice a month." (University of Vienna)

Here, with regard to the organization of extracurricular activities, it is obvious that educational institutions located in capitals or cities where many international organizations are based have a certain advantage, but one that can be evened out by study trips and other activities.

5.2.4. Internships

Most program coordinators interviewed considered internships to be a very important component of their program, as they provide a great opportunity for workplace learning and competency building and thus have a positive impact on the students' career development. Internships are seen as a bridge between the academic institution and the world of practice and between professional education and subsequent employment. As Table 5.1 indicates, many programs in our study have internships as a mandatory component in their curricula, as they aim to train students for the professional world and not for academia:

"We don't offer a research-oriented study program, but rather a practice-oriented one. We don't prepare our students to go for a Ph.D. They have ten months until they're done. That means that the practical element is very important. We have incorporated a required internship between the winter and summer terms." (Master of European Studies, University of Tübingen)

In virtually all programs where internships are not a compulsory component, students are strongly encouraged by faculty members and program managers to do one during their semester break.

All interview partners stressed that internships included in the curriculum as a mandatory component should (1) last at least a couple of months, (2) provide a real involvement in the actual work of an organization, (3) be undertaken in partnership with the experienced practitioners, and (4) be academically supervised to ensure the quality of the training results. With regard to the complexity of professional roles and settings, internships should be closely related to other course elements through supervision, tutorials, seminars, and written assignments. Program coordinators described it as follows:

"We tend to see internships as useful, if there is real involvement. We do not want to have an internship where people do photocopying. We really wanted to make sure that the internship would not be a constraint, but rather would be perceived by the students as an opportunity. In order to provide students with incentives to do the internship, we give credits for it." (University of Geneva)

"We opted for three months because we really want the people to get an in-depth look – not just to watch and follow the others, but rather to really do things themselves, such as working on a project. That of course isn't possible if it's only six or eight weeks long. So we chose the three-month option. But this is a bit problematic in that the breaks between the semesters are too short." (University of Konstanz)

However, our study revealed that not all institutions assist their students in finding an internship placement with a substantive assignment. Moreover, only few programs supervise internships academically

Table 5.1. Internship requirements

Institution	Program	Internship required
European School of Governance (EUSG), Berlin, Germany	Training for Public Servants	
Free University of Berlin, Humboldt University of Berlin, and the Technical University of Berlin, Germany	Postgraduate Program in European Studies	✓
Hertie School of Governance, Germany	Master of Public Policy	✓
Humboldt University of Berlin, Free University of Berlin, and the University of Potsdam, Germany	Master of Arts in International Relations	✓
Center for European Integration Studies (ZEI), Bonn, Germany	Master of European Studies	✓
German Development Institute, Bonn, Germany	Post Gradual Program	
University of Bremen and the International University of Bremen, Germany	Master of Arts in International Relations: Global Governance and Social Theory	
Collège d'Europe, Bruges, Belgium	Master of European Economic Studies	
	Master of European Legal Studies	
	Master of European Political and Administrative Studies	
	Master of EU International Relations and Diplomacy Studies	
Erfurt School of Public Policy, University of Erfurt, Germany	Master of Public Policy	✓
University of Geneva, Switzerland	Master in International Affairs	
	Master in International Studies	
	Master of Business Administration International Organizations	✓
University of Hamburg (Erasmus Mundus Program), Germany	Master of European Law and Economics	
University of Konstanz, Germany	Master of Public Policy and Management	✓
Zeppelin University, Ludwigshafen, Germany	Master of Arts in Public Management & Governance	✓

196

Institution	Program	Internship required
Ecole nationale d'administration (Paris), France and University of Potsdam, Germany	Master of European Governance and Administration	
Institut d'études politiques de Paris, France	Master of Public Administration	
University of Potsdam, Germany	Master of Public Management	
	Master of Global Public Policy	
Europa-Institut of Saarland University, Saarbrücken, Germany	Master of European Law	
German University for Public Administration Speyer, Germany	Master of Public Administration	
University of St. Gallen, Switzerland	Master of Arts in International Affairs and Governance	
University of Tübingen, Germany	Master of European Studies	✓
	Master of Peace Research and International Politics	✓
Diplomatic Academy of Vienna, Austria	Master of Advanced International Studies	✓
	Diploma Program	
	Special Program in International Studies	
University of Vienna, Austria	Master of European Studies ("Europastudien")	

Source: Authors

through tutorials and seminars. According to the information we obtained, students discuss their experiences with academic staff at the Professional Schools in Berlin and in Erfurt and at the University of Konstanz. In most programs, students are awarded credits for an internship if they write a final report on their experiences. In other programs, internships are a part of an applied project or academic course or the final graduation requirement:

"Students can earn up to twelve credits by doing internships: either an industrial placement or as a supplement to related coursework. Then it's possible. These elements are basically always linked to an academic seminar." (Master of Peace Research and International Politics, University of Tübingen)

The lack of time of the staff members who assist students in finding an internship placement is one main reason why some programs do not have a compulsory internship in their curriculum. Another reason our interview partners mentioned is that other components of the program, in particular academic modules, were viewed as a more relevant educational component than short internships. One program coordinator described it as follows:

"There is no required internship. We don't have time for one. That is something we discussed with the [German] Federal Foreign Office for a long time. Since we have such a tight program in nine months, we decided against it. We require more lectures than any other master's program, which means we of course have less time. And that rules out the possibility of a required internship." (University of Saarbrücken)

Some programs examined reduced the length of internships and give credit for just six weeks of work experience so that the students can do an internship in the semester break. Other programs assume that most students have already done internships – at some institutions it is also a basic admission requirement – and they therefore do not see the necessity to include them as a core component in the curriculum.

Some interview partners, for instance, at the Collège d'Europe, said that they do not require an internship in their curriculum as it is part of their training to teach students to act independently and proactively to arrange internships without being supported, awarded, or required by the university. This opinion is also shared by some educational experts who have included a compulsory internship in the curriculum. Here, the students are responsible for the application process:

"They [the students] must be able to proactively seek an internship, and we support that with letters of recommendation. We also have contacts. We place some people as well, but the alumni are a network. People have to get past their inhibitions and call the EU Commission, for example." (Center for European Studies, Bonn)

The experience shows that students are indeed creative and motivated when looking for internships and that they find appropriate, though mostly unpaid, positions.

"We have two or three offerings exclusively for our MIA students, where there are cooperation contracts between the MIA program and the internship organization. But that is still in the beginning phases, because we simply don't have the capacities required [to continue building it]. The students are very successful at finding their own interesting internship opportunities." (University of St. Gallen)

Finally, with regard to the whole process of arranging internship placements for their students, universities that are located in capital cities or places where many international organizations are based have a clear advantage, as they have easy access to a large number of international organizations and national administrations.

In our study, we also conducted a survey among young academics who carried out an internship at an international organization supported by the "Carlo Schmid Program for Internships in International Organizations and EU Institutions". As Table 5.2 shows, the majority of the young academics who participated in the Carlo Schmid Program considered their internship as having contributed to the development of social-com-

Table 5.2. Qualifications and skills acquired through participation in CSP

Skill type	Percent of responses
Soft skills (intercultural competencies, conflict management, ability to cooperate, etc.)	16.5
Expertise	14.9
Knowledge of specific IO	8.9
Knowledge of IOs in general	8.6
Improving/acquiring new language skills	8.4
Organization skills (administration skills, time management, planning competencies, etc.)	8.1
Work experience/knowledge of profession	7.8
Making important contacts/networking	6.3
Communication skills (presentation skills, rhetorical skills, etc.)	3.3
Knowledge of recruitment processes in IOs	2.0
Leadership skills (assertiveness, ability to delegate, motivation skills, etc.)	2.0
Flexibility in own work style	2.0
Knowledge of region of internship	1.8
(Professional) experience abroad	1.0
Self-confidence	1.0
Improving own CV	1.0
Cannot be evaluated at this point	0.5
Others and indistinct information	5.9
Responses in total	100.0

Source: Authors' data survey
Notes: 143 valid, 16 missing cases

municative, activity and implementation-related, personal, and professional competencies.

Young academics most frequently stated having improved their soft skills, as well as their professional expertise (45.5% and 41.3% respectively). Language skills and organizational or communication skills were developed as well. Learning more about international organizations in general and about specific organizations was also indicated as an important benefit of the internship by a large number of participants. Some participants considered the ability to work efficiently on new tasks and to acquire new knowledge rapidly (category "flexibility in own work") or learning more about the region where the internship took place as an important gain of knowledge and competence. Overall, our study has suggested that the Carlo Schmid Program is a good means of preparing young academics for positions in the international public service or for international work in general. 83 percent of the employed program graduates have a job with a substantial international orientation (in international organizations, research institutions, private companies, non-governmental organizations).[94]

5.2.5.   Studies abroad and joint or dual degrees

Only very few programs examined enable their students to study abroad. This is, in most cases, due to the short period of one to two years of study. This is usually possible in the scope of a semester abroad or in form of a dual or joint degree where students study at a partner institution for one year and then either earn a degree from both universities or choose one of them. A compulsory semester abroad is part of the program "Master of Arts in International Relations" in Berlin and Potsdam. This applies to all students who did not study abroad in their first degree. Furthermore, this program offers a limited amount of places in two dual-degree programs with the Moscow State Institute of International Relations (MGIMO University) and Sciences Po in Paris.

The Diplomatic Academy of Vienna also offers its students the opportunity to complete a dual degree and joint degree program. Its partner institutions are the Bologna Center of the Johns Hopkins University and the Fletcher School of Law and Diplomacy:

"We currently have a voluntary cooperation with Johns Hopkins, with the Bologna Center, where we have a joint degree, and with the Fletcher School, where we also

[94] Studzinski, J., Herz, D., Schattenmann, M., Dortants, S. L. & Linke, K. (2005). *Evaluation of the "Carlo-Schmid-Program for internships in international organizations and EU institutions"*. Retr. from http://nbn-resolving.de/urn/resolver.pl?urn=urn:nbn:de:gbv:547-200601395

200

have a dual degree program. That means that you can spend a year here and a year there and then choose which master's degree you would like to earn." (Diplomatic Academy of Vienna)

Dual degree programs are further available from the University of St. Gallen in cooperation with Sciences Po in Paris and the University of Vienna in cooperation with the University of Krakow. The program "Master of European Studies" at the University of Vienna is the only one-year program that offers the opportunity to spend half of the program at a partner university.

The program "Master of European Law and Economics" at the University of Hamburg is a unique program in German-speaking countries. This one-year program is offered in cooperation between nine European universities and is now part of the Erasmus Mundus Program. The program is divided into three trimesters, at least two of which are completed in different European countries. The academic title is awarded by the universities one attended.

Due to lack of time and other resources, all other one-year programs as well as some of the two-year programs examined in this study do not include studies abroad in their programs. They rather assume that students will have studied abroad during their undergraduate program. But many interview partners stressed that studies abroad are both important for the students' academic training and the development of certain professional skills, as students can learn about different educational systems and scientific approaches, as well as acquire essential intercultural and foreign language skills.

5.3.   Balance between academic and practical training

A particularly vexing problem for all programs examined in this study is the importance of theoretical training and practical training. The question as to which of these two aspects of professional education should be emphasized arises mainly during the processes of curriculum development and assessment.

Looking at the curricula of the educational institutions examined in this study, it is apparent that they vary in terms of the extent to which practical components are included in the core part of the program. The level of importance attached to academic and practical elements within the programs depends mainly on the educational objectives. Curricula of very practically-oriented programs consist of about 50% of courses that aim to train professional skills and knowledge application to students, whereas other curricula consist of only about 20-25% practical components.

In general, our interview partners felt that a healthy balance between theory-based modules *and* modules which aim for reflection, practical application, and competency development was very important for preparing students for the professional world:

"In my opinion, the combination of theory and practical usage is actually the important aspect here. Each person will have his or her own preferences as to what an ideal curriculum should be like. But the combination of theory and practical elements and interaction between scholars and practitioners should definitely be part of it." (Master of European Studies in cooperation between universities in Berlin)

"I believe that incorporating practical education in the program is very important, so that the students must deal with real-world elements within their program of study. And I also think independent work on projects, which we call 'Directed Study' and 'Case Study', is very important. I think the components we have included are also very useful for international organizations." (University of Konstanz)

"You must make sure that you have courses in the individual subject areas on the one hand, in which you include practical elements and develop the students. [...] Students should obtain knowledge about the EU that can be used in the real world. A look at the institutions, what they look like, and the ability to do networking." (Center for European Integration Studies, Bonn)

"In your research project, you will have often heard that project management skills, negotiation skills, soft skills, language skills, and all these things are of major importance and that academic aspects and content are not as important. We can only subscribe to this view in a limited manner, as an academic program also teaches analytical skills, as it must." (Erfurt School of Public Policy)

As German higher education institutions were traditionally designed to train students to do scientific and scholarly research, academic and disciplinary training is still a very prominent part of most of their curricula as opposed to the development of professional competencies and work-related training. However, all German programs examined in this study reported being open to new developments and reforms in the higher education system. They have made a move toward integrating skills development and knowledge application into their curricula to better prepare students for the labor market:

"Because we have not had and still do not have a certain proximity to the field, it is really up to the universities anyway to be somewhat more research oriented. And this tradition remains to some extent. We try to make up for this and also to increase the practical element by the teaching positions we fill or by elements in our program of study." (Master of Peace Research and International Politics, University of Tübingen)

"We try on the one hand to provide an academically-founded education and then basically try to give an overview of all theories, approaches, and studies of problems in the whole field." (University of Konstanz)

When analyzing the program design, it is apparent that academic training generally takes place at the beginning of each term, whereas practical and application-oriented courses are primarily offered in the second part of the program. However, there are also institutions that combine academic and practical training throughout the program. This might be the most effective way of preparing people for working in the international public service, as theory transfer, reflection, and knowledge application take place in one course or module and not in different stages.

5.4. Teaching and examination methods

Our study revealed that attempts to integrate courses on skills development and knowledge application into the curriculum have inevitably involved a shift from the traditional direct modes of instruction towards a more student-centered style of teaching and learning which often implies the use of interactive teaching methods. Two interview partners described this shift as follows:

"It is in fact our goal to distance our teaching methods as far as possible from the classic lecture. This is not an end in itself, but rather the objective is to – as much as it is possible in a demanding academic curriculum – simulate situations that are hopefully similar to the future situations students will confront at work. This can be done in different ways." (Hertie School of Governance, Berlin)

"Modern ex-cathedra teaching, meaning the classic lecture, which is still on the Bologna MA and BA agenda, is considered antiquated. Experts say so as well. The accreditation agencies clearly state that it is not contemporary. So interactive teaching is necessary. By the way, in other countries, it is already quite fundamental. The lecture only continues to exist on in Germany." (Center for European Integration Studies, Bonn)

Almost all programs in our study tend to use more interactive teaching methods, such as case studies, simulations, discussions and role-playing games, in addition to the traditional modes of instruction, as they enable students to apply their knowledge and develop important skills they need for their future professional life:

"These people have heard lectures for five years already. We want to prepare them for the work world." (University of Saarbrücken)

"Our seminars are always interactive, meaning from the first moment on. That means that there are not just lectures, but also working in small groups, phases of reflection, tutorials, and then of course guest lectures, round-table talks, and discussions." (European School of Governance, Berlin)

"You should definitely leave a lot of room for interactive teaching methods, like for role plays, so that students can also learn in a group. Such as acting out certain cases. Simulations of course require a great deal of preparation. But that's something

that is very well received among the students and which has a very good learning effect. [...] When you have put yourself in a certain role, you really remember that. Then you have learned something that you will always retain. Interactive teaching methods should have a significant role accorded to them – especially in the case of continuing education programs." (Master of European Studies in cooperation between three universities in Berlin)

"We have a variety of methods. I can show you this using the core course as an example. Although it does have individual elements of a lecture, there are also debates, Oxford debates, and seminar-style components. Then it also has practical skills, such as how to write a fact sheet or in general how to write down-to-earth reports that contain the most important information. Presentations also play a role: the people prepare something and present it. Simulations, too... so there's a whole number of methods just in the core course. But many different teaching and learning methods are also used in the other courses, though maybe not in such great variety." (University of St. Gallen)

"The students' motivation is 100% higher when such an element is included. That is quite simple. It seems to fascinate them more. And it is also clear when you're doing a simulation and suddenly have to take on a new role. That is exciting and you have to learn it differently, because you are representing it yourself. There's a nice diagram about this: you retain everything you do yourself much better in your canon of knowledge than the things you just see or hear." (Master of Peace Research and International Politics, University of Tübingen)

Interactive teaching methods are mainly used in applied courses, workshops, and team-based projects. The selection of the teaching methods, however, depends on the programs' educational objectives, the content that has to be taught, but also on the instructors' preferences. Programs with a strong practical orientation tend to often use interactive teaching methods, whereas research-oriented programs apply more traditional methods of instruction. Generally, it can be said that the higher the level of practical relevance is, the wider the variety of teaching methods is applied in the different programs. With regard to content, it is apparent that in theory-based courses that aim to develop a broad knowledge base, traditional direct modes of instruction are used, whereas for courses that focus on the application of knowledge and skills development, active learning/teaching methods are more appropriate:

"Of course, simulations do not lend themselves to the teaching of very dry administrative material. [But simulations are good] for showing what the decision-making processes are like and how something like this can work." (German University of Administrative Sciences, Speyer)

"We have a policy of methodic pluralism here. When you have a classic research-oriented MA program, then you will have lectures for the most part. Students must become familiar with the classics in their field and simply understand the texts and write research papers. That is obviously not possible at a public policy school. We try

to achieve as much of a pluralism and heterogeneity of methods in the classroom as possible. That means that we have elements of lectures. We have seminar discussions. We have case discussions based on case teaching, which are common at American professional schools. We have smaller simulation components." (Erfurt School of Public Policy)

One reason for using traditional teaching methods mentioned is the objective of bringing a very heterogeneous student body to one comparable level of knowledge. All students, regardless of their educational background, should develop a knowledge base that is relevant to the program. As described, interactive teaching methods are primarily applied in courses that focus on knowledge application and competency building.

As previously mentioned, *hands-on and team-based projects* are a mandatory part of many curricula examined, as they enable students to develop their project-management and teamwork skills and, more importantly, to reflect and apply theoretical knowledge gained in prior academic training.

In addition to team-based and hands-on projects, the method of *case teaching* is applied in many programs. This teaching method focuses as well on the development of skills such as problem solving, decision making, negotiations, and team work. Further, the use of cases, either alone or in combination with other techniques such as simulations, develops students' understanding of negotiation processes. Here, our interview participants at the Collège d'Europe, at Sciences Po, and at the University of Geneva mentioned the importance of "live case teaching" in which students are enabled to deal with real-world problems and focus on appropriate action rather than on the analysis of past events. Therefore, most cases used at these institutions are developed and taught in close cooperation with practitioners.

In the "International Organizations M.B.A." program at the University of Geneva, students even go directly to international organizations to discuss possible solutions with and receive feedback from professionals who have direct experience with the problem at hand. Sciences Po in Paris offers its students an excursion abroad, for instance to Brazil or Germany, to meet with local representatives of non-governmental, governmental, and international organizations and discuss a wide range of issues. After the excursion, students must write a paper on a particular case with which they dealt during the excursion.

Besides case teaching, a very common teaching method used to prepare students for the professional field is *simulations*. At the German University of Administrative Sciences in Speyer, for instance, practitioners are invited to speak about what it means to set up a civil administration in

Kosovo, to take care of public security, or to train and supervise the police. The highlight of this course is a simulation that takes place on a weekend:

"Then groups are created – say Group 1 PR China, Group 2 Russia, etc. And then the crisis situations are played out. The whole thing is partially supported by computers with a random generator. [...] What is also stressful for our participants is that we have a real TV journalist who carries out interviews under actual conditions. The students receive comments on this and can discuss it later." (German University of Administrative Sciences, Speyer)

The German Development Institute in Bonn conducts two large roleplaying games. In the "Development Cooperation Game", negotiations with different stakeholders are simulated. The participants are required to take on different roles and thus develop their communication and diplomatic skills. In the IMF game, participants simulate negotiations of the International Monetary Fund. Both simulations only last a few hours; that is why our interview partner called them role-playing games as opposed to simulations. Another interesting teaching method is a workshop called "Peace Boat" offered by the program "Master of Peace Research and International Politics" at the University of Tübingen:

"We have an element called the 'Peace Boat' in our civil war seminar. That is a ship chartered from a Japanese peace organization that is basically a tourist boat, but there are a few spots reserved for students. They travel to two, three, or four places and visit conflict constellations. And the seminar prepares them to do so. That means, 'Where are we going, and what kind of a conflict are we dealing with?' And then that has to be prepared and presented by the students." (Master of Peace Research and International Politics, University of Tübingen)

Some programs not only use a variety of teaching methods but also innovative examination methods. Our interview partners mentioned that programs which aim to prepare students for the professional world must also apply appropriate examination methods (e.g., policy recommendations, small presentations, minutes, project proposals, outlines, or similar assignments):

"You really have to consider teaching and testing methods together. When the goal of a course is just to impart knowledge and the acquiring of skills or competencies is not really the priority, then it's enough for students to take a written exam at the end. That does not work in a public policy program. We would like to enable the people to write good memos and make good, workable political recommendations. They have to be able to write a draft at a ministry that will eventually reach the minister. That is why we have corresponding types of exams in our program. We recently began requiring more fragmented exams: having them write many short memos in which they must analyze political problems in a very precise manner." (Erfurt School of Public Policy)

Although most programs examined tend to use a variety of examination methods in addition to the traditional written and oral exams, the final graduation requirement still tends to be a master's thesis. Only very few programs require their students to carry out an applied project, as is the common practice at most professional schools of public policy, public administration, or international relations in the U.S.

With regard to the application of interactive teaching methods and innovative examination methods, all interview partners stressed the importance of small classes to ensure the interactive concept of teaching and learning. Methods such as group work, role-playing games, and discussions are usually used in small-sized courses.

Many of the educational experts we interviewed said that the selection and proper application of teaching and examination methods can hardly be influenced by their institution, since it depends mainly on the instructors and their particular preferences in instruction methods. We received almost no information on whether instructors and their teaching methods and materials are systematically assessed by the institutions (besides or in addition to student evaluations) and whether training courses on new ways of teaching are offered. However, the Hertie School of Governance in Berlin did describe its measures in this area: All instructors are required to present a syllabus with selected teaching and examination methods to the head of curricular affairs before the semester starts. The head of curricular affairs revises the syllabus and the use of methods and materials if necessary. In a second step, this revised syllabus is presented to all other instructors to guarantee an exchange of teaching methods and materials:

"There is no specification concerning teaching methods. What we do have is a 'Syllabus Control Board', which actually works twofold: all instructors must submit their syllabus by a certain date. They first give it to me as a first screening. I look at it and pay attention to certain teaching models we have. I pay attention to the level of relevance to the field. I pay attention to whether guests are invited from the field. I pay attention to the teaching methods and how interactive the whole course is. I pay attention to the workload in comparison with other courses, which is important as well. That is the first step, so to speak. And the second step is presenting a revised version to the council." (Hertie School of Governance, Berlin)

Although none of the other programs seem to have any established assessment mechanisms, most of the program coordinators we interviewed indicated the necessity for such systematic feedback to ensure the use of the most appropriate teaching methods and materials in their programs. One of our interview partners mentioned that in particular those academic faculty members who are generally used to applying traditional methods of instruction and examination must learn how to integrate interactive teaching methods and innovative examination methods into their courses:

"The instructors also had to learn that they have to change their ways of teaching and that the type of interaction has to be different. We hardly have any written exams anymore. This is also understood among our colleagues. It is not always easy to convince our [academic] colleagues that you simply have to have different means of teaching and testing in a degree program like this. It is much easier to convince the field experts that this program requires a much different kind of proof of achievement. Some development has already taken place and I would say that it has been very positive. I also believe that it is important to keep moving in this direction." (Master of European Studies in cooperation with three universities in Berlin)

"It is of course not very easy to get this diversity of teaching methods into the instructors' heads. Even in our program, many of the instructors come from the very, very classical research-oriented tradition. But then many of them view it as a welcome challenge to try out different ways of teaching, such as with cases." (Erfurt School of Public Policy)

In contrast to programs that try to influence the instructors' method of teaching in some way, at the Collège d'Europe, it is a common policy that teaching staff can freely choose their teaching and examination methods. It is assumed that this policy contributes to the wide variety of different teaching methods, as the instructors come from more than 30 countries:

"That is actually not known, and it doesn't work any other way. We have quite a few – 120 or 130 – professors. How else are we supposed to get them all in line? That's simply not possible. So we make the best out of it and say, 'That's part of the education here." (Collège d'Europe, Bruges)

5.5. Faculty composition

In our study we were also interested in learning more about the composition of the faculty. Our results show that the proportion between permanent faculty members and adjunct faculty members, both academics and practitioners, mainly depends on (1) whether the program is traditionally integrated into a university or an institute and can thus fall back on a large number of permanent academic staff or whether it has just developed, (2) the financial resources available to offer teaching contracts for practitioners, and (3) on the level of practical orientation of the program. The "Master of Public Policy and Management" at the University of Konstanz and the "Master of European Studies" and "Master of Peace Research and International Politics" at the University of Tübingen emerged from traditional programs that have existed for many years. These programs cooperate with other faculties at the respective university and ex-

208

change academic personnel. At other educational institutions, adjunct faculty members provide between 20 and 50 percent of the instruction:

"There is a rule that we do not want to go below. 50% must be permanently employed, and we get about 50% from elsewhere. And not because we don't want to hire the people, but because we wish to constantly import fresh 'intellectual goods'. We want to have a relatively heterogeneous mix of thoughts as well as different theories and concepts." (Zeppelin University, Friedrichshafen)

"The directors are employed by the ZEI. The rest are from different universities. About two thirds or three quarters from abroad. You see that in our faculty, too. About eight or nine countries are represented there, too, from renowned universities in the rest of Europe." (Center for European Integration Studies, Bonn)

The adjunct faculty at the programs examined in this study consists mainly of scholars from other educational institutions in Germany or abroad; professionals in national, European, or international administrations; and experts from the private sector. Some of them teach on an academic-year basis; however, the majority of these adjuncts are employed on a semester- or individual-course basis. With regard to the educational and professional background of permanent faculty members, many interview partners highlighted that their instructors are primarily scholars with strong interdisciplinary and international backgrounds.

All educational experts interviewed considered it worthwhile to integrate practitioners into their programs, as they bring important real-world professional experience to the program. Both teaching and learning can then be based more on professional experience than on theory and abstract situations. Our interview participants described it as follows:

"I always include professionals from the field in my seminar to enrich the complexity of the class. A field expert does not simplify things, but rather brings in more problems than he solves. That's the beautiful part: that the theory can suddenly evaluate things that even the practitioners don't appreciate and vice versa – the practitioners can tell us things that we always forget. It is our goal to teach theory and practice equally." (Zeppelin University, Friedrichshafen)

"There are certain topics. If you deal with institutions and action areas such as the European Court of Justice or with human rights, for example, then it's better to take people from there than from mere law professors who see it from the academic point of view." (Collège d'Europe, Bruges)

"We always invite field experts, especially to our workshops. That not only has the purpose of including this content in our curriculum, like the point of view of a practitioner from the farmers' association or the tradespeople's union, but rather it also has the desirable effect that students can get in bilateral contact with these people. Some amazing things have come out of this, such as a job, [...] an internship, or help on their master's thesis." (Master of European Studies, University of Tübingen)

At many programs, the number of practitioners among non-permanent teaching staff is high (between 25 and 35 percent). This applies, in particular, to programs with a strong practical orientation, such as the "Master of Public Administration" at Sciences Po, "Master in International Studies" at the University of Geneva, the "Master of Public Policy" at the Hertie School of Governance, and the "Master of Public Policy" at the Erfurt School of Public Policy. At the European Institute at the University of Saarland, practitioners even provide the vast majority of the course instruction:

> *"We train them for the field. That means we don't just have professors. The minority is professors; the majority of our instructors – we have 70, so 70 instructors for 70 students – are practitioners. They are judges at the European Court of Justice, attorney generals, Commission officials, heads of department, directors. For us, it is very important that people from the field come here and say, 'This is how it works at the Commission,' 'This is how it works at the European Council or Court of Justice'. The students really appreciate that." (University of Saarbrücken)*

Most practitioners teach practical and problem-oriented courses or courses that focus on professional skills development, whereas solely theory-based courses are primarily taught by permanent academic staff. Two interview partners described it as follows:

> *"Similarly, if we do a class on communication skills – as we do – I really do not want an academic who has done his Ph.D. in advanced research on how people communicate. I want someone who is a consultant on communication." (University of Geneva)*

> *"There's only one exception in our content courses. We only let scholars teach our content courses. We don't believe anything else would be legitimate. The fact that some random practitioners teach content courses is in my opinion and in the opinion of the directorate absolutely out of the question. The only exception is for people from the European Commission. We have two people from the European Commission who teach subjects related to their jobs. These are only additional courses, however. The practitioners must concentrate on the Europe Dialogues." (Center for European Integration Studies, Bonn)*

However, in the opinion of many program coordinators interviewed, it is not only important that practitioners bring a high level of professional experience to the classroom, but also that they are good instructors. Many interview partners mentioned that practitioners often have difficulty with the mechanics of teaching and that their lack of teaching experience must be addressed. Therefore, the practitioners' academic qualifications and experience in the classroom is taken into account as well to ensure the quality of instruction:

"Practitioners, like theorists, must be selected according to pedagogical criteria and their competencies. I always bring a practitioner into my seminar in order to have a cross check and to enrich the complexity." (Zeppelin University, Friedrichshafen)

Yet our interview partners also said that it is not easy to employ practitioners with both sufficient professional and teaching experience.

"Our original objective was to have professionals. When trying to recruit them, however, we realized that it's not all that simple. It is especially difficult to recruit people with professional experience who also have a certain level of academic ability that allows them to earn a solid academic reputation." (Hertie School of Governance, Berlin)

"It is quite a funny experience that professionals are considered to be good per se at teaching. That isn't necessarily always the case. There are practitioners who are good instructors, but there are also practitioners who have held the highest posts but are terrible teachers." (Erfurt School of Public Policy)

It can be concluded that most programs examined in this study employ practitioners with a strong international and professional background in the field for which the program intends to train students. These practitioners mainly teach practically-oriented and applied courses, whereas permanent or non-permanent academic staff members are primarily responsible for academic and methodological instruction.

5.6. Student body composition

We were further interested in the composition of the student body, the program requirements, and the career paths graduates tend to follow.

The admission requirements are very similar among the programs examined. Potential program participants must have a first academic degree, which until now mainly included *Diplom*, *Magister*, and *Staatsexamen* degrees. However, in the course of the Bologna reforms, more and more students with a bachelor degree apply and are accepted to these programs. They are usually considered to be an adequate academic background and comparable to the traditional degrees.

The programs examined differ as to whether applicants must have a specific educational background. However, most programs do not make any restrictions regarding the educational background. Some of the programs examined even systematically recruit students from a wide variety of fields of study, as a diverse student body sets the context for an interdisciplinary learning atmosphere that most programs attempt to create:

"We recruit our students primarily from the social sciences and business and economics. We mainly have sociologists, political scientists, and economists in our program. But we're open to other backgrounds, too. We have computer scientists, for example. We even have a literature major, who is doing an excellent job because she

was able to show us in her application that she can quickly familiarize herself with new areas." (Erfurt School of Public Policy)

"You have to have a degree before you come here – at least a B.A. But we have no prerequisites with regard to the subject. We even got an application from a medical school graduate. It was very plausible: this medical school graduate had decided to work for the WHO. But the majority of our applicants is from the area of social sciences, from economics and law. That's just the way it is. These three disciplines are best represented. Neighboring disciplines as well – that's no problem." (Hertie School of Governance, Berlin)

"When we have someone from the field of agriculture here who says he wants to work for the FAO and has also done internships at the UN and EU, then he's predestined to get into the UN system. If he then says, 'I need these European Studies so I can work for the FAO or EU in the area of agriculture, but I don't have enough knowledge of the EU,' then he's the right candidate for us. Clear motivation. If he or she is very good and comes out of the system, then we know that the chances of getting into the EU and the UN are excellent." (Center for European Integration Studies, Bonn)

However, although some program coordinators pay attention to a wide variety of academic backgrounds, it is apparent that most students enrolled in the programs examined earned their first academic degree in political or social science, law, or economics. The program "Master of Arts in International Affairs and Governance" of the University of St. Gallen requires students who do not have any background knowledge in one of the program's core disciplines – law, economics, and political sciences – to attend specific courses in order to develop an basic understanding in the new disciplines and ensure that they can complete program.

Another selection criterion identified is work experience. However, most programs examined do not require extensive work experience, although it is regarded as very beneficial for the selection process:

"The second thing that plays a role is when someone has worked or done an internship for at least six months. We take that into consideration when making admissions decisions. We don't just say, 'He has a bachelor's degree and such and such a grade,' but rather, 'Okay, now he has spent three years working." (Master of Peace Research and International Politics, University of Tübingen)

At many practically oriented programs, the basic rule is that lacking professional knowledge can be compensated with work experience gained in the professional field that the programs intents to prepare. At some programs, applicants are required to write a letter of motivation where they outline their professional experience and the professional field that they are interested in:

"It is furthermore important – very important, in fact – that your Statement of purpose and résumé make us as the readers of your application believe that you have a genuine interest in politics, no matter what kind." (Hertie School of Governance, Berlin)

When comparing the programs examined in this study, it is apparent that none of the programs in the German speaking countries explicitly requires professional work experience, whereas the programs at the University of Geneva and Scienes Po demand that program participants have gained sufficient work experience. Our interview partners in German speaking countries mentioned that graduates usually apply for a master program directly after their first academic degree without having gained any work experience. This might be due to the fact that a bachelor degree is not yet fully accepted in the private and public sector as an academic qualification (e.g. a M.A. is still a minimum requirement for higher positions in the German public service). Therefore, it is not surprising that many German students do not plan their career entry after the B.A. but rather after the M.A. Even the reformed master programs have to accept this logic, although some interview partners stressed the importance of previous professional work for the students' professional development. At many programs in German speaking countries it is often the case that foreign students have already gained sufficient professional experience in their home countries after their first academic degree.

In addition to an academic degree and work experience, another important admission requirement is proficiency in English. As most programs are taught either entirely or partly in English, it is no surprise that students must be able to speak English fluently. Some programs also require proficiency in another language, mainly German or French.

With regard to the selection process, some programs conduct interviews or written examinations. The Centre for European Integration Studies in Bonn, for instance, conducts telephone interviews to evaluate the suitability of its applicants, whereas for the Diploma Course at the Diplomatic Academy of Vienna, applicants must run through a two-stage selection process. Here, basic knowledge in the disciplines of the Institute and the language skills are assessed. After that, a selection interview in the languages that the Institute requires follows.

Concerning the composition of the student body at the programs examined, it is apparent that a large number of international students (an average of 30 to 50%) is enrolled to set the context for an international learning atmosphere which is regarded as very useful for preparing students to function effectively in a multinational working environment. Students are enabled to deal with other nationalities and cultures during their studies. This trains their foreign language and intercultural skills needed for a successful job performance in international organizations.

At the Diplomatic Academy of Vienna and at the Collège d'Europe in Bruges students study and live with different nationalities:

"Another aspect is, moreso than at other schools, our students live in this building. We have our own kitchen and bathroom, which means they eat and sleep here. We currently have 150 students from approximately 50 nations from all continents – that means living for one or two years with other students from other countries and parts of the world in close quarters. That is a learning experience for the students in and of itself that may be more important than some of the theoretical things we do." (Diplomatic Academy of Vienna)

"If you ask the students what they got out of our program, all of them will say 50% was academic and 50% was living and working with others. That is a quite good experience. When they go to international organizations, the students then how to work with people from different countries or how to switch from one language to another without a problem." (Collège d'Europe, Bruges)

All programs examined in this study are highly demanded even if that means paying considerable tuition fees in some cases. However, students who must pay tuition fees can rely on attending small courses which are exclusively offered for the program. In programs that do not cost more than the general fees, it might occur that program participants must share courses with students from other programs and small groups of up to 15 people are rather seldom.

Although only a minority of the examined programs tends to prepare explicitly for careers in the international public service, this field of work is very popular among students. An average of up to 60 percent of the students in the programs examined study with the intention to work in the international public service or more general in the international field:

"It's not that 100% of the students in this program say they want to work at an international organization, but at the same time, most of our students are going for a job in the international context. [...] The students know that they can't plan enough to say that it will definitely be this international organization or that international organization. I think that most stay more flexible and open because they know they have to, and then it turns out to be an international organization or an NGO later on." (Master of Arts in International Relations in cooperation between the Humboldt University of Berlin, the Free University of Berlin, and the University of Potsdam)

However, according to our interview participants, very few graduates (between 10% and 20%) actually work in the international public service. As most programs examined in German speaking countries are still too young to show alumni statistics, we cannot refer to exact figures. However, the Diplomatic Academy of Vienna assumes that about one third to a quarter of their graduates work in international organizations. At the Collège d'Europe statistics indicate that about 30% of graduates work in international organizations, including EU institutions and NGOs, whereas all other program participants work in the national public service or private service. Most interview participants mentioned that many students change their opinion during their studies: They are either discouraged to find a proper job in international organizations or they do not value the attractiveness of a career in international organizations as much as they did at the beginning of their studies (e.g. because it is easier to find a job in the private sector and even the average salary is higher). A survey among this target group is highly recommended to find out more about students career interests'.

5.7.   Career services

Employees in international organizations highly recommended that higher education institutions should assist students in their career development. According to the information we obtained, most of the programs examined in Germany do not have career offices with permanent staff who is explicitly responsible for the students' career development, whereas all institutions examined in Geneva, Bruges, Paris, ST. Gallen and Vienna institutionalized their career services somehow, as they established career offices or centers. It is appears that the concept of "career development" or "career service" at higher education institutions in Germany has not become fully rooted, which is primarily due to the lack of financial and human resources. However, many educational experts regard it as very important for students' employability and make strong efforts to provide students with information on internship programs and job opportunities in international organizations. Some universities, for instance, established an official *internship pool* where all vacancies from different national and international organizations are collected and published either by e-mail or blackboard. The internship coordinator of the program "Master of Public Policy and Management" at the University of Konstanz, for example, collects all vacancies from different organizations and publishes them on a blackboard. Furthermore, internship reports written by former students are available to all students to inform themselves about internship opportunities:

"We have a lot of experience with long internships. In the 'Diplom' degree program, everyone had to do a seven-month internship. That was the same in the BA program. That means that we have thirty years' worth of contact to internship providers

where our students were placed. We have a big archive. Everyone has to write a report about his or her internship. The master students can view this archive and see where people from Konstanz were, what they did, and what their experiences were like. They can copy the addresses of the contact people and get in touch with them directly." (University of Konstanz)

The German Development Institute in Bonn, for instance, sends short CV's that provide basic information on the program participants' educational and professional background to potential employers such as the Federal Ministry for Economic Cooperation and Development (BMZ), GTZ or KfW:

"We help the participants create their profiles and short CVs that contain the main information about them: what and where they studied, what their academic background is, in which field their strengths lie, where they would like to further build their profiles, and where they see themselves in the future. That's all put together and then sent to many organizations that are already familiar with us. We don't send it to everyone, but rather there's a group of organizations that know us quite well and know that we educate very good people here whom they might be interested in. These organizations are the BMZ [German Federal Ministry for Economic Cooperation and Development], the GTZ, and KfW [Bank]." (German Development Institute in Bonn)

Furthermore, once a year they organize an informal meeting with different organizations in the Institute. Through this support, a vast majority of program participants (partly more than 90%) can be placed in different development agencies before the end of the program.

The Center for European Integration Studies in Bonn also has a career development element in its program: Professional trainers are invited to talk with students about their professional interest and assist them in their career development. Furthermore, the Center offers *special training courses* which aim to prepare students for the EU concours:

"We have a component of the curriculum that's called Career Development. We have training sessions that prepare them specifically for the selection procedure, meaning the EU Concours. [...] We have also had a personal training session for several years that the coaches call 'profiling'. A coach comes and talks to them about their goals, strengths, weaknesses, and how they can get where they want to go." (Center for European Integration Studies, Bonn)

At the program "Master of Arts in International Relations" that is taught in cooperation between universities in Berlin and Potsdam offers a course called "Introduction to the International Service" where students obtain insight into the field of work of international organizations:

"I brought the program of the event called 'Introduction to the International Civil Service', and you can see that the main function of this colloquium is to give the students an overview of the places they can work. I also do several introductory courses

and invite speakers from a variety of fields so the students can learn more about the different jobs and choose what type of internships they want to do." (Master in International Relations in cooperation between the Humboldt University of Berlin, the Free University of Berlin, and the University of Potsdam)

In the program "Master of Business Administration International Organizations" at the University of Geneva an informal mentoring program that brings together students and professionals who work in international and non-governmental organizations was created. Here, mentors share insider knowledge, job hunting tips, and any other helpful advice with students.

At most German universities alumni networks are still in process of being setting up. In programs that emerged from traditional programs, alumni networks can partly be used so that the institutions do not have to invest many years of work in setting up new networks. In particular, the program "Master in European Law" at the European Institute of the University of Saarland can refer to established contacts to alumni in the different EU institutions because of its long existence. Here, alumni assist with internship applications or are invited as guest lectures to give presentations on their work. Furthermore, they assist the Institute in planning and conducting field trips to EU institutions. However, it is not easy to develop an alumni network everywhere. Due to lacking financial and human resources at most universities in Germany, it is only possible to establish very selective and informal contacts between students and alumni.

Another important benefit of the alumni networks is not only the exchange of experience but also the feedback alumni can give on the program design: Some educational institutions receive feedback on the curricular design from their alumni. At the German University of Administrative Sciences in Speyer, for instance, meetings at which program alumni come together are organized. Here, former students are invited once a year according to their region, e.g. all African alumni are invited to Johannesburg in South Africa. There, they attend a two-day alumni seminar during which, among others, they evaluate the program after many years of graduation. From these evaluations new conclusions can be drawn for the current curriculum. The seminars are supported and financed by InWEnt and take place in different countries each year:

"We arrange regionally-specific seminars especially for our foreign students. That means a professor of ours goes somewhere in the Far East and chooses a country and a location somewhere between Korea, China, and Mongolia. And then we invite our Chinese, Korean, Vietnamese, Mongolian, and Japanese graduates there. Then we have a two-day seminar. [It's a good way of having] post-study contact and advis-

ing, which we want. They might also visit a graduate or two in their offices. It takes place basically every year, but only one region is visited each year. It's not that we can go to South America, the Middle East, and Africa all in one year." (German University of Administrative Sciences in Speyer)

5.8. Cooperation agreements

The analysis of the interview partners' responses revealed two types of cooperation agreements: those between two academic institutions that mainly focus on academic exchange and those between higher education institutions and non-governmental, governmental and international organizations.

5.8.1. Cooperation with IOs, governments, and NGOs

Our study has shown that formal cooperation agreements with international or other organizations do rarely exist. Most of the contacts are informal and mainly established by program alumni and instructors that have worked in international organizations before or practitioners who are invited for guest lectures:

"These are loose agreements. Sometimes there's a contract, such as when we want to have a state working group cooperate directly with the GTZ. Other than that, there's an informal, almost familiar behavior between the institutions. We know each other from research and consulting. We do a lot for the GTZ, including workshops. So that's more informal. But the contacts are relatively intensive." (German Development Institute, Bonn)

"There are lots of organizations that now have close cooperation, and where we know that people go there every year. The United National Fund for Partnership in New York is one example of a place where two or three students of ours go each year. We even do a small pre-selection round. It is very structured. We have lots of people who work for parliamentarians or for EU parliamentarians or in the periphery of the EU in other directions, where informal but established partnerships exist." (University of Konstanz)

It was stressed by many educational experts that their institutions basically do not aim to establish formal cooperation agreements with international organizations. It is more important to gain a good reputation so that the name of the university or the program becomes well-known and, thus, students are gladly accepted for internships or guest speakers for presentations and discussions can be easily found. Here, it was mentioned that trust on both sides is considered more important than formal contracts.

However, there are also few exceptions among the programs examined. All programs at the University of Geneva have close cooperation agreements with the United Nations agencies and programs placed in Geneva. Here, for example, the program "Master of Business Administration International Organizations" aims to set up a *strategic learning program* with the United Nations where UN officials and program participants study together. UN officials are further engaged in the evaluation of the program to ensure that it meets the demands of the professional world. Moreover, the program seeks close cooperation with social entrepreneurs, mainly non-governmental organizations, and with the private sector as well. The M.A. in International Affairs and Governance at the University of St. Gallen is in the process of setting up cooperation agreements with organizations and institutions in the private and public sector concerning internship placement:

> *"We have two or three offerings exclusively for our MIA students, where there are cooperation contracts between the MIA program and the internship organization. But that is still in the beginning phases, because we simply don't have the capacities required [to continue building it]. The students are very successful at finding their own interesting internship opportunities." (University of St. Gallen)*

The program "Master of Public Administration" at Sciences Po has already established so-called "Partnership Programs" with various national and international organizations and enterprises. Case studies and other teaching methods are developed and internship programs are arranged in the context of these partnerships. Furthermore, during the so-called "Capstone Project", students can work for two weeks on a certain project (typically in the area of policy analysis, evaluation, and implementation) in the respective organization. The program "Master of European Studies" at the University of Vienna cooperates with the Research Institute for Multilingualism in Brussels (one professor is member of the strategic staff) and the European Commission Representation in Austria.

To sum up, several programs have established close contacts with international organizations for career development and extracurricular activities as well as for quality assessment purposes.

5.8.2. Academic cooperation agreements

Almost all the programs we investigated have formal cooperation agreements with other national and international higher education institutions. The primary objective of these agreements is the exchange of students and, in some cases, also the opportunity to offer dual or joint degrees.

The program "European Law and Economics" at the University of Hamburg, which is an international postgraduate program, provides students with the opportunity to graduate at three universities within one year. Each trimester, students can attend courses at a different university, and the degree is then awarded by the universities attended. Students may choose between the Universities of Hamburg (Germany), Bologna (Italy), Rotterdam (Netherlands), Gent (Belgium), Aix-en-Provence (France), Haifa (Israel), Linköping/Stockhom (Sweden), Madrid (Spain), Manchester (Great Britain), and Vienna (Austria). Furthermore, all of these universities meet twice a year for so-called board meetings, one of which is even concerned with matters of curricular development.

The German University of Administrative Sciences in Speyer has cooperation agreements with the Budapest University of Economic Sciences and Public Administration in Hungary, the Katholieke Universiteit Leuven in Belgium, the University of Liverpool in Great Britain, and other institutions in Estonia, Finland, and the Netherlands. More agreements shall soon be established with universities in France, the Netherlands, and other European countries.

Due to its traditional programs, the University of Konstanz already has a large number of cooperation partners. However, according to our interview partner, the quality of programs offered at the partner institutions differ considerably and, thus, only few cooperation agreements are actually appropriate to the recently developed "Master of Public Policy and Management". Therefore, direct agreements for the program are currently being negotiated with a few select European universities. Cooperation agreements with Rutgers University in New Jersey and the University of North Texas – both in the U.S. – also already exist.

Both programs at the University of Potsdam maintain contact in particular to Scandinavian universities but also to universities in Italy, Mongolia, and the Sadat University in Kairo. Furthermore, they are integrated into a network of European public management programs. Through this network, students can, for example, participate in several summer schools that offer public management courses.

According to the information we received, only a few programs have formal cooperation agreements with professional schools in the U.S. As mentioned before, the Diplomatic Academy of Vienna offers its students the opportunity to spend one year at the Bologna Center of Johns Hopkins University or the Fletcher School of Law and Diplomacy. This example shows that it is possible indeed to cooperate with well-known American professional schools. Many of our interview partners showed interest in such exchanges but stressed the bureaucratic, financial, and organizational difficulties that go along with this type of close cooperation. However, they also believe that it is worthwhile to overcome these difficulties and provide students with the opportunity to study at a well-known educational institution abroad.

Moreover, only very few programs examined in this study are members of *professional networks*. The program of the Diplomatic Academy in Vienna, for instance, is a member of the International Forum on Diplomatic Training (IFDT), which organizes yearly meetings of deans and directors of diplomatic academies and institutes of international relations in order to discuss current developments in fields of international relations, international law, diplomacy, world economics, political science, and others.

"The directors get together for one week each year and discuss everything. But we're an atypical diplomatic academy: there are the institutions that you are now studying, but also the classic diplomatic academies that offer in-house training for future diplomats." (Diplomatic Academy of Vienna)

The University of St. Gallen and Sciences Po are members of the Association of Professional Schools of International Affairs (APSIA) which "is dedicated to the improvement of professional education in international affairs".[95] Members of the Transatlantic Policy Consortium (TPC), the goal of which is "to strengthen relationships between European and American scholars and professionals in the field of public policy analysis and education", include the Erfurt School of Public Policy, the German University of Administrative Sciences in Speyer, and the National School of Administration (ENA) in Paris.[96] The Hertie School of Governance in Berlin is a member of the Association for Public Policy Analysis and Management (APPAM), which aims to improve "public policy and management by fostering excellence in research, analysis, and education".[97] Because of how few institutions are members in such associations, it is apparent that it is not common a practice in Western Europe – and in German-speaking countries in particular – to join or create associations or networks or to hold meetings among program coordinators to exchange best practices in professional education. One interview participant suggested that a network should be established among programs that intend to achieve the same educational objective:

"That means that everyone who thinks they're good should get together and make cooperation contracts. Basically to reap the benefits from synergies, but the synergies must also be of network quality. Those lacking the level of quality don't get to take part. If that can be observed from the outside, then it is also high quality. Why shouldn't people have virtual exchange in certain areas? Like in research or teach-

ing, or student exchanges. You have to want it. It has administrative consequence, but then you can have a certain tradeoff of work: whatever you can't do but others can. Then you can also specialize a bit more yourself and develop your competencies even better than when you have to cover an entire area." (Zeppelin University, Friedrichshafen)

5.9. Conclusion on the European programs

As a result of the Bologna process and thus with the introduction of the three-cycle degree model (bachelor-master-Ph.D.), various efforts were made by educational institutions to internationalize and professionalize postgraduate education in the fields of "European Studies", "International Relations", and "Public Policy and Management". New educational programs offering internationally recognized certification have been created that now compete with long-established programs such as the Diplomatic Academy of Vienna or the Center for European Integration Studies in Bonn. Although our study revealed that the concept of professional education is not yet fully rooted in Europe, a wave of reform is currently taking place to "globalize" and "professionalize" degree programs and thus better prepare students for the national, European, and international public service or, more generally, for any professional field. Our study has further shown that processes of curricular development and evaluation are sensitive to the labor market and more geared to address the specific nature of the competencies needed for successful work performance in the (international) public service by taking into account a range of professional and other interests within the professional community, higher education, and society. Regular evaluations ensure responsiveness to new developments in the field by incorporating and building on the practical and professional experience of those involved. However, there is still room for improvement: On the one hand, professionals could be involved more systematically in both the development and evaluation of curricula to ensure that the demands of the labor market are taken seriously. Higher educational institutions and professional communities need to establish closer relations, and networks among educational institutions could be created in order to exchange best practices of professional education for the international public service.

Furthermore, it is apparent that all programs examined are committed to interdisciplinarity and characterized by a strong international orientation, whereas the latter varies considerably among the institutions. Many higher education institutions try to respond to the processes of globalization and Europeanization, which inevitably requires an international orientation in the education they provide. The programs have found different ways and means to face these processes and adjusted or are now adjusting their curricula accordingly.

Moreover, we were able to identify a growing emphasis on competency development and practical application in the educational objectives of the programs examined. In addition, the teaching of a broad knowledge base, the development of essential professional skills needed for a successful career in the national or international public service and, more important, the reflection and practical application of knowledge and skills gained in prior training is increasingly placed in the foreground of European study programs. Many of the curricula we examined were marked by the interrelationship of these educational components. A shift from theory-based and research-oriented to more practically- and application-oriented educational programs is apparent. Most programs in our study use various methods of teaching and learning to achieve their main educational objectives. In particular, teaching methods mainly concerned with inquiry, analysis, reflection, experience, problem-solving, and interaction are applied in almost all programs. Case teaching, simulations, and group work are used in most of the programs addition to the traditional direct modes of instruction. Furthermore, many programs include practical or hands-on courses, training courses for communication and teamwork skills and the opportunity for workplace learning (e.g., internships).

Professional education also typically entails providing some level of assistance to students in their career development. However, at Western European higher education institutions, career offices that support students in finding internships and jobs are more the exception than the rule. This mainly results from a shortage of financial and human resources.

Drawing conclusions from the results of this study, the educational institutions we examined are making major efforts to better prepare young academics for international work. As for Germany, the reform processes begun in the educational offerings for the international public service must be consequently followed in the future to produce more young graduates who are able to successfully complete the complex tasks in international organizations and thus achieve the long-term objective of increasing the number of German personnel in international organizations. However, in the end, it depends on how well universities and research institutes, the German government, and German professionals in international organizations work together to achieve this objective. This could be a greater challenge than improving the education for this professional field alone.

5.10. Overview of degree programs offered in Anglo-Saxon countries

As mentioned in the research design section, the main focus of the curricular study was to compare the educational offerings in the U.S. with those in Western Europe in order to search for best practice examples that could be transferred from one system to the other. In addition to these large-scale studies, smaller-scale studies were done to provide a general overview of the degree programs available in three other Anglo-Saxon countries: Great Britain, Australia, and New Zealand. While the findings were quite similar to those in the U.S., it is interesting to note that professional schools of public policy, government, and international relations do not exist in these countries in the same way as they do in the U.S. (or at least they do not call themselves as such). However, a wide variety of degrees are available that prepare students for the international public service and related fields. Among those included in the survey were:
– Development Studies
– Diplomatic Studies
– Environment Management and Policy Studies
– European Studies
– Global Politics
– International Law
– International Political Economy
– International Relations or Studies
– Public Policy and Administration
– Strategic or Security Studies (also: War Studies, International Conflict Studies, etc.)
– Other relevant programs, such as Refugee Studies or Management of NGOs

In comparing these programs, the same variety and range of options and offerings appears as among the U.S. professional schools. This applies to the amount of practical orientation, internationality, the sectors for which they intend to qualify their students, their areas specialization, and the numbers and types of students they (intend to) attract. In Great Britain, for example, many degrees can either be completed with a research orientation (MPhil/MLitt/MRes), which often leads to a D.Phil./Ph.D. and an academic career program afterwards, or with a more practical focus (MA/MSc), which is typically selected by students who wish to earn a terminal degree and then begin working in the field. A similar distinction exists in Australia and New Zealand with 'coursework' and 'research' streams for most master's programs. As with the U.S. professional schools, many public policy or administration programs tend to specialize in certain areas and train their students for careers in the private and public sectors without limiting their potential fields of employment. One notable difference between the offerings in these nations is that universities in Great Britain have many more programs in European Studies than those in Australia and New Zealand, which is to be expected considering the direct relevance of the EU to each. Finally, the student numbers (per year) range from 2 to 82, so the size – and therefore also the composition – of the groups of participants vary just as widely as those in the U.S.

In conclusion, the degree programs offered in Great Britain, Australia, and New Zealand for qualifying students for careers in international organizations are quite similar to those offered in the U.S. None of the institutions claims to educate students solely for careers in this field, and many are multidisciplinary and teach a combination of different types of skills.

6.   Recommendations on how to improve educational programs

The following recommendations drawn from the results of the PROFIO labor market study and curricular study can be useful to institutions interested in developing educational offerings to qualify students for careers in international organizations. They can also be used individually to improve upon existing programs. These recommendations primarily deal with the various aspects of study programs, such as the methods of instruction used, the composition of the faculty, and the structure of the curriculum. Less detailed information will be provided on the specific coursework such a program could or should offer, as German degree programs already, according to the results of our research, provide a solid substantive curriculum in the fields relevant to this study. However, there is still room for improvement in some areas. In the end, it is up to each individual institution of higher education to determine how these proposals should be realized. The structure or type of institution can vary, for example, from a department or cooperation between departments at a university to a private training academy to a separately established 'professional school' as in the U.S.

These recommendations are furthermore expected to be implemented in the form of a graduate-level degree program that can be completed by anyone holding a bachelor degree or higher, including those with a degree in natural sciences or other non-public-policy-related fields.

6.1.   Curricular development and evaluation

Curricular development and evaluation should take place in *cooperation with alumni and practitioners* in the fields for which the program intends to prepare students and should be market-driven rather than supply-based. Not much has changed in higher education since Mayhew and Ford wrote about such challenges in 1974:

"Too frequently courses have reflected chiefly interests of faculty, practices copied from prestigious institutions, unverified requirements of the professional community or accrediting bodies, or institutional interests. In a rapidly changing and expanding professional field as the international public service, these will not suffice."[98]

---

[98] Mayhew, L. B., & Ford. P. Joseph. (1974). *Reform in graduate and professional education* (1 st ed.). The Jossey-Bass Series in Higher Education. San Francisco: Jossey-Bass Publishers, p. 81.

Those responsible for designing and improving educational programs should be sensitive to changing labor market conditions. Of course, educational programs should not be governed by job descriptions or determined by practitioners alone, but it is necessary for the faculty to analyze the several roles that professionals in international organizations have to perform and which knowledge, skills, and competencies they need. Therefore, *higher education institutions and professional communities need to establish closer relations* and assume joint responsibility for curriculum development and evaluation. This would help ensure that the program designed produces graduates who are able to act independently and successfully complete the tasks in a professional field. The faculty should set up special committees for the purpose of reviewing the curriculum on an ongoing or intermittent basis, and educational institutions can consult with one another on their programs from time to time as well.

6.2. Educational objectives

First of all, in order to design a relevant degree program in the form of "professional education", it is essential to consider "*international public service" as a profession* and the program's target group as people who wish to pursue a career in a professional field rather than one in academia. One of the main differences that can be observed between the American and the European education systems is the extent to which they prepare their students to fulfill the expectations of their future employers. This is precisely the goal of "*professional education*": to impart the skills necessary to meet the demands of the job of one's choice. International organizations require personnel who can begin acting in their new working environment right away.

With regard to the competencies required by international organizations, the *first basic educational objective* should comprise the development and transmission of a systematic knowledge base, largely – though not exclusively – based on relevant academic disciplines, such social and political science, law, economics, and business. The study of these disciplines should be combined and courses with a strong international and interdisciplinary orientation should be offered. *The second basic educational objective* should involve the interpretation, reflection, and application of the knowledge base, including the development and application of analytical, methodological and basic management skills, the coverage of the range of professional activities and their contexts, problem-solving principles, and processes. The *third educational objective* should involve the opportunity for work-related learning (e.g., internships, community service). Here, students should primarily develop competencies related to their actions and behavior on the job that can be hardly taught at the university. These are the basic educational objectives upon which the curriculum development and selection of courses should be based.

6.3. Curricular components of the curriculum

The general structure of the different components that we would recommend is a pyramid (see Figure 6.1 below). At the bottom, a certain amount of theory (as determined in the curriculum design) should build the foundation for the students' knowledge of the field. On top of that, but to a lesser extent, the students must complete coursework that provides them with the tools for gathering and analyzing information on their own, presenting it to others, and using it to solve real-world problems. These courses can include qualitative and/or quantitative research methods, policy analysis, program evaluation, project and financial management, budgeting, decision making, problem solving, ethics and values, information technology, writing or speaking skills. The next level of the pyramid would generally consist of the field or fields in which the students choose to specialize. Besides these competencies and in addition to the area of concentration, students should acquire proficiency in a foreign language or complete a regional studies component. Above this – and quite often toward the end of the program or at least after completion of a set of basic courses – we find those elements of the program that should impart practical skills and expertise on the students. This may include an internship, pro bono consulting work, an assigned group project, or even smaller-scale training sessions in certain areas such as intercultural negotiation or presentation skills. In essence, these components should enable the students to put their knowledge to work and provide them the opportunity to learn and make mistakes within the program rather than on the job. This could be done through the use of case studies or simulations. Finally, the top of the pyramid consists of the final graduation requirements. Generally speaking, this should be a so-called capstone experience, which is a hands-on, problem-solving project related to the students' particular area of interest. Certainly not all curricula follow this pattern, but it is a common structure that allows for a great deal of flexibility, balance, and direction in the students' learning programs.

6.4. Areas of concentration or specialization

Concentrations should be offered that deal specifically with IOs or inter-institutional relations. Many concentrations already exist that deal with the relations between nations and regions. However, few are available that teach students about the structures, functions, decision-making processes of and relations between international governmental (and non-governmental) organizations. These could be limited to one organization (such as the EU), extended to include a whole group of organizations (such as the UN System), or designed broadly enough to provide basic information on IOs in general and allow the students to select organizations on which to concentrate. This course cluster could be complemented by seminars in other fields adjusted to deal with the specific role or impact of IOs in that area: International Law, International Economics and/or Development, and even Regional Studies (EU, African Union, regional development banks, etc.) or Environmental Policy (UNEP, etc.).

Furthermore, it is highly recommended to offer *regional specializations*: e.g., Latin America, the Balkans, the Caucasus, or Central and Eastern Europe, China and Southeast Asia. In order to enhance the understanding of the selected area of regional specification, students should be expected to satisfy the *foreign language requirement* in a language that corresponds to their chosen area of regional specialization. Study programs should be committed to offering additional *professional language training* to enhance students' employability.

The most effective method would be for programs to require their students to complement a *regional specialization with a thematic concentration* so that they combine a field of study or a thematic concentration such as economic development or religious studies within a specific region of the world. Students would gain an integrated and interdisciplinary approach to the complex issues faced by local and global communities. Therefore, all concentrations and specializations offered should be strongly interdisciplinary in nature.

6.5. Interdisciplinarity

For successful career development in the international public service, it seems that it is no longer sufficient to study a single discipline in isolation or obtain only one degree in a specific field of study. Therefore, programs which aim to prepare students for the international public service should be *intrinsically interdisciplinary*. Students should receive a multi-faceted picture of a topic through the exploration and synthesis of various ap-

Figure 6.1. Suggested curriculum structure for professional education for IOs

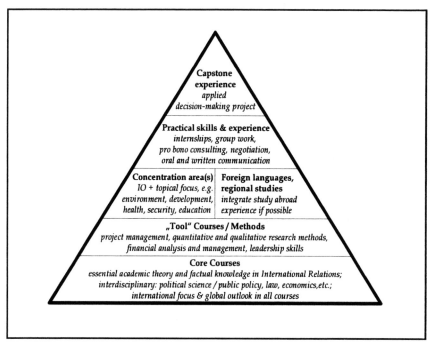

Source: Authors

proaches, methods, and views. These connections among disciplines require teaching staff with an interdisciplinary background and continuous dialogue within the faculty.

6.6.   International focus

National educational institutions and programs should be significantly *internationalized in substance and structure* to better prepare students for work in the European and international public service. The expansion of course offerings both geographically and by discipline as well as the introduction of comparative and multicultural materials into existing courses is one measure to enable students to deal with complex issues and global developments. The universities should sponsor lectures on international matters, faculty members should be encouraged to seek international experience, qualified foreign students and faculty should be accepted, and students and faculty should both be encouraged to learn foreign languages. They could initiate courses of specialized international character and could support faculty research of an international nature. The addition of *foreign students and faculty* also provides international enrichment and could be enhanced through *teaching the entire program in English*. *Offering exchange programs* also contributes to the internationalization of education, as it develops intercultural communication and foreign language skills.

6.7.   Program duration

Students should be allowed to study *part-time or full-time* and to opt for a heavy or a light course load each semester. This would enable them to *work or do internships during the program* if they wish. The minimum amount of time it should take to earn a master's degree is one year; at the same time, the program should not be unnecessarily long. When developing the curriculum, program faculty should take into consideration whether an internship and/or capstone experience will be required and plan accordingly.

6.8.   Foreign language requirements

Educational institutions should *enhance professional foreign language training*, as language skills are very crucial for a successful job performance in the international public service. English and French are no longer regarded as sufficient. Professional knowledge of other languages can give students a competitive edge when seeking employment.

6.9.   Practical, hands-on courses (skills/competency-building)

Study programs should facilitate the competency development of young professionals. This can best be done through coursework that teaches students *how to put theory to use* and by giving them the *tools necessary to solve real-world problems*. Exercises, labs, and application modules imparting skills needed in the international public service should be built into the curriculum. Examples could include international negotiation simulations, writing memos, role-playing games on conflict mediation, or practicing cost-benefit analysis for a real client.

6.10.   Extracurricular activities

It is recommendable for the coordinators of study programs to offer students a wide variety of activities they can participate in outside of the classroom. These can and should include *guest speakers, clubs* related to the fields of study and/or career goals of the students, and *excursions* to organizations or businesses of interest to the majority of the students. Any workshops organized by the educational institution should be open to the students as well. *Community service* should be another option available to interested students, and it could be mandatory for those receiving scholarships.

6.11. Internships

Work-experience programs if well planned and managed, can be of great benefit to students both in learning the art of application and in helping them to integrate knowledge and skills obtained through other methods. Workplace learning would provide a bridge between the academic institution and the world of practice and between professional education and subsequent employment. Therefore, it is highly recommended to integrate the opportunity for workplace learning – *internships, community service, and volunteer work* – into the curriculum. However, universities should make sure that the programs offered provide real involvement in the actual work of an organization, last several months, and are academically supervised through tutorials, seminars, and written assignments. Careful organization and supervision increases the *efficiency of work-experience programs*. The integration of workplace learning into academic programs requires close cooperation between higher education institutions, alumni, and employers. Furthermore, students should have the *opportunity to extend the duration of the internship* if possible, as this has proven to be very helpful in finding jobs later. Therefore, they should be able to defer their studies by a semester if they wish. Moreover, higher education institutions should not only assist students in finding internship placements but also help them to fund unpaid internships. They should hold annual fundraising mechanism to collect money for a so-called *"Internship Fund"* that can be used to give scholarships for unpaid internships.

6.12. Studies abroad and joint or dual degrees

The curriculum should allow students to *study for a summer or semester abroad* to let them improve their intercultural competence and, should they have a regional specialization or foreign language component, to gain a deeper knowledge of the country or area at hand. The exchanges can also be direct, which would enhance the international profile of the 'home' program. Another option is to *offer joint or dual degrees with other educational institutions* either in the area or abroad: Students wishing to earn qualifications in more than one field thus can do so in a shorter amount of time. Dual degrees between similar study programs in different countries would also benefit students, as they could study abroad and earn multiple degrees at the same time.

6.13. Balance between academic and practical training

There is no basic rule on how to balance broadly theoretical and more applied courses. Professional education should not narrow its offerings to training of practical skills. On the contrary: it should provide a solid combination of both academic courses and training seminars to equip students with thorough knowledge in a certain field of study/discipline, the intellectual and methodological tools necessary to analyze situations and shape responses accordingly, as well as a wide range of useful competencies and practical experiences. "This does not mean any reduction in essential basic theory or science, but it does suggest a different ordering of such work and in differing proportions."[99] Therefore, curricula should be fluid and comprehensive in nature by allowing students to take coursework that is focused on the delivery of broader and/or specific knowledge, while simultaneously offering courses for knowledge application, competency development, and workplace learning.

6.14. Teaching and examination methods

Preparing young academics for the professional world requires teaching and learning methods that encourage students to actively reflect and apply their knowledge and skills, and develop a greater personal problem-solving competence while learning. Interactive teaching methods are the best means for motivating learning interest by using real-world situations, which relate to the content of prior academic training and can give it relevance and meaning. *Case studies, simulations, workshops, and applied projects* can induce students to give more consideration to real-world situations and problems that they encounter in their future professional life and develop essential competencies required for a successful work performance: analytical and problem-solving skills, negotiation and diplomatic skills, as well as communication and teamwork skills. In this context, in addition to the traditional lecture-based teaching methods which should be applied to develop a specific knowledge base, great emphasis should be placed on *problem-based and practice-based approaches to teaching and learning*.

---

[99] Ibid., p. 13.

Programs which aim to prepare students for the professional world should also apply *appropriate examination methods* (e.g., policy recommendations, small presentations, summaries, project proposals, and outlines). The *final graduation requirement* should be adjusted to fit the career goals of the students taking part in the program. For those students hoping to work in the field after graduation, a more *hands-on or real-world-application project* is more appropriate than a purely research-based and academically-oriented master's thesis. However, a program can always have an oral or written comprehensive exam in addition if it wants to ensure that students have learned a certain amount of theory. When looking at the U.S. professional schools, one sees that the majority of them require so-called *capstone projects* in which students spend one semester or longer using the knowledge and tools from the program to analyze and solve a problem, either alone or in a team. The goal is to immerse the students into a situation as close to their future work conditions as possible in order to ease the transition from higher education to professional life (and thus expose them to the difference between the expectations placed on students and those placed on employees).

With regard to the appropriate application of interactive teaching methods and innovative examination methods, *small class sizes* are required to guarantee that students can work together in small groups.

To ensure that the most appropriate teaching methods are applied for the field of education at hand, programs should offer their faculty members (esp. adjuncts) *seminars on pedagogy*. Furthermore, all methods used in the program should be subject to *evaluation* and should be changed when it becomes apparent that other methods would be more effective or economical in guiding learning. Therefore, it is highly recommended to have external experts or a curriculum committee conduct *quality assessments* or accreditation.

6.15. Faculty and student body composition

Practitioners possessing a strong international and professional background in the international public service should be appointed to teach practical hands-on courses or applied courses which focus on professional skills development. Core courses which focus on development of a specific knowledge base or methodological skills should primarily be taught by permanent academic staff. It is not only important that practitioners bring a rich level of professional experience to the classroom, but also that they are good instructors.

Therefore, the *practitioners' academic qualifications and teaching experience* should be taken into account as well to ensure the quality of instruction. In general, a faculty member in educational institutions that focus on professional education must demonstrate knowledge of and work experience in the field for which the programs aim to prepare students as well as teaching ability and enthusiasm.

Higher education programs should recruit students from different fields of study and other countries. A diverse student body sets the context for helping students to develop a cross-cultural understanding of people and different perspectives and prepares students to function effectively in a multinational working environment. Therefore, special attention should be paid to a *wide variety of academic and cultural backgrounds* and the career goals. It would also be beneficial to require a minimal amount of work experience from the applicants to guarantee a certain level of reflection and understanding of the connections between theory and practice.

Interviews and written examinations to test their language skills could be conducted to ensure that the most qualified students are selected.

6.16. Career services

Higher education institutions that focus on training students for a professional field should have their own *career services offices* so that students can be assisted in their career development by *full-time staff members* responsible for the following tasks:
– Offering training courses in interview and presentation skills, as well as CV writing;
– Offering courses on selection procedures at international organizations;
– Job fairs;
– Internship placement;
– Alumni networking;
– Career events;
– Job placement;
– General cooperation with potential employers.

6.17. Cooperation agreements

It is advisable for educational institutions offering programs to qualify students for careers in international organizations to *join networks or associations with similar programs* in order to exchange best practices and discuss inter-institutional cooperation possibilities with each other. These can be formal or informal groups or networks, and they can be formed at the national, regional, or international level. For example, German universities may join the associations mentioned in the curricular study: *APPAM, APSIA, NASPAA, and TPC*. Similar associations could be founded in Germany, or an annual conference or meeting of program coordinators and administrators in this field could be established to promote an ongoing dialogue between them.

Another recommendation with regard to cooperation agreements is that programs seek out employers in the field in which their students hope to work after graduation and attempt to *establish direct partnerships to the benefit of their students*. The cooperation could involve having human resources staff speak to the students about career opportunities, working together with professionals in the organization on simulations or other course offerings, arranging internships for the students on a yearly basis, or other forms depending on the needs and demands of both sides.

6.18. Conclusion

In making the above recommendations to educational administrators and policy makers in Germany, we understand that their realization may be hindered (or may have been hindered in the past) by certain obstacles having to do with traditions, structures, and regulations of the German higher education system. For example, additional staff members and financial means would be necessary to implement some of the recommendations. This is only possible if the programs can charge tuition or raise funds in another manner, which in turn requires a greater level of autonomy of universities from the German states. The universities would also have to be free to design their curricula as they please and invite practitioners to teach courses. Finally, cooperation agreements with businesses or other organizations are not currently common, but it should be acceptable for program directors to pursue and conclude them with whomever they wish. These are important considerations for the stakeholders in this process, but it should not take too much effort to reduce the obstacles. It is already occurring with the Bologna Process reforms, and various steps have been taken toward granting universities more autonomy.

Changes can be made outside of the higher education system as well, as the PROFIO labor market study identified factors not directly related to the employees' educational backgrounds. The German government could expand the offerings of entry-level opportunities to international organizations such as the Junior Professional Officer (*Beigeordnete Sachverständigen*) program and internship opportunities such as those available through the Carlo Schmid Program and the *Stiftungskolleg für internationale Aufgaben*. In addition, volunteer opportunities abroad like the Peace Corps in the U.S. could be created for young Germans as well.

In any case, there are many opportunities to increase not only the number of Germans working for international organizations, but to raise the qualifications of IO staff members even further.

Bibliography

Bardach, E. (2000). *A practical guide for policy analysis: The eightfold path to more effective problem solving.* New York/London: Chatham House Publishers.

Ben-David, J. (1992). *Centers of learning: Britain, France, Germany, United States, Carnegie commission on higher education sponsored research studies.* New York et al.: McGraw-Hill.

Berliner Initiative. 2004. Ergebnisbericht 2003. Berlin.

Bines, H. (1992). Issues in course design. In H. Bines & D. Watson (Eds.), *Developing Professional Education* (pp. 11-25). Buckingham/Bristol: The Society for Research into Higher Education & Open University Press.

Blome, N. & Middel, A. (1999). *Deutsche Delle in Brüssel.* Retrieved July 20, 2007, from www.welt.de/print-welt/article578116/Deutsche_Delle_in_Bruessel.html.

Brinkerhoff, D. W., & Brinkerhoff, J. M. (2005). *Working for change: Making a career in international public service.* Bloomfield: Kumarian Press.

Bryman, A. (2004). *Social research methods* (2nd ed.). Oxford: University Press.

Carland, M. Pinto, & Gihring, L.A. (2003). *Careers in international affairs* (7th ed.). Washington D.C.: Georgetown University Press.

Claus, B. (2004). *Förderung deutscher Nachwuchskräfte für internationale entwicklungspolitische Organisationen: Chancen, Defizite und Reformbedarf (Analysen und Stellungnahmen (3/2003)).* Retrieved July 5, 2007, from www.die-gdi.de/die_homepage.nsf/FSdpub?OpenFrameset.

Deutscher Bundestag (1998-2004). Bundesdrucksachen 13/10793, 13/10300, 14/2158, 14/1937, 14/4952, 14/5048, 14/8347, 14/8185, 15/0517, 15/2652, 15/3635. Retrieved July 25, 2007, from http://dip.bundestag.de/parfors/parfors.htm.

Dietrich, S., Herz, D., Dortants, S. L. & Linke, K. (2006). *Careers with the World Bank. A study on recruitment strategies and qualification requirements at the World Bank.* Retrieved from http://nbn-resolving. de/urn/resolver.pl?urn=urn:nbn:de:gbv:547-200601351

Erpenbeck, J. (2005). *How new are the new types of competency development really?* Retrieved July 5, 2007, from www.scil.ch/congress-2005/programme-10-12/docs/workshop-6-erpenbeck-text.pdf.

Erpenbeck, J., & Heyse, V. (2004). *Kompetenztraining. 64 Informations- und Trainingsprogramme.* Stuttgart: Schäffer-Poeschl Verlag.

ESA (2006). *Core skills. ESA's Generic Competency Model.* Retrieved July 5, 2007, from www.esa.int/SPECIALS/Careers_at_ESA/SEMYRSXO4HD_0.html.

ESA. (2006). *Careers at ESA.* Retrieved July 5, 2006, from www.esa.int/SPECIALS/Careers_at_ESA/SEMV1TXO4HD_0.html and Secretariat, U.N. (2002).

Evers, F. T., & Rush, J.C. (1998). *The bases of competence: Skills for lifelong learning and employability.* San Francisco: Jossey-Bass Inc.

Hartigan Shea, R. (Ed.). (2004). *America's Best Graduate Schools* (2005 ed.). Washington, D.C.: U.S. News and World Report.

Herz, D., Dortants, S. L. & Linke, K. (2006). *Careers with UNEP. A study on recruitment strategies and qualification requirements at the United Nations Environment Programme.* Retrieved from http://nbn-resolving. de/urn/resolver.pl?urn=urn:nbn:de:gbv:547-200601348

Herz, D., Schattenmann, M., Dortants, S. L. & Steuber, S. (2005). *Working for the OSCE. Careers in a non-career organization.* Retrieved from http://nbn-resolving.de/urn/resolver.pl?urn=urn:nbn:de:gbv:547-200601330

238

Herz, D., Schattenmann, M., Dortants, S. L., Linke, K. & Steuber, S. (2005). *Careers with the EU. A study on recruitment strategies and qualification requirements of the institutions of the European Union.* Retrieved from http://nbn-resolving.de/urn/resolver.pl?urn=urn:nbn:de:gbv:547-200601351

Hoelscher, P., Herz, D., Dortants & Linke, K. (2005). *Studie zu Studiengängen und Bildungsangeboten Frankreichs, Belgiens und der Schweiz, die für eine Karriere in internationalen Organisationen ausbilden.* Retrieved from http://nbn-resolving.de/urn/resolver.pl?urn=urn:nbn:d e:gbv: 547-200601430

Karns, M. P., & Mingst, K. A. (2004). *International Organizations: The politics and processes of global governance.* Boulder: Lynne Rienner Publishers.

Krause, C., Tschirschwitz, C., Herz, D., Dortants, S. L. & Linke, K. (2006). *Bericht über Studiengänge und Bildungsangebote im deutschsprachigen Raum, die für eine Karriere in internationalen Organisationen ausbilden.* Retrieved from http://nbn-resolving.de/urn/resolver.pl?urn = urn:nbn:de:gbv:547-200601418

Mayhew, L. B., & Ford. P. Joseph. (1974). *Reform in graduate and professional education* (1st ed.). The Jossey-Bass Series in Higher Education. San Francisco: Jossey-Bass Publishers.

McGlothlin, W. J. (1964). *The Professional Schools.* Edited by G. R. Gottschalk, *The library of education.* New York: Center for Applied Research in Education.

Neuss, B., & Hilz, W. (1999). *Deutsche personelle Präsenz in der EU-Kommission.* Retrieved July 5, 2007, from www.berlinerinitiative.de/materialien/2001_europa.pdf.

Nidiffer, J. (2001). *Postsecondary education.* In *The Encyclopedia Americana.* Danport: Grolier Incorporated.

OSCE (2005). *Are we identifying and preparing mission members correctly? Managers talk back.* *The 2nd OSCE Meeting on Training and Recruitment.* Vienna: OSCE.

OSCE (2005). *Guiding principles and recommendations for the revision of the training standards for preparation of future members of the OSCE field operations. The 2nd OSCE Meeting on Training and Recruitment.* Vienna: OSCE.

OSCE. (2006). *Employment.* Retrieved July 5, 2007, from www.osce.org/employment/1310 9.html.

Ritchie, J. & Lewis, J. (2004). *Qualitative research practice: A guide for social science students and researchers.* London: Sage.

Robert Bosch Stiftung (1999). *Stuttgarter Appell an Bund und Länder, Wissenschaft und Wirtschaft: Für mehr Internationalität in Bildung, Ausbildung und Personalpolitik.* Retrieved July 5, 2007 from www.berlinerinitiative.de/materialien/1999_stuttgarter_appell.pdf.

Rychen, D. S., & Salganik, L. H. (2003). A holistic model of competence. In D. S. Rychen & L. H. Salganik (Eds.), *Key competencies for a successful life and well-functioning society* (pp. 41-62). Göttingen: Hogrefe & Huber Publishers.

Sherrington, P. (2000). *The Council of Ministers: Political authority in the European Union.* London: Pinter.

Sklaroff, S. (Ed.). (2004). *America's Best Colleges* (2005 ed.). Washington, D.C.: U.S. News & World Report.

Studzinski, J., Herz, D., Dortants, S. L. & Linke, K. (2005). *Qualification requirement strategies at the European Space Agency (ESA).* Retrieved from http://nbn-resolving.de/urn/resolver.pl?urn=urn:nbn:de:gbv:547-200601376

Studzinski, J., Herz, D., Schattenmann, M., Dortants, S. L. & Linke, K. (2005). *Evaluation of the "Carlo-Schmid-Program for internships in international organizations and EU institutions".* Retrieved from http://nbn-resolving.de/urn/resolver.pl?urn=urn:nbn:de:gbv:547-200601395

Tyler, R. W. (1971). *Basic principles of curriculum and instruction. Open University Set Book.* Chicago and London: The University of Chicago Press.

United Nations (2001). *Targeted strategies could help boost U.S. representation.* Retrieved July 5, 2007 from http://www.gao.gov/new.items/d01839.pdf.

United Nations Secretariat (2002). *Administrative Instructions. Staff Selection System.* Retrieved July 5, 2007, from http://www.un.org/staff/panelofcounsel/pocimages/stai024. pdf

Voncken, M. (2004). *Being competent or having competences. Social competences in vocational and continuing education.* In A. Lindgren, & A. Heikkinen. *Studies in vocational and continuing education.* Bern: Peter Lang AG.

Weiler, H. (2003). *Professional Schools: Ein Bündnis von Anwendungsbezug und Wissenschaftlichkeit.* In *Hochschulreform in Europa - konkret. Österreichs Universitäten auf dem Weg vom Gesetz zur Realität,* edited by S. a. S. H. Titscher. Opladen: Leske+Budrich.

Westlake, M., & Galloway, D. (2004). *The Council of the European Union* (3rd ed.). London: Harper.

Pirkko Vartiainen

The Legitimacy of Evaluation

A Comparison of Finnish and English Institutional Evaluations of Higher Education

Frankfurt am Main, Berlin, Bern, Bruxelles, New York, Oxford, Wien, 2004.
150 pp., 3 fig., 5 tab.
ISBN 978-3-631-52415-2 · pb. € 34.–*

Evaluation is an important issue in all European societies: it concerns all organisations and institutions whether they like it or not. Organisations in higher education are not an exception; on the contrary, during recent years, university evaluations have moved in a formal and routine direction. This book's hypothesis is that this development has strengthened the institutional tendencies of evaluation. By looking through the lens of legitimacy, this study analyses the ideologies, models and practices of English and Finnish higher education evaluations. The central question is: what gives modern higher education evaluation its legitimacy? This book shows readers the many-sided elements of legitimate evaluation and ends with conclusions that show the similarities and differences of institutional university evaluations in Finland and in England.

Contents: The Legitimacy of Evaluation · Higher Education · Institutional Evaluation · Comparative Evaluation

Frankfurt am Main · Berlin · Bern · Bruxelles · New York · Oxford · Wien
Distribution: Verlag Peter Lang AG
Moosstr. 1, CH-2542 Pieterlen
Telefax 0041(0)32/3761727

*The €-price includes German tax rate
Prices are subject to change without notice
Homepage http://www.peterlang.de

Peter Lang · Internationaler Verlag der Wissenschaften